WEISER ♀ CLASSICS

THE WEISER CLASSICS SERIES offers essential works from renowned authors and spiritual teachers, foundational texts, as well as introductory guides on an array of topics written by contemporary authors. The series represents the full range of subjects and genres that have been part of Weiser Books' over sixty-year-long publishing program—from divination and magick to alchemy and occult philosophy. Each volume in the series will include new material from its author or a contributor and other valuable additions to the work whenever possible and will be printed and produced using acid-free paper in a durable paperback binding.

Pure Magic

A COMPLETE COURSE IN SPELLCASTING

JUDIKA ILLES

FOREWORD BY MAT AURYN

WEISER
BOOKS

This edition first published in 2022 by Weiser Books, an imprint of
Red Wheel/Weiser, LLC
With offices at:
65 Parker Street, Suite 7
Newburyport, MA 01950
www.redwheelweiser.com

ISBN: 978-1-57863-760-7
Library of Congress Cataloging-in-Publication Data available upon request.
Typeset in Arno Pro
Printed in the United States of America
IBI
10 9 8 7 6 5 4 3 2 1

Series Editors
Mike Conlon, Production Director, Red Wheel/Weiser Books
Judika Illes, Editor-at-Large, Weiser Books
Peter Turner, Associate Publisher, Weiser Books

Series Design

Kathryn Sky-Peck, Creative Director, Red Wheel/Weiser

Disclaimer: This book contains advice and information for using herbs and other botanicals, and is not meant to diagnose, treat, or prescribe. It should be used to supplement,
not replace, the advice of your physician or other trained healthcare practitioner. If you
know or suspect you have a medical condition, are experiencing physical symptoms, or
if you feel unwell, seek your physician's advice before embarking on any medical program
or treatment. Readers are cautioned to follow instructions carefully and accurately for the
best effect. Readers using the information in this book do so entirely at their own risk, and
the author and publisher accept no liability if adverse effects are caused.

FOR ADELE, MY WITCH SISTER

Contents

Foreword xi

Preface. xv

Introduction xix

PART ONE
Magic 101

Earth Mother Magic 8

Communicating with Earth 10

What You Won't Find in This Book 13

A Psychic Glossary: Some Magic Vocabulary Words. 14

The Four Elements 22

    Earth. *23*

    Air *23*

    Water. *24*

    Fire. *24*

Colors 25

Supplies 29

    The Most Important Ingredient. *31*

    The Enchanted Grocery List. *39*

    Amulets. *44*

PART TWO
Other Powers: Your Magic Allies

Tools *47*

Allies *48*

Animal Allies 53

Animal Allies: What Do I Do with Them? 54

Threshold Animals 62

Familiar Animals 65

Spirit Land 70

The Yoruba Model for Practical Spiritual Interaction 72

Why Do Spirits Help Us? 73

Altars as Vehicles of Communication 75

Ancestors 77

Spirit Sponsors of Magic 78

Minerals and Metals 85

Crystals. 85

Metals 91

Botanicals. 95

True Oils 96

Essential Oils 97

Flower Essences 99

Incense 103

Potpourri 104

Whole Plants. 105

The Magic Garden. 107

Fragrant Night Garden 108

Dreams 119

Remembering Your Dreams 121

Having the Dreams You Desire 122

PART THREE

Spells

The Magic Calendar. 136

Where to Practice Magic. 137

Words of Power. 139

CONTENTS

Let's Get Real: Realistic Expectations of Magic 140

Aura-Cleansing Spells 141

   Florida Water 145

Protection Spells 154

   A Magic Garden of Protection 154

   The Body 160

Psychic Enhancement Spells 172

   Magical Exercises 179

Divination Spells 185

   Daphnomancy 186

Lucky Wish Spells 189

Beauty Spells 201

Love Magic 210

   Aphrodite's Bower of Love 210

   Love Sachets and Bags 224

Aphrodisiac Spells 229

   Love Beads 230

Marriage Spells 232

   The Celestial Spirit of Marriage 232

   An Enchanted Wedding 234

   Magical Wedding Gifts 239

   The Wedding's Over and the Party's Begun! 240

Fertility Spells 240

   Spirit Allies 241

Antifertility Spells 247

Pregnancy Protection and Enhancement Spells 248

   Childbirth 248

Protection for Infants and Children 251

   Henna for the Baby 252

   The Baby's Pillow 252

Money Magic 255
   Animal Allies 255
   A Money Garden 255
   Spirits of Financial Prosperity 258
   New Orleans Money Magic 263

Enchantment to Heal Body and Soul 271
   Animal Allies 271
   A Healing Garden 271
   Spirits of Healing 272
   Candle Healing 272
   Crystals 274

Dying, Death, and Funerals 277
   Baron Samedi Altar 277
   Aids to Transition 277
   A Bower of Comfort and Grief 278
   Animal Allies 279

APPENDIX

Botanical Classifications 281
Bibliography 289
Acknowledgments 292
Index of Spells 293

Foreword

Being asked to write this foreword is one of the greatest honors of my life. Words hardly suffice to express how much respect and admiration I have for Judika Illes. While our backgrounds and life stories are quite different—being from different generations and different cultural backgrounds—I have always felt some deep comradery between us. Beginning at a young age, Judika was a voracious reader, eagerly devouring any books she could get her hands on, particularly books on folklore, divination, mythology, magic, and other esoteric topics. This passion for books on these subjects is something we share and has remained constant throughout our lives. It's a love affair for books on the unseen that would eventually shape both our individual paths into adulthood, both spiritually and professionally. My hope is that as I grow older and gain experience that I can transform that book knowledge into lived wisdom as fully as has Judika.

I first met Judika several years back at a witchcraft festival where she was the keynote speaker. I had read her books and was excited to hear her speak in person. Her lecture remains one of the best I've ever attended. But what impressed me most about her was her manner when she approached me later that day. At that time, I hadn't published any books, didn't write for any magazines, and my blog had yet to gain any semblance of popularity. Yet, she spoke with me with friendliness, love, hospitality, and respect. This is how I have seen her treat everyone, regardless of who they are. For me, that is more impressive than any accumulation of knowledge, publishing accomplishments, or magical power that one can possess; all of which she has an endless abundance. It speaks to the spiritual core of who she is, what her magic is centered in, and what she is about.

Judika Illes is one of the most influential magical practitioners of our lifetime. Her influence is intertwined throughout the works and lives of the magical community. This isn't due solely because of her prolific work as a writer and teacher on esoteric topics but also because she has worked with authors as the editor of hundreds of books that have been published by the historic occult publisher Weiser Books. Not only has she curated and preserved folklore, myth, and magic on literal encyclopedic levels, but she has tirelessly devoted herself to helping those in our community, wanting to see everyone succeed. Whether it is her desire to see authors and teachers within our community be successful (regardless of which publishing house their books come from) or her desire for her readers to be successful in all areas of their lives as proficient spellcasters, Judika has always been consistent in sharing what she knows and what she can do, to better the lives of everyone with whom she comes into contact. Sometimes this is through her written words, at other times it's through her integrity of interpersonal interaction. This book that you are holding is one of the countless examples of Judika's eagerness to share her limitless knowledge and wisdom

Finding an entry point into learning the art of authentic magic can be a daunting task for the newcomer, particularly during this time when we have such a massive surge of information and books on the practice of magic—many of which are brilliant and many others that, to put it nicely, may not be worth the trees that were sacrificed to print them. Even more confusing can be the bombardment of self-appointed and often self-important experts on the magical arts in the age of social media; often with contradictory voices asserting opposing views. While there are definitely some brilliant occult content creators doing great work, there's also a lot of bad advice and teachings out there, often ineffective at best and dangerous at worst. Because of this it can be difficult to find an entry point into the magical arts that strike the sweet spot between a practice that is spiritual, practical, and effective while not dumbed down. Judika's *Pure Magic: A Complete Course in Spellcasting* meets these criteria perfectly. In it she leads the reader through the basic concepts, terminology, theory, and praxis of magic, as well as a complete spell book.

Pure Magic explores the ins and outs of magic in a manner that is approachable for the beginner, but there's also a rare depth of practical wisdom for successful magic and spiritual partnership which may not be obvious on the first reading. Like all of Judika's books, this is one that I've returned to periodically over the years, and each time I'm struck by insight and perspective that continues to enhance and level-up my own magic and relationship with spirits.

Many of these spells that Judika shares have been cherished tools in my magical arsenal for many years, ever since my first reading of this book, not only due to their efficacy but also the pure practicality of them. Most of these spells are quick and easy to perform, requiring only accessible materia that you probably already have in your kitchen, can grab at your grocery store or your local botanica or metaphysical shop without having to pay a fortune. As stated, the book's magic is extremely practical; there's a rare depth of rich spirituality interwoven throughout it, one that is sure to not only enchant your life, but brings you closer to the Earth, its forces, and the myriad of spiritual beings residing here—both physical and nonphysical. In my opinion, this is exactly how spirituality should be, completely integrated into our daily lives, not something separate or purely mental or reserved for only a special type of person. This is exactly the spirit of *Pure Magic,* a book brimming with magic that is accessible to everyone, magic that works regardless of one's level of experience or background.

This book contains some of the soundest practical advice that a magic worker can come across, and the reader would be wise to not skim through the first two sections—particularly the second section—but rather savor and reflect on the words you read. Judika takes her experience of street smarts, everyday common sense, and observations of nature and then brilliantly shows how these insights apply to our magical work and spiritual interactions. These insights serve to not only strengthen our magic and connection to the spirit world but more importantly, to help us be in the proper relationship of respect and honor with them, just as she is with the people in her own life. She never dresses up her writing in false pretense or obscure language. Instead, she shares from a place of personal passion in a tone that makes you feel like a close friend is having a chat with you because she truly wants to help you to learn how to help yourself through magical empowerment.

This authentic appreciation, sincerity, and enthusiastic passion for magical practices, folklore, and mythology from all over the world and how she respectfully approaches it, shines throughout each page of this book awaiting to enchant your life with its pure magic.

—MAT AURYN, author of *Psychic Witch: A Metaphysical Guide to Meditation, Magick, and Manifestation*

Preface

There are books that one returns to over and over, partly for love and pleasure but often also because there always seems to be something new to discover at each reading. This is not an uncommon experience. I can't even begin to guess how many times I've re-read *The Master and Margarita* by Russian novelist and playwright Mikhail Bulgakov or George MacDonald's *The Princess and the Goblin*, but each time I do, they bring fresh insights. It's a completely different situation, however, for authors revisiting their own works. That's an experience more akin to time traveling. Memories flood back in intense detail regarding *who* you were and *where* you were when the book was first written. This is especially true when re-reading your first book, which in my case was *Pure Magic*.

My attempts at being published had been frustrating prior to *Pure Magic*, as I had run into many brick walls and received plenty of rejections for other works. But one such rejection actually led to the writing and publication of *Pure Magic*. Although enthralled by witchcraft for as long as I can remember, I had not set out to be a metaphysical writer. My love of the magical arts was, back then, something very private. Instead, I had assumed in my youth that I would write about music, as I was inspired by the great music journalists of the time, such as Greil Marcus and Peter Guralnick. Reading them taught me to write with my heart on my sleeve and not to be afraid to share my passions.

Despite this ambition, the first book I actively attempted to publish was devoted to traditional methods—magical, spiritual, herbal, and other holistic therapies—of overcoming infertility. The lack of interest from publishers depressed me. Eventually, however, I encountered a publisher who liked my writing and, in particular, the chapter I had written on magic spells. While rejecting my original manuscript, he asked whether I'd like to expand that chapter and write a book for him on spellcasting instead. I jumped at the chance. It was a sad time in my life, and this was the first piece of good news I'd had in a while.

I was, by then, quite aware that the doors of publishing did not swing open easily. I did not assume future opportunities were guaranteed, and so I filled *Pure Magic* (which was actually first published under the title *Earth Mother Magic*) with what I most sought to share with readers: my love for spells, spirits, Tarot, essential oils, and flower essence remedies, as well as what might have seemed to be unexpected sources of magic, at least back in those days: cooking, blues music, and the city of New Orleans. As a result, *Pure Magic* is probably the most personal of all my books.

Because I did not assume that I would ever publish anything else, I determined to write the most authentic, truthful book I could—a book that shared the practical spellcasting information that I had learned over the years, much of its material not readily found in books or at least not back then.

Of course, this was years prior to the current enthusiasm and growing acceptance of witchcraft. Now in the 21st century, many wonderful and authentic books devoted to the magical arts are published and receive wide exposure. *Pure Magic* was written in 1999 and first published two years later, an era when folk magic was still very much a niche topic that was frequently considered to be unsavory. The books that were available were largely geared toward Pagan practice, witchcraft as religion, and ceremonial magic, but spellcasting was what I really loved. My goal was to share that love with readers, to treat both readers and material with the respect I believe they deserve, and to provide an honest, realistic, guide to magical practice that would be accessible to anyone who wished to learn about it. Because, as I write in *Pure Magic*, the ability to practice magic is our birthright, our common human heritage.

I was very pleasantly surprised by the positive reception that *Pure Magic* received upon publication, which led to the writing of further books. As I write the preface to this new edition, my ninth book *Daily Magic* has just been published, and so it is extremely gratifying for *Pure Magic* now to become part of the esteemed Weiser Classics series. As with magical spells that at first may not seem to work, end results are often breathtakingly more satisfying than initially anticipated.

In re-reading *Pure Magic* now, I recognize the seeds planted there for my future books, although of course I did not know it at the time. My devotion to Michael Archangel and Marie Laveau is a thread that begins here but continues through all my other books, as does my love for the rose—the Queen of Flowers—and the metaphysical meanings of numbers. I find myself continually returning to the topics that fascinate me, trying to delve deeper. Like great archaeological sites, there are always more exciting levels to excavate. Some of the seeds planted in *Pure Magic* surprise me. The references to saints, for example. If you had asked me when I was writing *Pure Magic* if I would ever write an entire book devoted to saints, I would have laughed. It would have been inconceivable to me, and yet, as I re-read my own words, I can see the groundwork for *The Encyclopedia of Mystics, Saints, and Sages* already taking root in *Pure Magic*.

This new edition of *Pure Magic* has been only lightly updated. I have resisted the temptation to update pop culture references which were current and relevant when this book was first written, such as those to *Sabrina the Teenage Witch*. I imagine that whatever I replaced them with would also eventually fade from popularity and be superseded by something new. The crucial point is to comprehend the distinction between *true* magic—the magic that is real and your birthright as a human being—and fantasy magic that is, at best, fun, entertaining, and inspiring but, at worst, can causes false expectations, despair, and may be detrimental to accessing and maximizing personal magical powers. Fantasy witches come and go, but true magic—is timeless.

Some things have changed since I first wrote *Pure Magic*. For example, "Botanicas"—the magical shops that were once so common in and around New York City and where as a teenager, I learned so much from so many generous people—are now endangered. Even before the lockdown associated with the Coronavirus, the cost of real estate and competition from online sources had already pushed these shops to the brink of survival. Meanwhile, our beleaguered spiritual allies, the endangered plants, animals, and other living beings discussed in *Pure Magic* remain endangered, the only change in many cases being a worsened situation.

I have *not* resisted the impulse to modernize the text of *Pure Magic* a bit, in the desire to increase its inclusivity. All the spells and rituals in the original edition remain, however. Many of them derive from ancient, traditional, and sometimes culturally conservative sources. Various schools of herbalism, for instance, posit that certain plants possess different affinities for different genders. For example, onions are frequently perceived as "male" plants, while roses are "female." This is intended to be understood in the context of the Chinese philosophical concept of the yang and the yin, as a way of classifying and comprehending Earthly energies.

Ultimately, *all* magic is personal. *Pure Magic* was written with the intention of assisting in the discovery and enhancement of your magic. Feel free to experiment and tweak the material as suits you best. Listen to your intuition. Exert your will. Whoever you are, whatever your needs, find the magic that empowers you and improves your life. Take your magic into your own hands and claim your power. The practice of magic is the key to entering a world of wonders, a world that never grows old, boring, or irrelevant, regardless of whether you are an adept or just starting on your path. May this book bring you joy, success, and increased personal magical power.

—JUDIKA ILLES, September 6, 2021,
beneath the Virgo new moon.

Introduction

When I was a little girl, *Bewitched* was among my favorite TV shows. Samantha was my role model, and who could blame me? Who wouldn't want to be Samantha? She was beautiful, poised, charming yet sensible, extremely intelligent and articulate, completely at home in everyday society but also secretly filled with magical powers. Her magic appeared effortless. A wiggle of her nose and she could do anything. Ironically, while so many watched rapt with envy, the central theme of the show was how badly Samantha wished to be just like us regular folks. It was the one feat she couldn't accomplish. No matter how hard she tried to live our mundane, tedious lives, washing dishes by hand rather than by wiggling her nose, she couldn't help it. Samantha was innately magical.

Jeannie, star of *I Dream of Jeannie*, found herself in much the same boat. Her magical powers, which, of course, all the viewers longed to share, were a burden to her and a source of embarrassment to her true love. While everyone but the object of her desire looked on enviously, Jeannie only wished to be an ordinary woman so that Tony would truly love and accept her.

Television shows like *Bewitched, I Dream of Jeannie* and more recently, *Sabrina, the Teenage Witch*, have delivered hours of entertainment but have also been a source of frustration. The magical powers that so delight us are clearly completely unattainable to mere mortals. The powers depicted are very special and very unique. Typically, they are hereditary; passed down through bloodlines, an accident of birth. Jeannie, Samantha, Sabrina: the girls can't help it.

The girls aren't alone. The best-selling books in the Harry Potter series also deliver this message. Although Harry and friends are shown studying diligently to perfect their skills, ultimately those skills are innate. Once again, some are magically gifted and some, unfortunately, simply aren't. Just as the "magical" people can't help their powers, so the nonmagical are left permanently outside the enchanted circle. Some protest that these books and television programs tempt children (and adults!) by glorifying "dark arts." The protest seems pointless: they're missing the message. The underlying theme of these works is that if you're not born a member of a witchly family, there is no sense in trying. Your longings cannot be fulfilled. Harry Potter, like Baby Tabitha, was born with his power. The rest of us humans can only stand apart wishing wistfully, consoling ourselves with the notion that magic isn't real. By dangling the possibility of a special separate magical world before us, a supernatural existence, the ultimate insinuation is that it is all only a lovely fantasy. Magic doesn't exist. Enjoy the fantasy for half an hour and then get back to real life.

I don't mean any disrespect. I would still love to be Samantha. I love *Bewitched* as much as ever. I love Harry Potter, too. *I Married a Witch* starring Veronica Lake is one of my favorite movies. Stick a fantasy witch into a movie or television show and I'll watch it, *Bell, Book and Candle,* you name it. At heart, these entertainments acknowledge our deep and frustrated longing for magic. They are wonderful fantasies, but fantasies are truly what they are because their implicit message is incorrect. There is magic. Real magic. You can do it and I can do it. Magic is not unique or elitist, or reserved for those with special mystical blood. Magic is as common as dirt.

Part of our problem involves limitations of language. Languages function as more than just communication tools. They also reveal much about their cultures of origin. In the same way that English is limited to only one word for snow versus the twenty-seven-odd words in the Inuit tongue, we have only one word, *magic,* to express so many different concepts. That word, *magic,* is used to delineate tricks, sleight-of-hand, sorcery and television fantasies, as well as the timeless Earth knowledge that helps us connect to the energy of our Earth Mother, fulfill our desires and destinies, and protect ourselves and our loved ones from harm.

Regarding real magic, real practical, functional, down-to-Earth magic, I have good news and bad news for you. Bad news first. As far as I know—although believe me, I would love to be the one to tell you different—there is no effective spell for redecorating your entire home in a quarter of an instant just by wiggling your nose. Get away from the mirror, girls.

Practicing the Jeannie nod doesn't help. Our longing for this sort of television magic prevents us from seeing the real magic at our own fingertips.

The good news? Magic is your birthright. It is open to all. Yes, Harry Potter is not alone, nor is he unique. The aptitude to practice pure Earth magic is present in all humans at birth. It is not culturally specific nor is it dependent upon your IQ. The ability exists for all gender identities and sexual preferences. Are some more magically gifted than others? Sure, but we're not all great dancers, either. Talent is but one factor; effort and desire play major roles, too. You already possess the building blocks to create the magic that is right for you. What's stopping you? Challenges to your magical gifts tend to be insidious ones, but with a little awareness and effort can be overcome. Beyond false expectations of magic, and the defeatism that this fosters, the major obstacles for most are our severed connections with Earth.

What is magic anyway? What is this Pure Magic?

Real magic, the magic of the Earth, is Pure Magic. Magic in its purest form consists of a dialogue between Earth and yourself, a dialogue whereby you are able to express your desires, receive and recognize a response and are then able to make your wishes and desires come true. Earth's gift to her children, it is the simplest, most basic and most ancient magical art, open to all. Expenses are minimal. No specialized metaphysical training is required. You don't even need to understand what *metaphysical* means. What is required is an awareness of the natural rhythms, energies, powers and patterns of Earth and her diverse inhabitants. These rhythms and powers are then manipulated in a harmonious and conscious manner to help manifest your goals. In simple language, Pure Magic encourages you to take your dreams and desires and translate them into concrete reality.

The bottom line is that magic is communication: communication between yourself, Earth and all the other life forms with whom we share our Earth Mother. Easier said than done? Well, unfortunately, unlike fantasy magic, real magic is not completely effortless but, on the other hand, it *is* completely attainable. Your own goals and desires will determine the level of effort that you need to fulfill your birthright and become a magical practitioner.

The first step is simple. Buy a cauldron? Find a familiar? No. Just be kind to yourself. This is real life, not television or literature. Forgive yourself for being unable to master unattainable and unrealistic goals and start afresh. (Magic and reality? Oh, yes. More about that later.)

There are so many reasons that people assume that they can never become a magician, witch, wizard, warlock, practitioner, adept, whatever word you prefer. Perhaps you feel that it is hopeless because you've never been able to master the nose wiggle, let alone *do* anything with it. Or perhaps you work as an accountant, and what kind of magic is that? Or maybe once you tried a candle spell and it didn't work. Maybe once you tried a Ouija board and you think maybe it *did* work and you got scared and threw it away, so how magical are you? Maybe you tried to read someone's cards and your predictions were completely off the mark. That's all old baggage. Throw it away. None of it prevents you from achieving your full potential now.

There is one aspect of magic that all of these TV shows and novels did get right: those actively practicing magic do have more fun. Magic will put a sparkle in your eyes. It will put a lift in your walk. You will begin to see things in ways that you have never seen before. Loneliness and boredom will be banished. You will feel stronger and radiant with energy. You will not feel purposeless but competent to fulfill your own destiny.

No, I can't teach you how to turn your mean boss into one of the less attractive mammals, but magic does provide some invaluable gifts. Magic can get you out of trouble. No, not everyone comes up with winning lottery numbers, but magic can ensure financial well-being. You can achieve peace in your family and gain the love that you've always wanted. Magic can provide spiritual and romantic fulfillment, not to mention improving your sex life. It can also improve your appearance, bolster health and vitality, and help you become the person you've always secretly known you could be.

PART ONE

Magic 101

By definition, magic is mysterious and effective. The effective part is crucial: magic is a practical art. There are spells that have lasted for millennia. If they absolutely didn't work ever for anyone, they wouldn't be remembered. The converse is also true: no one thing works for everyone. This goes for conventional medicine, traditional medicine, educational theories and magic, too. Because your headache defied that aspirin doesn't mean that aspirin never works. It just wasn't the right tool for you at that moment. "But that's real life," you protest, "not magic!" Well, magic is real life, too.

There is a power that radiates from all living beings in varying degrees of force and clarity. Different languages have different words to identify this power. The Polynesians refer to it as *mana*. Among the Yoruba, a prominent language group of Western Africa, it is known as *axé*. In Morocco, this power is called *baraka,* and in other areas of the Islamic world some variation on that word may be used.

I offer you words from different languages because English has no specific word for this concept. I can describe this concept for you in English but I can't name it. The closest approximation is *force* or *power* but these are imprecise because there are so many types of forces or powers. One could say spiritual force but that, too, is imprecise. It *is* a spiritual force but this force also expresses itself in very physical ways. The spiritual aspect cannot be separated from the physical. This force is a holistic power. It does not acknowledge the splits between spirit and matter that humans may perceive but transcends these divisions.

This concept lurks in the English language, perhaps for safety's sake, demonstrating our cultural ambivalence to magic and reflecting the reality that for centuries, those who openly and effectively practiced Earth magic were persecuted and suppressed. Interestingly, the cultures that do possess an explicit and specific term to identify this force rarely possess just one generic word for *magic*. Their languages may instead contain something more like those twenty-seven Inuit words for snow, assorted various, specific words that describe specific acts, intents and practices that would in English all be lumped together under the category, *magic*. There is no one blanket **word** to distinguish magic from real life because in these cultures, magic is incorporated into real life. It isn't *supernatural* but a part of the way *natural* works. One is encouraged to be aware of the various forces because contact with them strengthens, protects and improves quality of life.

Just because we lack a specific English name for it doesn't mean that this concept isn't at home in America. It just doesn't reside out in the open. You will most likely encounter it outside the cultural mainstream, most easily in ethnic enclaves. The most publicly accessible place to find acknowledgement of these forces is within blues music, if you know what to listen for. When the great Chicago blues singer Muddy Waters boasts of "all the powers in his hand," this, not merely his physical prowess, is what he is singing about.

Although anything may contain a spark of this power, the quantity and quality varies. Certain species of plants and animals contain greater quantities than others. A human science that analyzes and studies these powers has developed over the ages, although cultural perceptions vary. Universally, horses are recognized as possessing tremendous quantities of *baraka*. How each individual horse measures up to the standard of potential varies but the potential always exists. In Polynesia, the *ti* plant also possesses the potential for vast quantities of power. It is placed near the front door to bring protection to the house and its inhabitants. No one anticipates that in the event of a burglary, the plant will transform into an armed response guard. Instead, inherent in the *ti* plant is a radiant force that magnetically attracts good fortune and spiritual protection. The *tulsi* plant, holy basil, is used similarly in India.

In North America, when sage is referred to as a power plant, when it is burned so that its smoke cleanses and purifies an area, this is the concept that we are trying to express. The concept may be expressed with a certain awkwardness, but this is on account of the inadequacy of language, not some failure of the power itself. There are no traditional cultures that did not recognize that there were plants that were especially powerful and that provided an immediate link to the sacred. In fact, wherever sage has been in contact with people, it has been recognized as being extremely powerful and used for similar purposes, not only in North America but also throughout North Africa, Asia and Europe.

Baraka, this force, this power, possesses a sacred aspect. It is defined as a positive power, a benevolent force. This power can be transmitted. It is contagious. It can be expanded. It can also be lost. (Traditional Hawaiians believed that misuse of *mana*, manipulating it for selfish, unethical purposes caused one's own personal power to decrease.)

The closest image that I can give to you, although it is a negative image, is radioactive radiation. Like that type of radiation, this power is formless, has no scent or sound but is absorbed and stored just the same. You will witness its absorption by its effects upon you. If you consistently feel drained or frustrated, if things just don't ever work for you, if life lacks a spark of joy, you very likely suffer from a deficiency of this power. You can attain and balance this power by selecting, arranging and manipulating the powers that surround you.

Although certain species inherently contain specific powers, the actual quantity and quality varies according to the individual. In other words, a sage plant growing wild and free in pristine wilderness contains immense power. A sage plant cultivated in a garden with love, consideration, respect, reasonably clean water and sunshine also contains immense power. Whose power is greater is a toss-up. The wild sage's power may technically be greater, however, the cultivated sage may have developed a relationship with a specific human. Working together as a pair, they may be a formidably powerful unit. A sage plant growing along the roadside, processing toxic fumes daily is using its power for its own survival; it doesn't have any to share with you.

People, too, contain this power, some more than others. Sometimes this power is innate; sometimes it's learned or acquired. Different cultures maintain varying views on exactly which individuals are most likely to be extra blessed. Blues music, for instance, extols the wonders of the seventh son, whose order of birth ensures extra power. (And the seventh son of a seventh son! Wow! That power should radiate right through the roof!)

You can recognize this power in another person: having been in their presence, you emerge feeling strengthened and empowered. Sometimes an individual's power is so strong, it doesn't terminate at death but can still be accessed by others in need. To this day, people travel to Voodoo-Queen Marie Laveau's grave in New Orleans to beg her assistance and leave testimonials to the miracles she still accomplishes.

In some areas of Earth, power of this magnitude, extending beyond the grave, is the chief, intrinsic requirement for sainthood. The behavior of these saints may not always be exemplary, however it is expected that they will use their powers to benefit others. Although in the United States, the word *saint* is tied somewhat exclusively to Roman Catholicism, this broader concept of sainthood exists in many cultures, including African Diaspora, Buddhist, Jewish and Muslim traditions. The power of these saints can be so immense that it permeates the very ground in which they are buried. It is the desire to access this power, usually for healing or good fortune, that stimulates pilgrimages to holy people and their shrines. In Morocco, the dirt surrounding a saint's tomb is sprinkled upon newly created fabrics and textiles to imbue them with added *baraka*. This is because not only the works of nature contain this power but also the creations of people. The intent of many tribal artisans is not merely to create something beautiful or functional but also to infuse it with as much positive force as possible.

> *Every year, thousands venture to Marie Laveau's grave at St. Louis Cemetery Number One, New Orleans' oldest cemetery, to beseech the self-proclaimed Pope of Voodoo for favors, especially those related to money, health and legal matters. Attempts to contact her are made by knocking three times on the front of her tomb marked Marie Glapion, her married name. Offerings of petition and gratitude are also left: traditionally salt water, seven dimes or her favorite, red anisette.*

Transmission of this power is constant. Transmission occurs independent of your mind and control. You can choose to be aware of these forces and manipulate them for your benefit and that of your loved ones. Because you don't acknowledge them doesn't mean that they do not affect you, any more than not acknowledging the flu guarantees that you won't get sick. Awareness of these forces shouldn't make you feel passive or hopeless but energized. The healthy presence of this power on Earth can only be good for us. There is an infinite quantity. Because someone else has a lot doesn't mean you get less.

These powers are not generic. Because a horse has power and a camel has power doesn't mean that they have identical or interchangeable powers. The beauty of this power, the beauty and power of magic, comes in the details. Your power is unique and by expressing that power positively, you are a valuable asset to Earth. No two powers are exactly identical, although many share characteristics, and the most powerful, whether belonging to humans, plants, animals or spirit beings, are amazingly versatile. The key to magic is recognizing the existence of these powers, determining which ones are most beneficial for you and manipulating them in a positive fashion to achieve happiness and success.

You already possess the ability to recognize those powers and to distinguish between them. Consider, for example, the rose. Since ancient times, roses have played a major function in healing, cosmetics and spirituality. Roses were associated with some of the grandest female divinities: Aphrodite, Cybele and Juno. Sufi poets used the rose to represent the highest spiritual ideals. In medieval Europe, roses were considered so powerful that one was expected to beg permission from the plant before daring to pluck a blossom. The rose was picked neither haphazardly nor carelessly but with respect. Indeed, roses do not give themselves easily. The family of roses is characterized by visual beauty, heavenly fragrance *and* thorns. Those who have only received florists' roses, all thorns carefully removed, have not experienced the full power of a rose.

This power is holistic. Roses have something to give humans on every possible level. Their therapeutic oil preserves and protects aging or delicate skin. As used in modern aromatherapy, essential oil of rose is indicated for a wide range of physical ills. Rose's spiritual and emotional effects are equally profound. The scent of rose assuages grief. The worst, most painful grief, grief beyond the realm of language, can be soothed by the healing fragrance of roses. This doesn't mean that just smelling or beholding roses will instantly make everything fine and whole again. Those are the false expectations that lead to inertia. Healing, like magical aptitude, is accomplished in increments, step-by-step. A walk through a fragrant rose garden or the scent of rose attar serves as an elevator, uplifting the spirit at least one level from wherever it was, for most individuals. (Remember, *nothing* works for everyone!)

You may or may not have been aware of the technical properties of roses or their spiritual history before you read them here, but I guarantee that you do not need anyone to tell you this: a bouquet of roses is not the same as any old bouquet of flowers. Roses indicate love, romance, desire. How do you increase the power? By number. Whether you receive five, seven or eight roses may be immaterial but make that number a dozen and a powerful message is sent.

Alternatively, one single rose speaks very loudly of love and admiration. A desperate, yet often successful bid to win back a lost love is to fill an entire room with roses. In fact, roses are invaluable components of love spells from all over Earth.

In the metaphysical science of numbers, twelve signals completeness, totality.

Let's consider another plant now, one that's also probably very familiar to you and which is also universally prized for the strength of its power. This plant, too, communicates with you via your olfactory senses, although this plant is far more modest in cost and appearance than the luxurious rose. It's garlic.

One question: knowing nothing else, would you use garlic as a chief component within a spell for romance? If you couldn't afford roses, would garlic be your substitution of choice? I think not. You don't need anyone to tell you that, in fact, garlic is rarely, if ever, a component of romantic spells.

Garlic's chief magical role is as a protective device. Hmong householders use the number four to enhance that power, hanging four heads of garlic at the door for protection. Other communities prefer braids—often of twelve garlic heads rather than just any random quantity.

Interestingly, while garlic is not used for romantic spells, it is often a prime component in sexually oriented ones. Whereas roses can help you capture your true love and assure them of your devotion, it's that humble head of garlic that can help you keep those home fires burning bright. In situations where love and romance are not an issue but sex is problematic, garlic has proven beneficial, especially for couples of long standing where the existence of love and commitment is beyond doubt, but the male partners may be overworked, physically tired and/or emotionally drained.

Garlic is famed for reviving men's vitality and stamina and revitalizing their sexual energy. Records show that the workers who built Egypt's great pyramids were fed a daily ration of garlic to increase productivity. Pharaoh's rations of garlic may have kept construction of the pyramids on schedule; it also helped give him a plethora of baby Israelites to worry about.

Visualize your personal reaction to receiving a dozen beautiful, fragrant roses from the individual of your choice. Visualize also your reaction to sharing a single plate of a warm, delicious, garlic-redolent meal with someone whom you love, desire and, of course, with whom you feel completely comfortable. They're not identical feelings but both bring a glow of happiness and the sense that you are where you are intended to be.

Can you substitute plastic roses for that bouquet? Will handing your beloved a garlic tablet, carefully engineered to remove all trace of taste and smell, achieve the same ends? You knew those answers before you read the questions. So many have been trained to respect only the wisdom that comes through accredited formal education. You already possess the ability to recognize those magic powers in your bones. Learning to access and manipulate these powers is a sensuous intuitive process akin to cooking and, in fact, many of the most powerful magical practitioners are wonderful chefs as well. Not for nothing are witches so often depicted stirring a cauldron! Putting together an effective magical spell is a little like planning a great meal: determining which powers best complement which others in order to produce your desired effect. Are you creating a meal to impress future in-laws, ingratiate yourself to a boss or seduce a lover? You need to understand your intent and the power inherent in your tools. This is the basic theory of magic.

Garlic and roses can both be characterized as friendly, gregarious powers. They don't withhold information, it doesn't have to be coaxed out of them, they communicate loud and clear. Not every power is like that. The good news is that you don't have to discover each one for yourself. A vast library of traditional knowledge exists from which you can avail yourself of desired information.

EARTH MOTHER MAGIC

Some fifteen hundred years ago, the Teuton tribes of Northern Europe held an annual ceremony. At night, under the rays of the moon, a veiled statue of their preeminent female divinity was placed in a wagon. Her sacred cows were hitched to this wagon, which was pulled through the fields, as people assembled to greet and salute them. While this ceremony itself has obviously not been performed in centuries, vestigial memories of Herta or Eartha, as her name is sometimes spelled, remain. Her name resonates in our language as the name given to our planet, Earth.

We can't presume to understand all that this specific ritual meant to the Teutons nor precisely what their expectations might have been. Much of what we know about Teutonic ritual comes to us via descriptions written by Romans, themselves outsiders to the culture. The Romans tell us that this was a joyous time for the Teutons. Destruction and warfare were consciously and deliberately ceased, placed on hold, at least for the duration of the ritual. What we can recognize from our current distance is their attempt to unify and harmonize all the components of nature, all Earth's children, including plants, animals, spirits and people.

The Teutons did not confuse Herta with Earth. They were agricultural: they could distinguish between a spiritual entity and the dirt beneath their feet. Nor was she merely a personification of Earth. Rather, Herta served as an intermediary, a broker between Earth, humans and all Earth's other inhabitants, seeing to it that everyone's needs were met. Neither did the Teutons, or other early people, confuse the statue with the spiritual entity. They understood that humans created the statue. If the statue was damaged or destroyed, they realized that it did not destroy or damage the spirit. Rather this damage might indicate something significant about the relationship between people and spirit, perhaps one reason why conquerors destroy the representations of their enemies' spiritual allies with such force and glee.

Attitudes toward Herta changed over the centuries. From a benevolent intermediary, Herta evolved into a Queen of Witches, a spiritual entity to be feared and avoided. Earth's image evolved as well. No longer a *she* but an *it*, Earth became something to be conquered, mastered and controlled. No longer perceived as beneficially linked guides, providers and protectors, Earth and Herta became instead a source of danger and temptation.

This was paralleled in changing attitudes toward Earth's other children, the plants and animals. Animals became witches' familiars rather than potential friends and allies of all. As the witch craze overtook Europe, plants that had given healing and pleasure became illicit objects of fear. People became increasingly afraid to communicate with these forces that had served them so well for so long, although the true danger, in the form of torture, repression and murder, came not from plants or animals, but from other humans.

Attitudes toward women were shifting, too. Once considered a repository of holy fertility power, the ultimate magic, women's bodies became a source of shame, danger and sin. Jumping forward to the present day, the effects of these attitudes are palpable. Earth is badly damaged. Many species of plants and animals are extinct or endangered. Creatures who remain on Earth are having difficulty reproducing. Sperm counts among many species, including our own, have fallen drastically. Earth, abused and caged to the point where she cannot provide for her children, may be practicing her own birth control.

The damage to humanity transcends the physical. In the United States, as elsewhere on the globe, to be human now in the 21st century typically means to be lonely and disconnected. Modern child-rearing practices are wary of the influence and power of the mother. From the first breath, the infant is encouraged to separate from its mother, and vice versa. Attempting to foster independence, we have fostered isolation instead.

> The Lakota people, whose ancestral territory covered a large swath of
> the North American plains, possess a spiritual concept encapsulated in
> their phrase Mitakuye Oyasin. This translates into English as "all my
> relations." Implicit in this phrase is an affirmation that all creation
> is connected. The two-leggeds, the four-leggeds, snakes with no legs,
> birds, fish, plants, rocks, minerals, spirits: we are all relations.

Tribal peoples, and that counts for all our ancestors, some just a little farther back than others, recognized that in addition to a specific human mother, we all share a common mother. Earth, the planet, is the ultimate mother. Just as the child is separated from the human mother, we have camouflaged our Earth Mother with concrete and fences. However, just as the weeds continuously break through the concrete, so Earth continues to reach for us in the manner of the good mother who never stops trying to reunite with her missing children.

Although we have limited information about pre-Christian Teutonic society, we do know of another ceremony they possessed, a childbirth ritual. This was a ritual of immense simplicity. Immediately following birth, the cord having been cut, the baby was taken and laid upon the ground. The intent was to formally introduce the child to his or her own other mother, Earth, the mother whom we all share.

There are practitioners of herbal medicine who believe that Earth provides solutions and remedies for all our ills, if only we can discover them and understand how to apply them. Would-be magicians will find the same to be true: Whatever you require is already available within you or has been provided by Earth. Recognizing our tools and learning to use them are the true challenges.

COMMUNICATING WITH EARTH

If pure magic involves a dialogue between you and Earth, the most obvious question is how do we speak to her? How do we make ourselves heard? How do we receive our answers? How do we know that anything really transpired?

Although you may certainly speak to Earth, or any part of creation, in English or any other human language, it may not be the most efficient way, nor should you necessarily expect your response to come in that manner. There are various methods of shared communications that are far more effective:

- *You can communicate through fragrance.* Fragrance is the most primal, elemental form of communication, the one shared by plants, animals, humans and spirit beings. Smell remains the most mysterious of our senses, defying scientific explanations. The olfactory system, the part of your brain that processes scent, is lodged near the most ancient part of the brain. Fragrance stimulates the limbic system, which integrates mind, body, emotions and memory. This most mysterious of our senses is also typically the last to leave us, remaining active until the last breath. Humans communicate with each other through scent, signaling our romantic intentions through scents that we no longer have the aptitude to consciously smell with our noses, the pheromones. Fragrance transcends language. It bypasses the language filter; the message arrives directly in our hearts, bones and brains. The part of your brain that processes smells is intimately connected with the part that catalogs memories. Some find fragrance to be the key that opens hidden past life memories.

- *You can communicate through dreams.* The dream state refuses to be stifled and bound by the rigid literal confines we have imposed upon the rest of our existence. Dreams transcend language although dreams also delight in word games. Dreams are the threshold between concrete and psychic reality. Dreams are where spirits most willingly reveal themselves. Dreams are where you are most likely to receive communiqués from the Earth Mother and the relatives. You've very likely been receiving signals all your life, whether or not you consistently understood them, whether or not you sent back the response that you would have liked to. Remember, lack of response is a response, too.

- *You can communicate through symbols.* Symbols are the language you need for dreams and for two-way communication with the spirit realm and with those living beings among us who lack speech but still have something significant to say. Symbolic language transcends speech. You understand it as a reverberation in your brain, a knowing in your bones. It is fluid and simultaneously multilayered, rather than precise and rigid. You have the aptitude to relearn this language. I say relearn because once upon a time, all our ancestors possessed this capacity and somewhere, deep in your genetic code, the ability remains, waiting to be tapped.

Scientific studies indicate that literacy, beyond just teaching the ability to read, encourages the brain to function in different ways. Different areas of the brain are accessed and exercised while others are left to lie fallow. Both forms of thinking, linear literate and fluid symbolic, are necessary. Humans need access to both in order to be whole. We need essentially to be bilingual. You need literate thinking while you're driving. That traffic signal isn't a true symbol, it's shorthand, developed by literate minds, as well it should be. Imagine the disaster if that traffic signal meant something unique to everyone. Strictly literate thinking, however, limits your dreaming and magical capacity.

Symbols come in minute details and often use repetition as a means of showing emphasis. Magic doesn't accept the concept of coincidence, although every single repetition doesn't have equal significance. Symbols are not about what is but *what could be*.

To think symbolically is to read one's environment as carefully as a road map. Is that rabbit you suddenly see just a bunny? Well, yes it is, but maybe it's also the harbinger of fertility that you've been waiting for, the message from Earth that your body is ready, go home and make love. Perhaps that rabbit is an omen of good luck: rabbits have strong associations with gambling. If that rabbit is lying dead in the road, maybe this isn't the weekend for that Las Vegas trip. Is that rabbit a messenger from the Siberian spirit Kaltes come to tell you that your petition has been received? Perhaps it's Kaltes herself coming to see you, in the form of her sacred animal. You don't have to look very hard for these signs. Once you get a dialogue going, they'll come to you.

> *Harming none includes not harming yourself. No matter what kind of a human mother you may have had, your Earth Mother wants you to fulfill your potential, be healthy, comfortable and happy and be a source of pride to her and all your relations.*

Even if you feel unable to express yourself through symbols, you should at least be able to recognize symbolic language because this is likely how Earth will talk to you. Perhaps she's been speaking to you for years but you haven't been able to pick up the messages. If you've previously attempted some magic and found yourself unsuccessful, this is a common cause. If you are putting out requests, but then seemingly ignore the reply, ultimately the reply stops. It is important that you realize that you are not inconsequential, that you're worthy of two-way dialogue with Earth and all her powers. Every power has its place in the cosmos, including yours.

Sometimes symbols embody our hopes and dreams. Imagine the woman who wants to lose weight and has taped a picture of a very skimpy bathing suit onto her refrigerator door. That symbol is more than just a reminder. Gazed upon, it may have the power to prevent the dieter from opening the freezer door and eating that ice cream. The symbol translates the dream into concrete form and can help make the dream a reality.

WHAT YOU WON'T FIND
IN THIS BOOK

There are no spells included in this book that intentionally set out to harm others. There are no revenge spells, no "getting back at people who've hurt you" spells. If you're looking for those spells, there are plenty of other places to find them. They are published in many books but, frankly, save your money: with only a little magic under your belt, you'll fast find that knowledge within yourself.

Resist the impulse. The most powerful magicians have always been characterized by self-restraint and for good reason. Another universal magical tenet is that magical energy possesses something of a boomerang effect. Whatever sort of energy you put out into the atmosphere comes straight back to you, multiplied several times over. Imagine, once you really get powerful, the force of your magical returns. Wouldn't you really prefer to have positive energy bombarding you rather than the opposite?

Habitually sending forth destructive energy ultimately has dangerous and unpredictable repercussions for you and yours. So, even if you can, desist. If you fear malevolent energy has been invoked against you, there are good, effective methods for simply blocking the hex and returning-to-sender that will not incur any further damage to you. Check this book's section on Protection Spells. The other spells that have been deliberately excluded are spells that involve sacrificing animals or that use their body parts as materials. It's not necessary to point the finger at specific cultures: more cultures than not share in this tradition. Nor is this the moment to discuss whether these spells even work. Their effectiveness or lack thereof is not the point. That discussion veers dangerously close to the rationale frequently presented about how awful it is that the tiger may soon be extinct because poachers kill them for primitive medicines that don't work. Would it be any less tragic if these items did work? Isn't the loss of the tiger's presence enough? Whether those items or products or spells work or not is irrelevant; they will no longer work for us. The damage to Earth and the damage that humans have caused other species has wreaked havoc upon a sacred balance. The potential for long-term harm, for you as well as the animal, is greater than any short-term success.

A PSYCHIC GLOSSARY:
SOME MAGIC VOCABULARY WORDS

Alive: In the hospital, heartbeat, pulse, breath and EKG measure life, the quality of being alive. In magic, when something is referred to as *alive* or *living*, that isn't necessarily what is meant. While water is "living," no one is suggesting that you search for a literal pulse. The magical definition is broader:

- If something occurs naturally on Earth, whether plant, animal, human, element, stone or metal, that something is considered *alive*.

- If something radiates any degree of magical force or energy (*baraka*), that being is considered *alive*.

- Anything that is alive is unique, has a potential for power and cannot be totally predicted.

- If something can be recreated so that there are identical, indistinguishable specimens, and if that something is completely predictable, it is *not* alive, it lacks life. Lacking life, it contains no power, no innate magic.

Aphrodisiac: Something (usually food or fragrance) with the power to stimulate and enhance sexual desire and/or performance. Don't confuse these with love potions or fertility brews: Aphrodisiacs are about sex, pure and simple. Anything else is just an added bonus.

The concept of the aphrodisiac is named in honor of Aphrodite. Aphrodisiacs were considered to be her gifts to people. The finest are considered to share something of her essence, her power and her energy.

There is also such a thing as an **anaphrodisiac**, which has the opposite effect. Anaphrodisiacs reduce sexual interest, thoughts and sometimes ability. Anaphrodisiacs may be beneficial to those walking a celibate path, temporarily or not, voluntary or not.

Some substances can go either way. Lavender, for instance, has a reputation as both an aphrodisiac and its opposite. Some schools of thought claim that men find the scent of lavender irresistible, while others recommend that lavender be used when you wish to *discourage* someone's attentions. The truth is that aphrodisiacs, like so much magic, are highly specific and individualized. Chemical interactions are highly personal and so you will find individuals to vouch for either affect.

The only way to discover the effect of a specific aphrodisiac upon you or your intended is to try it out for yourself. Have fun playing. Personal tastes and experiences influence which aphrodisiacs are best for you. If the object of your affections has allergies to seafood, forget about oysters.

Some Famous Aphrodisiacs!

Caviar	Henna	Mint	Saffron
Champagne	Hibiscus	Onions	Shellfish
Chocolate	Honey	Radishes	Sushi
Garlic	Jasmine	Roses	Vanilla

Botanica: Latin-American stores offering a variety of spiritual, herbal and magical supplies. Often a good source for herbs, oils and candles. Not long ago, botanicas were confined to immigrant enclaves, but it's now difficult to find an urban area without at least one. Botanicas have become sufficiently mainstream that in many communities they have their own category in the phone book. To some extent, botanicas now fill the marketing void left by the demise of the once-thriving hoodoo mail-order industry.

Evil Eye: Oh, that Evil Eye! Is there such a thing? Well, if there isn't, an awful lot of energy is exerted worldwide trying to avoid and repel it. The Evil Eye is the name that embodies the generic evils and dangers that threaten humans on Earth. It doesn't necessarily have anything to do with eyes literally. The Evil Eye is jealousy and malice, a destructive, negative force. Sometimes it originates in spirit sources; however often humans are to blame. The Evil Eye isn't necessarily meant malevolently: those who cast it may do so inadvertently and unwillingly.

There are two paths to avoiding the Evil Eye.

1. Avoid bragging and boasting about one's good fortune so as not to attract dangerous attention.

2. The best defense is a good offense: a powerful, deflecting amulet. Wear, hang or carry as needed.

Fertility: In industrialized Western societies, much emphasis is placed on women not getting pregnant at the wrong time. Historically, and even today in much of the world, the emphasis is otherwise: this is reflected in the multitude of magical spells and rituals whose goal is to allow women to conceive more-or-less when they choose. Fertility spells are not limited to literal pregnancy, however: use them to remove any creative block or achieve any creative goal.

Infusion: The process by which one medium is encouraged to permeate another, usually herbs in water or oil. The most famous infusion of all is your basic cup of tea, and if you can make a cup of tea with leaves rather than a tea bag, then you already know a good deal about making an infusion. Infusions allow you to insert true botanical powers into your magic potions, enchanted bath or floor wash.

The standard recipe for a water infusion is one teaspoon of dried herb or one-and-one-half teaspoons of fresh herb to every cup of boiling water. Maintain that same proportion **even if** using a combination of herbs, unless otherwise advised. Put the herbs into a nonreactive pot or container, pour the water over the botanical material and leave it to brew for a period of time, usually between five and fifteen minutes. Following the brewing period, the herbs are usually strained from the water.

The process of creating **infused oils** is slightly more complicated but still easily adaptable to your kitchen. The standard proportion suggests that for every cup of oil, you will need one ounce of fresh herbs or one half ounce of dried. Unless otherwise advised, do not exceed that proportion, even if using a combination of herbs, as a balance needs to be maintained.

1. Pour the oil over the herbs into a stainless steel bowl.

2. Heat over simmering water, either in a true double boiler or an improvised water bath, a saucepan one-quarter filled with water. The bowl with the herbs must not sit on the bottom of the pot but float in the water. The process needs constant supervision for safety. Keep the

oil covered. Stir once in a while and simmer gently for thirty minutes. Make sure the oil doesn't get too hot because if it smokes, bubbles or burns, an acrid fragrance can develop, spoiling your infusion.

3. Allow the oil to cool and then strain out the herbal material through four layers of cheesecloth or another fine nonmetal strainer. Strain twice if necessary: all herbal material must be removed to prevent the oil from turning rancid.

4. If an infusion-spell includes essential oils or flower essences for enhancement, they should be added at the end, when the oil has been strained and is cool.

- A crockpot can be used instead of the water bath. Maintain the same proportions and leave on low heat for two hours. Strain as above.

- If you can depend upon some consistently warm, sunny weather, you can go real low-tech but high power and create an infusion through solar power. Place the herbs in a jar with a tight-fitting lid and pour the oil over them. The herbs must be completely covered. Add one tablespoon of apple cider vinegar. Leave the jar to sit in the warm sun all day and in a warm cupboard at night for two weeks. Strain as above.

Psychic Shield Infused Oil

Rub this oil into your body or add it to your bath, to bestow psychic protection before embarking on any magical work and also to replenish psychic energy or to repair a damaged aura.

> ¼ ounce dried St. John's Wort
>
> ¼ ounce dried yarrow
>
> (if using fresh herbs, increase proportion to ½ ounce of each herb)
>
> 1 cup sunflower oil
>
> 6 drops essential oil of rosemary
>
> 4 drops angelica flower essence (FES, Green Hope, Pegasus)

Use any of the three methods above (water bath, crockpot or solar) to create an infused oil. Strain the botanicals well. If St. John's Wort blossoms (rather than just the dried leaves) have been used, your oil may display a pretty, red hue. Pour the infused oil into a bottle. Add up to six drops of essential oil of rosemary as well as the flower essence. Close the bottle and roll gently to blend.

If you are making large quantities of infused oils that you wish to store, it's best to add a natural preservative. One-quarter teaspoon simple tincture of benzoin, available from many pharmacies, can be added per cup of infused oil. Benzoin is prepared from the gum of the styrax, an Indonesian tree, considered to have sacred properties and often burnt as cleansing incense. (Make sure that you have simple tincture of benzoin, not compound tincture, also known as Friar's Balsam.)

Occult: *Occult* means "hidden" or "secret." Occult usually refers to some magical or spiritual knowledge that may not be well-known. It is a neutral term, neither positive nor negative and certainly not a synonym for "evil."

Oracle: *Oracle* means "answer," the ability to receive needed information about the future right now in the present. There are spiritual entities who possess this power and can provide direction and answers. Some are also able to bestow this ability upon a person. In the most famous case, Apollo gave this gift to the Trojan princess Cassandra, with the proviso that no one would ever believe her impeccably accurate predictions.

The simplest oracle of all comes courtesy of the Greek divine spirit Hermes, a ruler of communication. Centuries ago, people would enter his shrine, make an offering, carefully phrase a question, then stop up their ears and leave. At some point, shortly after, they would open their ears and the first words they heard were considered the oracle's response. Hermes no longer has active public shrines, but you can still utter a petition or make him a small gift. A pyramid of stones calls him. Give yourself a cue for when to open your ears. Count to 100, for instance, and then open your ears or look for a visual cue. When you see the color red or see a bird fly, that could be your signal that the oracle is ready. Words uttered by children are considered extra powerful and prophetic.

Prosperity: A common goal of magical spells, prosperity doesn't mean that you're guaranteed to win millions of dollars and do nothing but what pleases you for the rest of your life. Prosperity indicates that you have enough to fulfill your needs, beyond bare-bones needs, enough to feel comfortable and relaxed even if you're not rich beyond your wildest dreams. Prosperity doesn't have to mean cash; there are spells for when you specifically need money. Prosperity indicates a level of material comfort and independence. Prosperity has always been considered a reasonable and realistic magical goal.

Root Magic: Different spells use different parts of plants, but roots, which lie buried in Earth, are considered particularly magical. The most powerful plants have the most powerful roots and some are extremely potent indeed. Different roots are used for different purposes. **Adam and Eve root,** for instance, which resembles its namesake, is used to draw love, while **Angelica root,** also known as **Archangel root** because knowledge of its use was a gift from the Archangel Michael, bestows healing and protection to all, as well as extra power for women. You'll find some other roots, the **Devil's Shoestrings** and **High John the Conqueror,** discussed in greater detail in the Spells part of the book.

Root magic is tremendously ancient. The Jewish Bible records Leah and Rachel's squabble over possession of a prized mandrake root, said to draw both love and fertility. (The Bible incidentally records mandrake as a success story, attesting to its power.)

Today many magical root plants are terribly endangered. Because it's easier to destroy the plant to obtain the root, indiscriminate harvesting has decimated many of these species. In addition, many spells require roots to be chopped into small pieces. In this form they are fairly unrecognizable. Dishonest merchants prey on people's desires by substituting other plants. If you've purchased what is marketed as mandrake in the United States, it's most likely you've actually bought mayapple, also a plant used in enchantments but not the same thing, not as rare and certainly not worthy of mandrake prices. Even worse, artificial and/or petroleum products are frequent substitutes.

The best way to be confident that your roots are genuine is to be familiar with its aroma and appearance. What *should* it look like, what *should* it smell like? **Lucky Hand Root** *(Dactylorhiza orchids)*, for instance, looks like a tiny human hand with too many fingers. Those extra fingers are believed to help you catch whatever it is that you need. For complete security and power, cultivate your own root plants or purchase roots only from reputable vendors.

Shaman: Don't be confused by the last three letters of the word. *Shaman* names a function, not a gender and the earliest shamans were women. A shaman is not synonymous with witch or fortune-teller although some individuals may be all, or some, of the above. The magical abilities possessed by a shaman are among the most profound. A shaman can soul-travel to different dimensions, the spirit land, the realm of the dead. Through this ability, which may take years to master, they can perform healings and soul retrievals, receive and deliver messages and, very importantly, return safely.

Threshold: A *threshold* is a border area where one force, power or element meets another. There are borders and thresholds everywhere. The seashore is the most prominent example, the transitional area where ocean meets land. There are thresholds in your home: the windows and doors, for instance. There are thresholds in time: New Year's Eve, your birthday, midnight. Twilight and dawn are thresholds: you can feel the energy of the incoming power but the old power hasn't departed yet. There are thresholds on your body: your mouth is the threshold between thought and speech.

Women's Thresholds

In many cultures, the time immediately preceding menstruation is considered a powerful threshold. Rather than negative associations of "PMS," traditional cultures perceived the premenstrual period as a time of great psychic potential. A young girl's first period, as well as the entry into menopause, are also considered powerful, yet vulnerable, thresholds, a time to expand one's power but also to nourish one's well-being. The Warundi people from East Africa have a ceremony that celebrates a girl's first surge of female power: upon the occasion of her first menstruation, the girl's grandmother leads her through their home so that she may touch every object in order to imbue it with the special holiness now upon her.

Thresholds are simultaneously areas of great power and extreme vulnerability. A tremendous percentage of amulets and rituals are created specifically to protect thresholds.

Wicca: Deriving from the same source as *wisdom, wise* and *witch,* "Wicca" refers to the modern Earth-centered spiritual traditions based upon ancient Celtic roots, and focused upon enhancing personal power through harmonious existence with all of nature.

Vodou, Voodoo, Hoodoo: Confused? Well, although some people do use these words synonymously, no, they're not the same. *Vodou* literally means "spirit" in the Fon language of West Africa but the word is now commonly used to name the spiritual traditions of the descendents of the Fon people who were enslaved in Haiti. Because their faith has been ridiculed, vilified and stereotyped by outsiders and because the word *Voodoo* is often used pejoratively, some practitioners prefer the spelling "Vodou" to "Voodoo." *Voodoo,* however is also used to distinguish the specific traditions that emerged in New Orleans following the emigration in the nineteenth century of many Haitian refugees and the word has been used in that sense within this book.

Hoodoo, on the other hand, is American magic. Based largely on African practices, Hoodoo evolved in America's melting pot. Enslaved African magicians, healers and shamans unable to access their old materials, learned a whole new botanical repertoire from Native Americans. Eventually, elements of Freemasonry, Kabbalah and Spiritism were incorporated, too.

The first half of the twentieth century saw the rise of Hoodoo as a business enterprise. Although rural populations may have easy access to botanical materials, urban dwellers typically do not. In response to massive urban migration, commercial manufacturing and marketing of Hoodoo magic products developed. Specific, generic formulas developed: "Boss Fix" if you were having trouble at work, for instance, or "Kiss Me Now!" for those feeling lonely. Formulas were available as oils, soaps, powders and floor wash, in much the same way as if you were to go to a perfume counter, a fragrance might be available as perfume, cologne, dusting powder or soap.

> *Floor washes are botanical infusions, which are strained and then added to a bucket of rinse water along with some vinegar for cleaning your floor. Different recipes serve different purposes: cleansing, protection or romance, for example. Check among the spells for some samples. If you're looking only to freshen the atmosphere a bit, you can allow someone else to clean your floor, but if you need real magical energy, you must do it yourself.*

Many of the old formulas are still available, although they are often sold as novelty products, complete with lurid packaging. Because the creators may not take the product seriously, there's no telling exactly what's in those cute little vials. If you really want the stuff to work as intended, buy from a reputable dealer or go back to the roots and mix up your own. Formulas are easily concocted at home. You'll find variations of some of the most popular among this book's spells.

THE FOUR ELEMENTS

In the West, Earth's power is traditionally broken down into four components known as the elements: air, earth, fire and water. (Okay, in China they count *five* elements, including metal, but let's not worry about that yet.) Air and fire are usually considered masculine energies while earth and water are most typically perceived as feminine. Life springs from earth and water, but air and fire are necessary to spark the process and to provide health and vitality. From a magical standpoint, the power of each element is unique, specific and alive.

Each element, separately or in combination, can serve as a vehicle for spiritual and physical healing. Power comes in the interplay of the elements. Power is enhanced when the elements intermingle and form a threshold: air and fire, fire and water, earth and water. Thus steam, emerging from the marriage of fire and water, is a particularly potent vehicle of healing energy.

Earth

Earth is the battery, the generator. She provides stability, security, a grounding influence and the capacity for growth. In a wide selection of multicultural traditions, Earth is the material from which humans are created. Unfortunately, in English, there is confusion between the dirt that is "dirty," unclean, a must to avoid, and the dirt that we trod upon. Avoiding Earth depletes our energy, as Earth is a cleansing force that revitalizes and purifies.

Simply being in physical contact with Earth can be healing and grounding. There are also many traditions of packing an ailing individual into hot dirt or sand for spiritual and physical healing. Mud packs can do more than improve the complexion. Although not yet as popular as aromatherapy or hydrotherapy, the ancient use of clay as a therapeutic material is currently undergoing a revival.

Anything alive is unique and distinct. Just as each person is an individual, Earth's dirt is not generic and identical: Dead Sea mud is used to soothe aching joints, moor mud for cleansing toxins from the body, whereas bentonite clay is used to soothe assorted skin ailments. Dirt can be pure magic, too: Thousands of pilgrims flock annually to New Mexico's Shrine of Chimayo to gather small quantities of the miraculous earth found there whose healing powers are reputed to fix everything from broken bodies to broken spirits and even, on occasion, broken computers.

- Plants and botanicals contain the concentrated essence of Earth Magic. Create magical gardens outside on Earth or inside in pots to further your magical goals.

Air

Air serves as a transmitter and messenger. Air affects health, creativity and the capacity for hope. Magical philosophy (and some schools of upper physics, too!) asserts that nothing truly disappears, so the phrase "vanish into thin air" is meant somewhat literally. When you burn a candle, thin air is where the energy goes; your wish enters the atmosphere with the smoke.

Fragrance is the language of air. Direct inhalation of essential oils or the smoke from botanical materials is the simplest method of using air to heal. Smoke from a smoldering dried herb bundle cleanses the aura and soothes an uneasy mind. Fueled by water and fire, saunas, steam baths and sweat lodges nourish the soul as well as healing the body.

- Use fragrance via oils and incense to send smoke signals to your magical allies.

Water

Water is where life originates, not just as an abstract concept but literally for each of our individual lives. We first emerge into consciousness in our mothers' wombs, floating in water and salt. Our first experience of sound is filtered through amniotic fluids. Our first familiar motion, ideally indicative of safety and security, consists of rolling waves of water. Babies carried on their mother's hips or backs transition gently to solid Earth.

Fairy tales recount adventures searching for the "water of life." Many of Earth's most ancient shrines have been located near sacred springs, the mineral content of the water providing therapeutic benefits while the element itself nurtures body and soul. Hydrotherapy, healing through water, is a universally ancient practice currently in revival. Each source of healing water is distinct and unique, nor do they all serve the same function. Celtic water shrines were once famed throughout Europe for healing eye diseases. The Moulay-Yacoub shrine, at the foot of the Rif Mountains of Morocco, is now updated with modern medical facilities, to take advantage of its venerable reputation for healing gynecological disorders. On the other hand, a stay at the cold springs of Jesenik in the Czech Republic is prescribed for soothing neuroses, psychoses and psychic disorders. You may have your own favorite wishing well, proven to grant your secret desires.

- Water magic is performed in your bathtub and by creating magical floor washes and room sprays.

Fire

Fire, too, purifies but in a very different manner. Fire heals and energizes and is profoundly independent. Fire defies human illusions of control. Fire possesses a transformative energy and must always be treated with respect. Fire can be a beneficial, helpful, healing element but the potential for danger always exists. The fact that you're engaged in magic doesn't mean you can ignore standard safety rules.

When you are cleansed with the smoke of with burning herbs and you can actually see, hear, and smell the fire, not to mention feel the occasional spark, it is not only the botanicals that are performing the healing. Fire, too, revives and recharges us, albeit from a greater distance than the other elements.

- Create enchanted candles to further your magical goals.

Though the human body is composed largely of water, your psychic nature may be linked to any of the elements. Ultimately each individual's chemistry is unique. As you are inspired to do magic, you may find yourself pulled toward working with specific elements. You will be drawn to your allies. For many, magic is candlework, while others can only envision enchantments performed in the tub. Some call their desires through fragrant smoke signals while still others are drawn to Earth, creating patches of transformative, healing energy. The elements that you are drawn to indicate something significant about your own power.

COLORS

Repeat after me: *There are no bad colors.* There are no inherently negative or positive, good or bad colors. Each radiates with its own power and energy. There may be colors that you prefer over others. There may be colors that resonate most deeply for you. There may be colors that are more or less beneficial for you personally, but colors themselves are neutral in value. Each has its place in the cosmos. Each has its place in magic. It's important that you have an understanding of the powers that radiate from each color, so that you'll know which to choose for your own personal spells. All colors have a protective aspect, although each may be most effective protecting different areas. Each color also serves as a magnet for different gifts. Need to burn a money candle? You need a green candle, right? But what about a justice candle? Choose colors for candles but also for color-baths, crystals, gemstones, clothing, surroundings and amulets.

A specific color may mean something special to you. A color may have associations that resonate only for you. It's your magic: allow your instincts and intuition free reign.

Black: Comfort. Associated Element: Earth.

Black indicates fertility, the promise of the richest, most powerfully fertile Earth. Black is the color of regeneration and life eternal, indicating potential for future growth. The Egyptians painted statues black to indicate the immortality of the subject. Black absorbs and blocks pain and evil, providing a protective cloak of comfort and safety.

- Harness the power of the color black for fertility spells and for petitions to heal those who are chronically ill. Black candles are considered the most beneficial for repelling evil intentions while black crystals create psychic shields.

Blue: Protection. Associated Elements: Air and Water.

Blue protects, heals and relaxes. Blue provides peace and tranquility. Blue soothes psychic and emotional pain, in particular, traumatic stress. Blue is not only for boys; traditionally it's the color associated with the power of the Great Mother, from Mary's cloak to Yemaya's beads.

- Blue is traditionally the most important protective color, particularly in regard to thresholds. A blue bead worn at your throat protects you from saying "the wrong thing."

- Borrow a household custom familiar from the Himalayas to Native North America, the Middle East to the Mediterranean: Paint your doors, window frames and/or ceilings blue for spiritual protection.

- Blue assists in breaking the chains of bad habits. Burn blue candles to reinforce your commitment to terminate a detrimental addiction.

Brown: Stability. Associated Element: Earth.

Earth comes in an endless palette of colors, from pure black to red to pink to yellow to pure white. However, Earth most typically appears in some variation of brown as does skin, bark and fur. Brown is a color of tremendous force and potency. Brown is the color of stability and gravity, the literal kind, the kind that keeps you attached to Earth. Brown is the color that embodies hard reality; it's an essential color for those who practice extensive psychic or intellectual work because it keeps you grounded. Brown heals, nurtures, empowers and is the color of creative potential.

- Surround yourself with brown energy to preserve and reinforce your personal power in the midst of long, draining projects.

- Brown is the color of justice. Brown candles are traditionally burned for assistance during legal procedures.

Green: Growth. Associated Elements: Earth and Water.

Green indicates fertility, prosperity and growth. Green also has the power to heal. It has close associations with blue, and there are many ambiguous shades, such as teal or aquamarine that blend their energies. However, while blue is used to soothe psychic and emotional trauma, green is resolutely physical. Its power is often invoked for healing serious physical ailments including cancer.

- Use green candles, baths and crystals in spells for employment, to get cash and, in general, for anything that you wish to increase in your life.

Purple: Power. Associated Element: Fire.

Purple is the color of royalty and spiritual authority. Long ago, natural purple dye was painstakingly coaxed from murex snail shells along the Mediterranean coast. Rare and expensive, the color purple was reserved for royalty or for those held in the highest esteem, the high priestess of a spiritual cult, for instance. Today, anyone can wear purple to bolster and enhance psychic energy.

- Purple is also associated with sexual pleasure. If you can't decide what color silk sheets to buy, you might consider purple. Purple candles are used in the most amorous of love spells.

Red: Luck. Associated Elements: Fire and Earth.

Many consider red to be the most profound magical color. Certainly, it's the color most associated with luck. Red is the color of birth and death. In Western culture, red is often associated with men and with violent imagery: blood indicating injury and death. Yet red belongs to the female principle most of all as the color of blossoming life. Red is the color of primal female power, of menstrual blood, whose arrival indicates that the gates of fertility are open. Babies arrive amidst blood, although no injury exists. Red indicates strength, vitality, health, passion, courage and sex.

Red beseeches the blessings of the Earth Mother as well as your personal ancestral spirits. Red is a defiant color, proclaiming survival and demanding attention.

- Harness the power of red to enhance your personal power, your vitality and to protect as you transition over thresholds, particularly those having to do with marriage, birth and children.

- Pink demonstrates red's gentler aspects. Pink is especially beneficial for spells involving children and new romance.

> *Different colors are associated with specific spiritual entities. Here are a few examples:*
> **BLACK:** *Baron Samedi (Haiti), Kali (India), Lono (Hawaii), Min (Egypt)*
> **BLUE:** *Tanit (Berber), Yemaya (Yoruba)*
> **BROWN:** *Babalu-Ayé (West Africa), Ochossi (Yoruba)*
> **GREEN:** *The Green Man (England), Neith (Egypt), Wadjet (Egypt)*
> **PURPLE:** *Dionysus (Eurasia), Maman Brigitte (Haiti), Oya (Yoruba)*
> **RED:** *Pele (Hawaii), Set (Egypt), Shango (Yoruba)*
> **WHITE:** *Artemis (Greece), Ix Chel (Maya), Mami Waters (West/Central Africa), Obatala (Yoruba), Poliahu (Hawaii)*
> **YELLOW:** *Amaterasu (Japan), Aine (Ireland), Laka (Hawaii), Lakshmi (India), Oshun (Yoruba)*

White: Creativity. Associated Elements: Air and Fire.

White is a color, not the absence of color, in magical terms. White is, in fact, a very intense color, the color of bone, the color of extended exposure to the hot sun as well as the color of ice, snow and intense cold. Just as a white piece of paper beckons your creative instincts, white offers you the power of a blank slate upon which to project your desires and dreams.

- White is especially beneficial for candles and spells to initiate new projects. Keep a healthy stock of white candles on hand for spontaneous spells, as white may also be used for any purpose in candlework, substituted for any other color, if necessary. If you don't have the time to run out and get a purple candle, for instance, use a white one.

- White is traditionally the color of the moon. Use white crystals, candles and clothes when you wish to draw down some moon magic.

Yellow: Romance. Associated Elements: Earth and Fire.

Yellow is the color of the sun. It's a joyous, happy color indicative of growth, communication and intellect, a color of wealth and spiritual harmony. In ancient China, the color yellow was reserved solely for the emperor. The yellow dye obtained from saffron is used to indicate spiritual maturity in Asia.

- Yellow is associated with romance as it's the color most frequently associated with the most powerful spirits of love. Harness the power of yellow for romantic enchantments. A yellow candle will kindle new love. A yellow color bath can help you learn to love yourself.

SUPPLIES

What are you likely to find in a well-stocked magical pantry? What's really on a witch's grocery list? Now that you know you can do magic, do you need to buy anything? Probably not! Odds are, almost everything that you need is already on your shelves.

This doesn't mean that you shouldn't travel to all ends of Earth, searching out rare and precious treasures. If you have the means and the time and desire for some adventures, pack up the caravan and hit the road! However, don't ever feel that your inability to do this presents roadblocks to your magical career.

Magic is intended to improve your finances, relieve your stress and make you happier with yourself and your life, not create any of the opposite reactions. If you *can* spend a lot of money on your magic, feel free. There's a lot of fun, powerful stuff you can buy. It's very tempting to spend a fortune on flowers and oils. There are precious gems whose price is well beyond the range of most, but potent magic can still be made from what are to us the most mundane of materials. Don't ever let the assumption that you need rare and expensive ingredients and accoutrements prevent you from accessing your magic power.

There are sources that will advise you that in order to truly perform magic, you will need special equipment. You may need a special cape, a special knife, a cauldron or a special type of broomstick. If this suits you, fine. If this information resonates for you, collect whatever supplies you need but be aware that this represents only one of Earth's many magical traditions. There is no one right way to practice magic. Every culture on Earth has developed valid and powerful magical techniques. What these techniques have in common are a way of seeing, a way of perceiving and benefiting from Earth's energies. What *things* they use, what ingredients they possess, depend upon a lot of circumstances.

There are sources that will tell you that it is imperative that you have specially consecrated tools only to be used for magical purposes. There are sources that will tell you that it's vital that you have specially consecrated space only to be accessed for magical work. These sources may be in possession of some very powerful magic but I'm not sure which planet it's from. It's certainly not from Earth where an urban witch may share a small apartment with her family, where economics may necessitate that one tool serve many purposes. That sort of magic also encourages the false view that magic is somehow not part of real life, but separate, apart and distinct.

The reality is that there is no traditional culture on Earth, the cultures that have preserved so much Earth Magic, that bestows as much private space as we in the industrialized West already possess. So don't worry: whatever privacy and space you already possess will be sufficient for your magic.

As for special magical tools, well, there may be times when you need them, but in general, consider that any magical work that you do imbues your daily tools with a sanctity that will spread into any other area where you use them. The magical knowledge of the nomadic Wodaabe people is renowned throughout Western Africa. There are no U-Hauls for the Wodaabe. All the possessions of even the wealthiest Wodaabe tribesman must fit on the back of a couple of camels or donkeys with room left for the kids to ride.

Don't worry too much about finding space for your work. I have seen beautiful altars squeezed onto bathroom counters and onto car dashboards, too. The majority of your work will likely be accomplished in either the kitchen or the bathroom. A corner of any other room can work, too.

Not only do we have more space and privacy than ever before, we also have greater access to a wider variety of rare and magical ingredients than ever before. We have powerfully charged items right under our noses. The trick is in recognizing them. Part of the problem is that our concept of the exotic has become distorted. Many of the magical items that once were found only at the ends of Earth are now so readily available that they seem downright ordinary. Shopping for magical ingredients has become easy. Once upon a time, salt was an exotic item. True honey was obtained only at great physical risk. Columbus sailed the ocean blue looking for a better way to obtain spices. Today, even frankincense and myrrh, once the world's most precious substances, can be purchased in most good health food stores.

Most of the power objects that you need are already in front of you. You may handle them daily without recognizing them for what they are. There are very few magical necessities that cannot be purchased from a reasonably well-stocked supermarket or toy store. What can't be bought often can be grown. Seed catalogs offer us a variety of plants previously available only to royalty.

Magic is not compatible with multitasking. If you perform your spells while simultaneously walking on the treadmill, talking on the cell phone and keeping an ear cocked for the fax machine, it may not be the quality of the materials that prevents your spell from succeeding. This is the reason emergency spells work so well: your intense desire, focus and fear turn the key to success. Ideally, you can train yourself to harness that intensity of focus without requiring an emergency to spark your fire.

The Most Important Ingredient

There is only one ingredient in your magical work that brooks no substitutions and that is *you*, your energy, your presence. You are the most vital component of any enchantment. What you bring to magic are your own desires and focus and no price can be placed upon them. Your energy and power are unique. No one else can substitute for you. The more you give of yourself, the greater your success will be.

Following is a list of the basics that you are most likely to use in your magical practice.

Don't let the lack of any one article or item create a hurdle for you. You can almost always make substitutions. Improvise. Your own goals determine what you really need versus what would be kind of fun to have. For instance, those wishing to work extensively with plant allies may need some gardening tools. If that path isn't for you, then neither are the tools.

The most crucial magical tools of all are your hands. They transmit your personal energy and receive it from others. They can't do this if you keep them at a distance from your materials. Wherever it's possible and safe, touch your materials, handle them, let your hands do the mixing and sorting, rather than resorting to other tools.

CANDLES

For many, magic is candle work. Candles range from tiny tea lights to large 7 Days (their name reflects how long it's anticipated they'll stay lit). They come in a variety of colors and a variety of shapes. Occult supply stores sell candles for specific intents: reversible candles to return an evil spell, candles shaped like men, women, couples or cats for assorted enchantments. The ubiquitous skull candles you see aren't meant for any evil purpose: they're intended to "get inside someone's head" when you need to implant an idea or you need them to hear your side of a story.

Some prefer to take their magic from the ground floor up and make their own candles, for a list of good reasons:

- Candles are reasonably simple and inexpensive to make.

- You can control the contents of your candle.

> Figure candles may be used if their image resonates for you. Use female candles to represent women, male candles for men. You'll also find joined couple candles for love spells and when your magical goal involves two of you as a unit. Candles in the shape of witches and cats are also very popular. Traditionally, witches enhance any magic while cats bring good luck, but use them in whatever way your inspiration guides. Any shape candle can serve a magical purpose.

- You can imbue the candle with your intent right from the start.

- You are not limited to the shapes that are commercially available.

- Candle-making is fun, creative and relaxing.

If you enjoy crafts, you can indulge your passions with candle-making. Many cookie cutters and old-fashioned chocolate molds can be used to personalize the shapes. Another option is beeswax. Beeswax candles are easy and quick to make. You can get sheets of pure beeswax in various colors from craft stores as well as from candle-making supply houses. The sheets should not lack fragrance but be redolent of bees and honey. You can leave the fragrance as is (the scent of beeswax is considered propitious), or before you shape the candle, place some fragrance oil onto your palms and smooth it onto the wax. Line up a cotton wick and then just roll sheets into the desired shape: tapers are easiest, but you can also make pyramids and squares fairly simply. To make them thicker, just add more sheets of wax. You can also use cookie cutters to cut shapes from one sheet to attach to a larger rolled candle.

There *is* one exceptionally good reason for not making your own candles and that, of course, is that making candles is time-consuming and few people consistently have that kind of time. No need to content yourself with a generic candle, however. A store-bought candle can easily be doctored to imbue it with your own energy and intent. In magical parlance, this is known as "dressing a candle."

- Carve initials, birthdays, prayers, astrological symbols and incantations into the soft wax.

- Add fragrance by rubbing scented oil onto the candle.

- Decorate and personalize your candles. Enhance the power by adding small shells, glitter, herbs, pinecones or any sort of small treasure, just always keep fire safety in mind!

- It was once customary for 7-Day candles to slide out of their glass sleeves for easy dressing. It's getting harder to find these, but don't despair. If you can't remove the candle, drill holes into the top of the wax and insert your fragrance. After the candle has burned out, reserve the glass sleeve to create future candles.

Choosing Your Candle: Before you choose a candle, determine what you wish to do with it.

- If you want to carve an entire incantation, you will need a candle of appropriate size.

- If you need to watch the whole candle burn without extinguishing it, use a tea light or small votive.

- Tapers are notoriously hard to carve, they tend to split in half, although they are easily rubbed with fragrance. Rub tapers with a romance-drawing oil for a seductive candlelit dinner. (Check in the Spells section for some examples.)

- Match the color of your candle to your magical goal. Check back a few pages to the Color section if your memory needs refreshing. Remember, a white candle suits any goal.

Tips for Successful Candle Magic:

- Make the goal of each candle as specific as possible.

- Remain focused on your desired intent while dressing your candle.

- Hold the candle in your hands to transmit your energy. Make your wish with the candle in your hands before lighting it.

- Use common sense around candles. Because you're doing spiritual work doesn't mean that the laws of nature don't apply. Never leave candles unattended. In most cases, it's perfectly fine to extinguish a candle before it's finished, before you fall asleep, for instance, or if you have to leave your home.

- Repeat your wish and intensify your concentration every time you relight the candle.

- If a spell requires that a candle burn out entirely by itself, wait until you have sufficient time for initiating that spell.

- Candles, children and animals are a volatile mix. When faced with any combination, use extra caution.

CARVING TOOLS

If you do candle work, you will need something with a sharp point to cut into the wax. Every rule has an exception and here's mine. This is the one area where it is beneficial to keep separate tools. Candle work often expresses your most secret, private wishes. Your tool can be as luxurious or inexpensive as you choose. Some witches use intricate knives but others use metal skewers. You could use a craft knife, a sharp pointed pen or even a pointy twig. Rose thorns are traditional carving tools. The edge of a key works well, too.

CHARCOAL

You'll need these if you'll be burning herbs or incense. Unless you're doing really big rituals outside, you won't need the large bags of charcoal that are used for barbecuing. The charcoal of choice is small and round and has an indented surface where you can sprinkle the incense. These are usually sold in packs of ten in occult supply stores and in botanicas.

CHOPSTICKS

One pair of wooden chopsticks is versatile, finds many magical uses, and lasts quite a long time. They are excellent mixing tools, particularly for salts, herbs and oils where metal tools should be avoided. Chopsticks can also be used to retrieve fallen matches from the bottom of 7-Day candles and unclog your drains should you neglect to strain the herbs from your bath infusion.

Boxes are easily transformed into magical containers. The very shape of the box embodies the concept of reproduction and what is magic, after all, but creating something new from existing energy? Use whatever sort of box resonates most for you. Magic boxes may be made from wood, stone or metal. They can be of any size, from a walnut or matchbox to a steamer trunk. Store your prized amulets and tools in a special box for protection and place herbs and crystals inside to enhance their power. For extra enhancement: use henna or decoupage to adorn the outside or glue shells and feathers to surfaces.

CONTAINERS

What you need depends upon what you wish to store. Most likely you'll need glass containers or containers of some other nonreactive material. Salt and essential oils interact poorly with plastic. Darker glass protects oils and herbs and extends their shelf life. Seashells and coconut shells add their own power to whatever they hold. They're especially good for things that don't need to be enclosed.

You can also use boxes more actively by creating a spell box. Spell boxes are enclosed altars, miniature wishing tableaux. Fill your box with the power items that will assist you to achieve your goal: money, a new job, romance, good health. Keep the box shut except when actively performing rituals or visualizations to ensure the success of that specific goal. (Make as many boxes as you need but use only one for each purpose.)

GRINDING TOOLS

A **mortar and pestle** is ideal. It is an ancient instrument and is readily available in a multitude of materials: stone, clay, metal or glass. Because this incorporates a physical process, you are actually grinding your intent and desire into the materials, this is a particularly beneficial tool. In addition, the mortar and pestle is designed to echo male and female energies and the procreative act, hearkening back to the most ancient magical ritual of all. A *molcajete*, the Mexican stone mortar, works great, too.

If you don't have a mortar and pestle, a small food processor can provide what you need, although because just pushing a button doesn't allow you to contribute as much of your personal energy as the older instrument, you should compensate with extra strong visualizations. Spice and coffee grinders can also be used but be aware that the flavor of whatever you are grinding may infiltrate your coffee grinder forever.

PAPER

Paper is a common canvas upon which to create enchantments. The magical uses of paper are virtually unlimited. Paper can be enhanced and preserved: it can be folded, pasted upon or somehow made to resemble another object. Paper can be drawn upon or written upon. Charms and amulets are commonly made from paper.

Some spells require that paper be destroyed for the magic to be released; typically a wish or secret desire is written upon the paper. Following a ritual or just some plain intense concentration, the paper is then burned or dissolved in water. For maximum efficacy, when burning paper for spells, make sure every tiny bit, every last letter, is reduced to smoke and ashes.

Sometimes magic is on the paper but at other times, magic is *in* the paper. The quality and quantity of your paper is up to you. If the paper will be preserved whole, the content of the paper itself may not be too important. However, if you're burning paper, you need to be aware that you are releasing the paper's chemical components into the air side-by-side with your expressed desires. Releasing toxic chemicals may distract the powers-that-be from paying attention to your spell—or it may attract the wrong kind of powers! One way around this is to make your own paper. You can control the color and reinforce its power with flowers and fragrance. If you're unfamiliar with the process, craft stores and toy stores sell simple kits. Otherwise, try to buy unbleached paper, as chemical-free as possible. Typically, for a spell, only a small square is needed.

Spirit Mail

China is the ancestral home of burnt-paper magic. The theory behind this practice is that by burning special paper, messages are reliably sent to the spirit realm. Thousands of varieties of mystical paper (known as joss, fu, paper horse or spirit money paper, among other names) exist. Spirit money, which resembles cash bills, is relatively easy to find in stores that cater to traditional Asian clientele (or to tourists in Chinatown); finding other varieties is like searching for treasure. You never quite know what gems will turn up. This practice also extends to other areas. Special magic wishing paper, often beautifully handcrafted, comes from Nepal. Write a wish and burn.

POTS AND PANS

Finally, here's your cauldron! The fairy tale image of the witch stirring her magic cauldron isn't far from the truth. In the language of symbols, pots represent the womb of creation, women's primal power. None of this symbolism means that the pot as a tool is restricted to women's use. In

West Africa, an iron pot is among the accoutrements of Ogun, the *very* male spirit of metal, tools, agriculture and war, who remains today's active patron of soldiers, surgeons and taxi drivers. An iron pot is one of his symbols; inside that pot you would find carefully cultivated red rust as recognition that even when representing this most male of entities, the pot still echoes the creative female womb.

You can use any pot or pan that you already own, however, be aware that the concept of completely nonreactive cookware is an illusion. Every item contributes, at the very least, its energy and probably a lot more than that. A cast-iron pot or pan is ideal. Iron has traditional associations with magic. Cast iron is durable, improves with age and puts you in touch with the healing powers of metal. A plain ten-inch or smaller cast-iron pan has a vast variety of uses, from cooking to roasting spices to burning incense. The more you use it, the stronger its power becomes.

The tools listed here are standard equipment for most, but don't feel limited to them. Many cultures have evolved specific magic tools. If you follow a tradition faithfully, some may become necessities. The Celtic practitioner may be unable to envision magic without her specially consecrated athamé, her ritual knife. The Saami shaman may not need a knife; her magic is incomplete without her sacred drum. Among other items commonly used in magic are bells, masks, musical instruments, wands and, yes, brooms. There is no single right way to use these tools. Access the childlike, magical part of you and play!

Communication and interaction with nonhumans is difficult for many of us. The farther away from human language we get, the more difficult it becomes. In other words, communicating with a dog may be plausible for many but a plant, a rock, a *pan?* Cast iron is a good teacher with which to begin this process. For most people, the visual sense is strongest and cast iron communicates very visually. When it's happy and feeling its power, a cast-iron pot is sleek, black and shiny, although it may take years to build up to this level of experience. An inexperienced pan has a grayish tinge; its color is metallic rather than shiny. An ill-used pan or a tired one will develop rust and needs to be reseasoned and fed some fat, the equivalent of sending cast iron to the health spa. You won't have to work very hard to build up an alliance with a cast-iron pan. It's a willing ally if well-treated and will speak up promptly when mistakes are made in its treatment.

The Enchanted Grocery List

Some of the strongest powers masquerade as mundane food items in the supermarket: honey, milk, salt, spices and water. All are potentially alive and filled with power, however, in order to best retain and preserve that power, always try to obtain the purest, most unadulterated items possible, preferably with no additives and minimal human adjustment. You'll find the following ingredients to be among the most common components of magic.

HONEY

An ancient culinary, medicinal and magical ingredient, honey is a gift from the bees, ancient allies and sacred creatures of many divine female entities. Bees and their products are among the most primeval reflections of divine feminine power. One legend says that bees are the returning souls of Aphrodite's priestesses. Honey shares something of the essence of the most beautiful female spirits, those who provide humans with love, beauty, prosperity and good health. Honey is used for healing and for love spells.

Sweetness is not always associated with power but honey is truly potent. Internal consumption is not recommended for children under one year or for those with suppressed immune systems as honey contains spores that can be potentially fatal for them, although it is among the safest foods for others.

Honey is a living, protective substance. One type of honey is not identical to another. It will taste slightly different and radiate slightly different powers, based upon which flowers were used to create it. The nature of the flowers, whatever powers they themselves contain, permeates the resulting honey and exponentially increases its power.

- Lavender honey is a favorite of occult practitioners, as it's believed to contain a particularly strong reservoir of power. If you were to have but one jar of honey in your cupboard on standby for enchantment, this would be it.

- Manuka honey is favored for physical healing and as an aphrodisiac.

- Orange blossom honey is favored for love spells.

- Rosemary or thyme honey is favored for protection spells.

MILK

The very first food of all, milk is the only substance that exists purely to nourish. Milk comes from mothers. All mothers of mammal species produce milk that is the perfect first food for their babies. No two species have chemically identical milk. Fat and sugar content, among other components, varies by species. Milk isn't even always pure white: human milk sometimes has a faint blue tinge, while kangaroo milk is pinkish. No two women produce identical milk either. Again, this is a living substance. Milk changes in subtle ways daily. Milk reflects the mother's diet but as if by magic, mother's milk also adjusts to her baby's needs. The milk from a mother whose nursing baby is ill can transmit healing and immunity-boosting substances. Milk is used for physical healing and for protection. Milk is used in many spells that involve bathing; it benefits your skin as well as your aura. The powers inherent in the producing species are transmitted through milk. Ancient spells specified different types of milk, from the fantastical (lion's milk was reputed to have miraculous life-giving powers) to the more mundane (ancient Egyptian magic prized milk from women who'd borne sons). The selection of milk available in your supermarket may be limited, however, you probably have at least a few choices: goat or sheep's milk tends to be tampered with less than cow's milk and may thus contain more power.

- If you add milk to the bath, organic whole fat milk is most beneficial for your skin.

- Powdered milk may be used as well. It's convenient and stores easily, but its power is lessened.

SALT

A universal protective agent, salt not only possesses antiseptic properties to cleanse and protect the body, but also provides spiritual protection and cleansing. A handful of sea salt added to a tub full of water will quickly cleanse you of the day's ill vibrations. The very simplest protective spell is a circle made from salt; sit in the center until you feel it's safe to come out.

Salt comes from all over Earth and isn't necessarily white. A legendary purple salt comes from Libya. There is a salt available now from Hawaii that has a reddish tint, reflecting the color of Hawaiian earth. Like water, honey, milk and earth, salts from different areas are unique. If the spiritual properties are similar, the physical gifts differ:

- Dead Sea salts soothe skin disorders.

- Epsom salts relieve muscular aches and pains.

The less that salt is tampered with, the more power it retains. For magical purposes, sea salt is considered to have the most power, as it carries the power and essence of the sea. The exception is if you're concocting a salt scrub. Although in theory, sea salt is available both finely and coarsely ground, coarse ground may be the only one readily available. In that case, table salt's smoother grain may be gentler and less likely to irritate sensitive skin. You can also grind salt yourself using a salt mill or mortar and pestle.

SPICES

Once among Earth's most precious, expensive substances, most spices grow only within a narrow belt between the Tropics of Cancer and Capricorn. Although their price has dropped, their power remains. Spices are generally associated with the sun and with the fire element. Many spices are available in the supermarket; purchase them whole and grind as needed. Once ground, their fragrance and power dissipates quickly. Essential oils extracted from spices are also available but use with caution. Many can irritate even the least sensitive skin, so dilute them *extremely* well, whether in oil or in water, if ever they are to be in contact with your flesh. (They may be added to candle wax undiluted.) Because their fragrance is so heavenly, it's a temptation to wear them as perfume: perhaps the safest method is via a spice necklace. Different spices serve as magnets

PURE MAGIC

for different desires (love, money, easy childbirth, etc.); a spice necklace also serves as an amulet. Later on in the Spell section, we'll look at spice necklaces to further each goal.

WATER

Many creation traditions begin with Earth emerging from primordial waters. There is rarely an explanation for how the water arrived. Water just *is*. The tradition of healing, rejuvenating waters is as old as Earth. Every spring, every river or lake, every body of water has one or more presiding, inhabiting spirits; the water contains and transmits their aura, essence and power alongside its own. Immersion in water cleanses human souls and auras and initiates spiritual rebirth. For as many people as associate magic with fire and candles, there are an equal number who cannot imagine magic without water. Magical herbal and perfumed baths are integral features of many spiritual traditions.

Unfortunately most of the water you are likely to come into effortless contact with has been so processed and tampered with that its spiritual energy is lacking. The most powerful water is water from a living source: ocean water, water from a lake, stream or river. Each type of water possesses a slightly different energy. For magical uses, carry containers to collect water—remember to take only what you need. Easier yet, collect rainwater. Bottled, pure spring or mineral water possesses more energy than tap water. A lot of magic is accomplished in the bathtub. Unfortunately, both ease and expense precludes most of us from using anything other than tap water. Add as much rainwater as you can collect. In addition, adding just one glass of pure springwater to your tub creates a powerful gesture. The addition of that one glass of springwater will positively empower the water in which you bathe.

Among the popular ingredients of spells are specific types of water, especially "holy water" and flower waters. These different types of water provide different powers and energies.

- Holy water technically refers to water from the Jordan River, sacred in many traditions. Basically what the spell is calling for is spiritually charged water. Any water can potentially be holy water. Where a formula calls for holy water, use Jordan River Water if that suits you (available from occult suppliers, Israeli and Jordanian

42

exporters as well as some local parishes). If not, consider what would be *your* holy water—water from a stream near your home perhaps? Water from the tap of the restaurant where you spent your happiest moments? If in doubt, just double the proportion of springwater in the spell.

- Ideally, flower waters combine botanicals and water to create a power greater than the sum of its parts. There are three possible sources for these waters:

  1. *The supermarket*, where they are usually displayed among the spices and baking supplies. However, be aware that many of these products are diluted and weak; they may be little more than flower-scented water. Stores that cater to Middle Eastern cooks may carry stronger flower waters as it's a popular component in their cuisine.

  2. *Hydrosols* are the other product created by extracting essential oils: the water left over from the distillation process. True hydrosols are infused with actual plant molecules: there's really some plant in there. Hydrosols are magically powerful although therapeutically very gentle. Once rare, hydrosols have become quite popular and may be obtained where aromatherapy and herbal products are sold. Refer to the Appendix at the back of the book for sources.

  3. *Your kitchen*. Simple flower waters are quickly and easily made. If the flowers are from your garden, it's an inexpensive process and you can be confident about the lack of pesticides. In addition, although you may find a wide variety of hydrosols, flower water from the supermarket tends to be limited to rose or orange blossom. At home you'll have access to any blossoms that you choose: make jasmine blossom water or primrose water, for instance. Use any flowers you like, provided that the flowers are not poisonous.

Rose Water

Use this formula to create orange blossom or other flower waters, too.

1. Take the petals from 2 or 3 roses, place them in a small pot and cover them with a quarter inch of springwater.

2. Let simmer gently.

3. After a few minutes, you will observe a change in the blossoms: the color will become pallid, the textures of the petals may become limp. It's a visual change: you will know it when you see it. If in doubt, let the petals simmer a minute longer.

4. Strain and allow the liquid to cool.

   • If you do not use it up at once, refrigerate the rose water.

   • Do not use flowers that have been sprayed with pesticides.

Amulets

Many anthropologists believe that the origin of all jewelry and beads lies in the amulet. Amulets by definition are power objects used to either draw a specific good fortune (money, love, glory) or to serve as a general protective device. Once you start carrying a power object for a specific intent, it becomes an amulet.

Amulets may be objects left just as they are found in nature: cowrie shell girdles, necklaces and charms are among the earliest amulets, discovered in Paleolithic graves. Cowries are used to draw fertility, health, wealth and spiritual protection.

The word *amulet* indicates that an object's inherent power is being used for the benefit of a person. Cowries exist independently; it takes a person's recognition and intent for them to be transformed into an amulet. The simplest amulets are nuts, shells, rocks and botanicals in their original form. Carry a hazelnut in your pocket to attract desired wealth.

> *Perhaps the most common "species" of amulet, known virtually everywhere on Earth, consists of a small container holding at least one highly charged item. This type of amulet answers to many names: mojo hand, charm bag, huangi bag, conjure bag, medicine pouch—or for those in an anthropological mood, phylactery. The simplest consists of a few nuts or rocks carried in a knotted handkerchief. The most sophisticated are intricately bejeweled containers. The container itself becomes part of the charm, the color and material carefully chosen to incorporate the correct power. The standard American charm bag comes in a red flannel bag.*

Amulets are also fashioned by human hands. As soon as humans perceived the existence of power objects (pretty early in our history, based upon burial evidence), we set about to take advantage of that power, to control it, isolate it and enhance it. The finest amulets manipulate objects, putting them together to create something more potent than merely the sum of its parts. There are professional amulet makers, skilled in the magical arts who not only manipulate materials but are able to infuse the finished product with their own personal power, imbue it with that extra boost of magic.

Once created, an amulet becomes an independent force: it radiates its own energy. Most amulets can be transferred from one person to another; they benefit whoever carries them or is in contact with them, somewhat akin to Aladdin's genie, in service to whoever possesses his lamp.

Amulets are not identical with each other nor are they completely interchangeable. They tend to have very specific purposes, they're luck-drawing specialists, so to speak. In order to know which amulet is right for you, you need to know what you are trying to attract. A gambler's charm for success can't be counted upon to help you retain your boyfriend or vice versa.

POPULAR AMULETS

- **Protection:** Blue Eye Beads • Peacock Feather Fan • Magic Hands: Horned Hand, Hand of Fatima, *Hamsa*

- **Wealth:** Horseshoes • *Maneki Neko:* the Beckoning Cat • An image of a frog kept in your wallet

- **Romance:** Mistletoe • Charms in the shape of doves or dragons • Wishbones

- **Fertility:** Bivalve shells and cowries • *Akuaba* Doll • Russian Nesting Dolls

- **Health:** The Endless Knot • Pomanders • Lion-shaped Charms

PART TWO

Other Powers:
Your Magic Allies

Every living being on Earth has its place in the cosmos and its own specific, unique powers. In addition to the human realm, Earth's children fall into some basic categories or realms:

Animals
Spirit Beings
Metals and Minerals
Botanicals

There are basically two ways to approach and work with these powers: as tools and as allies.

Tools

Appropriate when you need something or someone to simply perform a specific service for you.

> *Remember, we're talking "alive" in the magical sense, not in the hospital sense. If you need to refresh your memory about the difference, check back to the glossary.*

> *A basic magic spell is the manipulation of these powers to further your*
> *goals. The spell section that follows includes precise and specific details*
> *and directions as to which powers may be best approached for your*
> *goals and desires.*

Maybe this analogy will help: You have a toothache, so you go to the dentist. If the problem can be corrected quickly, perhaps you only need one visit. If the problem is more complex, repeat visits may be required. A few individuals may develop a personal rapport with the dentist, an alliance that transcends the specific treatment, but for most a simple transaction is all that occurs.

On the magical level, let's say you need to stimulate some cash flow quickly, so you invest in some basil, among the most powerful money-drawing plants. Maybe you'll create a basil floor wash, sprinkle some basil infusion near your cash register, take a basil bath or rub basil oil onto your wallet. (Don't worry: instructions follow in the Money Magic section.) Depending upon the complexity of your situation and the depth of your need, perhaps you'll only need to do this once or perhaps a series of spells is in order.

There are three basic steps to incorporating other powers into your magic as tools:

1. You choose a power based upon its ability to perform a specific function or service for you.

2. You use it correctly and respectfully.

3. You store the item, or knowledge of that item, for future use should the need arise again.

Allies

An alliance involves a deeper relationship. You may consider it a partnership or you may consider it akin to acquiring a personal teacher, mentor or counselor. The relationship is ongoing and mutually beneficial. Creating an alliance with a power is more personally fulfilling and rewarding than the previous approach, however it's also more demanding than using a power as a tool.

You may use hundreds or even thousands of powers as tools, depending upon the extent of your magical repertoire. The number of alliances is inevitably far smaller, although you are not limited to any set number of alliances. Some people's needs are met with one ally; others accumulate three, five, a dozen or more.

> *Consider the tool-approach as having talented acquaintances whereas allies are your closest friends, with perhaps one or two as your very best friends. Just as everyone's social needs are different, so the need for magical alliances varies. There's no competition. It doesn't matter how many alliances someone else has. There's no one right number.*

Some of your alliances may be life long. Others may involve brief intensive relationships followed by similar alliances with other powers. You may have one at a time, you may maintain several simultaneously. You will accumulate different alliances as you need, desire and/or earn them.

HOW DO YOU PICK AN ALLY?

In general, they pick you. A specific power, whichever it might be, recognizes something about your power and initiates the alliance. There are various reasons for why you were chosen. Any or all of the following might be the cause:

- The power perceives that you share something of its nature or essence.

- There is some historic basis for affection, assistance and loyalty. This might be based on all sorts of factors: ethnic, familial, professional or other.

- The power perceives a need in you that it is able to fulfill, in much the way that humans provide assistance to each other. Dentists and other specialists make themselves available to you when you need them, while good Samaritans may proffer favors spontaneously, so do allies and other powers.

- The power just likes you and enjoys your presence.

- Knowingly or unknowingly, you've called upon this power and they've responded.

> *You may also discover information regarding your past lives by examining and studying your allies, as many believe that alliances never end but continue over many lifetimes.*

SPIRIT PROTECTORS

Some allies may have been hovering near you since your very first moments on Earth. General metaphysical wisdom is in agreement that every human is born with a cadre of spiritual helpers. These include representatives from each of the realms: mineral, animal, spirit and botanical. Perhaps they've been waiting silently. Perhaps they've been making overtures toward you, waiting for a gesture or response. Perhaps they've served as guardian angels. Their role is to provide guidance and protection along your life journey. Some reveal themselves easily, particularly animal allies. Others may help silently until they perceive that you are ready to be an active partner. The most powerful relationships are always mutually beneficial: Your role is not merely to be the recipient of their kindness but to provide honor and empowerment to your allies as well.

CLUES TO IDENTIFYING YOUR ALLIES

- Be aware of images that repeat in your life. Magic refutes the concept of coincidence, considering them instead to be signals requesting your attention. Was there a birthday when everyone gave you the same type of stuffed animal? Did everyone laugh when you received twelve stuffed chipmunks? What sort of jewelry enters your life—is it funny that you're always accumulating pearls? Whatever house you live in, does there always seem to be a particular plant nearby?

- Your allies are likely to appear in your dreams. Do you ever dream of flowers or of precious stones? Spirit beings may speak to you in your dreams or approach you in various forms. These may or may not be pleasant dreams. Sometimes our allies inadvertently scare us. It's not necessarily their intention, more likely faulty communication, misunderstandings or even prejudice on our behalf. You may have a recurring dream of a wolf chasing you. You run, fearing it will harm you. That wolf keeps returning, frustrated in its attempt to reach you, its intent merely to offer advice and assistance.

> The Kabbalah suggests that although guardian angels can assist us anonymously, their powers are limited unless we specifically request help. When we explicitly ask for assistance, they are free to perform ever-greater services upon our behalf. This applies to other powers as well.

- Often, we know our allies because we love them and long for their presence. Something about them attracts our attention. As the old saying goes, "that which you are seeking is causing you to seek." There's a lot of chemical interaction involved in alliances with other powers. It's like going to a crowded party, looking across the room, making eye contact with someone and just knowing that the potential for a valuable, special relationship exists. The key word is *potential*. You could leave the party immediately, with no interaction. No relationship would have begun although there's always the chance you'll have another opportunity at some later date. Or you could go greet that someone or make some sort of welcoming gesture, letting them know you welcome their approach.

An alliance is intended to be mutually beneficial. Although you may be receiving overtures, if it's not a relationship you desire or find appealing, you're not obligated to enter into that relationship. This is your magic. You set the boundaries. It may be that you're not interested in alliances, period. Tools are what fit your needs. It may be that you'd like to work with crystals but not with spirit beings or vice versa. Those are your choices. Consider what's being offered to you and make your decisions based upon your needs and desires. If something doesn't appeal to you, you can always just graciously decline.

> *When someone or something chases you in your dreams, stop and ask*
> *what they want. If you repeatedly tell yourself while you are awake that*
> *you will do this while you're dreaming, eventually you will find that you*
> *do. If you are very fearful of what pursues you, also repeatedly remind*
> *yourself, while awake, that whenever you wish to you can wake up and*
> *escape. You may also wish to examine the protective dream crystals and*
> *charms discussed in depth a little further on.*

Okay, so in theory you know how to signal to someone at a party to let them know you're interested, how do you do this with a rock, an animal, a spirit?

We'll examine each realm in turn, but at the most basic level, you start by making them feel welcome. Anything that is "alive" in the magical sense has certain preferences, certain things, colors, foods and especially fragrances that serve as signals and sometimes as magnets. By creating a conducive atmosphere, you signal that their presence is desired.

Although experimenting can be fun, rest assured that there is already a fairly encyclopedic occult canon regarding the care and feeding of powers. You don't have to figure it all out by yourself. Despite the association of the word "occult" with secrets, the most powerful, knowledgeable practitioners have always made the effort to share and pass down their wisdom, and so it exists for our benefit.

> *There are also certain welcoming fragrances that consistently call in*
> *beneficial, powerful spirits. Luckily, these tend to smell pretty wonderful*
> *to us, too; cinnamon, frankincense, gardenia, rose and sandalwood.*

Don't be discouraged if it takes a little while for a response. You may have to keep trying. Sometimes powers don't realize the invitation is for them the first time or the second time but eventually they'll get the message. Some powers are more gregarious and eager than others. The more you know of your chosen power's nature, the easier communication becomes and the more likely you are to recognize a response.

It is crucial to remember, especially in a society where hearing voices or communicating with nonhumans can be considered grounds for commitment, that you are not obligated to obey any instructions or recommendations from your guides, any more than you are obligated to take advice from Dear Abby. If they suggest something you're not comfortable with, just say no. Respectfully, as always, of course, but decline. This is ultimately your magic, your life, your choice, your responsibility.

Part of the danger comes from the misconception that other powers don't belong to real life, to our day-to-day existence, so that any communication is treated as either innately evil and to be avoided at all cost or the opposite, something so sacred that it must be blindly obeyed. Remember that all life forms, whether mobile like humans or animals, rooted like trees or existing in some spiritual dimension that humans don't completely grasp, all share our Earth Mother.

Jewish folklore refers to a wide array of demons, angels and assorted spiritual beings of varying levels of power as living *on the other side, our other side,* the other side of our own existence, not some completely different reality. These forces aren't from some other Earth. They share our Earth with us and we all have a place. There is no different plant world, no separate animal planet. For better or worse, we all share this one.

Each living being has its own individual powers and its own individual skills to teach. Earth provides allies for every purpose. There are plants, animals, minerals and spirit powers ready to assist you in the acquisition of literally any skill or experience. Crucially, there are some specific powers that serve as magical ambassadors from their respective realms. They will teach you to sharpen your psychic skills, they are your finest teachers for learning how to access and work with other powers. They will teach you how to tap directly into Earth Magic. Let's examine each realm, in the order of easiest accessibility.

ANIMAL ALLIES

Animals are our most beloved allies. We all have personal allies in the plant, spirit and mineral realms but animal allies are our most accessible spirit helpers. Animals provide us with protection, knowledge and psychic inspiration.

- Your animal ally may take the form of an actual individual living, breathing member of a species, with whom you actually have some level of concrete, physical contact: your cat or a bird that visits you periodically, for instance. This is what the ancients used to refer to as a *familiar*.

- Your animal ally may also appear to you in spirit form. Each species has a presiding spirit: the Spirit of the Dog versus Fido, the basset hound down the street. This enables you to acquire wisdom, skills and protection from animals with whom it might not be safe, practical or even possible to have actual physical contact. Communication in this case is usually via dreams, visions and symbols.

> *In magical parlance, animal is not limited to mammals but encompasses many biological classifications including birds, fish, reptiles, amphibians and insects as well. In the simplest terms, **animal**, in magic-speak includes anything that is "alive" in the same way that we understand human beings to be alive: breathing, pulsing, visibly eating and excreting, etc.*

Animal Allies: What Do I Do with Them?

Just as every couple's marriage may be slightly different, so is every alliance. The nature of your personal animal alliances—and the allies that you attract— depends upon your needs, desires, potential for growth and your expectations. Animal allies provide guidance, comfort and spiritual direction and protection.

- An animal ally can provide guidance and comfort. Its ability to provide for you is based partly upon your cooperation and conscious interaction. An ally may appear in your dreams to cheer you during a difficult period. If before you went to sleep, or during a ritual, you were to ask for specific advice, your ally might then be able to provide you with the needed information.

- Your ally may have come into your life to teach you skills that you may need or that will be beneficial for you, either explicitly or by example. Perhaps you have a hard time setting emotional boundaries, causing consistent relationship problems for you.

Armadillo, the master boundary setter, may be waiting in the wings to protect you and teach you how to acquire the skills that you need. Do you live in fear of physical danger? Do you find yourself in potentially abusive situations? Rabbit may enter your life to teach you how to use your wits to escape, survive and thrive.

- The most concrete way to work with animal allies is to increase their presence in your life. Start by focusing your concentration upon them: studying their habits and nature.

- Surround yourself with them, either an actual animal, if safe and practicable, or its image or ideally both. Your ally will respond to your eagerness and friendliness, increasing its efforts upon your behalf.

- The goal is the eventual absorption of something of their nature and power, so that you are able to infuse your own personal power with their essence and positive qualities.

Animal allies are the most prevalent spirit allies and often the easiest to access. Everyone has them, usually several. If you've had limited or no contact or awareness of these allies, be a little patient. The animal spirits may have been hibernating near you, waiting for your call: Sometimes it takes a little while and a few approaches before they'll broach contact. This is particularly true if your ally's nature is shy and cautious or if it's what might be considered a "scary" animal. They don't wish to overwhelm or scare you. Let them know if you're ready.

Pay attention when that animal or its image enters your life, even momentarily. Dreams of your ally are significant: consider what they mean. When pondering a dilemma, have you ever flipped open a magazine and just "coincidentally" found an image of your ally? Pay attention to the context. You may be receiving advice and clues for solving your problem.

Reflect upon your animal's nature; learn all you can about your ally: you'll find an endless source of significant information. Line up all your allies and consider what they have in common. Do they eat similar diets? Perhaps there's a health recommendation for you here. Do they live in similar climates? What kind of personal relationships do they have? Most canines like to live in packs, whereas cats, with the exception of lions, are solitary. Deer mothers are solely responsible for their children, whereas with other species, the father is involved. You share something of your essence with your allies. Within this information there will be a spiritual path for you to follow, should you choose.

> *Animals are particularly beneficial allies when we're unsure of our proper path. Animals invariably know the right path for themselves, they lack the conflicts we possess. Skunks don't long to live the life of a beaver or vice versa. They are secure in their identity and if you allow them, they will assist you to become secure and confident with your own power and identity.*

How will you know your allies? On some level, you already do. The key is bringing that information to the surface, recognizing and identifying them. Think back to your favorite childhood animals. Which animals intrigued you, delighted you, comforted you most in childhood? Which animals appeared most vividly in your dreams? Do certain animals or their images keep appearing in your life? What animals do you really love? When you go to the zoo, who do you *have* to visit? Conversely, which animals do you really fear or hate? If you catch even a random glimpse of a drawing of a snake, does it ruin your whole day? I hate to tell you, but any extremely powerful emotion tends to indicate some sort of an alliance.

In some traditions, if you've been bitten by an animal or survived an attack, that species is now obligated to provide you with spiritual assistance. In some shamanic traditions, if an animal attacks you, it was sent to see if you are strong enough to handle its power.

> *Remember: we may not be referring to each individual member of a species, but the presiding spirit of that species, Big Coyote versus just any old coyote running down the street. You can demand that that spirit fulfill any obligations; whether each individual member of the group will be amenable is debatable.*

Animals are divided into prey and hunters. Hunters follow prey. If a prey animal is your ally, assume that the predator most associated with that animal has entered your life as well. If a rabbit is your ally, a lynx may be around the corner. This isn't meant to be threatening. If needed, you can call on its power, too. These animals share a spiritual symbiosis and will share their power and equilibrium with you.

PAYING FOR SERVICES RENDERED

Healthy relationships are mutually beneficial. Earth's balance is also dependent upon your reciprocity. Alliances are based on energy transfers. If your ally always gives of its energy without receiving a return transfusion, eventually its power will suffer. In addition, your reciprocity, your "payment" if you will, becomes a part of the give-and-take of communication.

- Personal tributes and testimonials may be created, by building an altar, for example, or by creating artwork. Some individuals reciprocate by acquiring a tattoo of their ally.

- When you receive a favor, return a favor. Do this by demonstrating kindness and concern for an individual of the species or for the species as a whole. Do something that will please the presiding spirit. The presiding spirit's sole function on Earth is not merely to be your ally; its main function is to protect the welfare and survival of individual members of the species.

You can:

- Feed hungry individuals or provide a home.

- Discover if their natural habitat is endangered and if so, find out what you can do to help.

- Become an ally on their behalf.

To earn an alliance, perform services on behalf of the species and wait for a signal or approach from the presiding spirit via dream, gesture or symbol.

For every good turn done for you, do one in return. Whenever you feel your life has been enriched, do a good turn in return. You will reap the benefits: the more you do for them, the more positive attention will be turned toward you.

Allies can also be revealed through divination. Excellent divination systems, mainly based upon Native American or Celtic traditions, exist for this purpose. The one problem with these systems, which are mainly presented as cards, is that you are limited to a preset, preselected variety of animals. Use them as they help you but don't allow yourself to be limited by them. There is no rigid number of animal allies. Let them reveal themselves to you via divination, in your dreams or in your daily life. You can also retrieve knowledge of your allies from within yourself by using guided visualization.

Prepare yourself before you initiate the visualization process.

- Arrange sufficient time, privacy and comfort.

- Prepare your area by using the spiritual cleansing and protective techniques offered in the Spell section. Use these techniques to cleanse your own aura as well.

- If you're apprehensive or wish for extra assistance, choose an appropriate crystal. (See page 85 for the section on crystals.)

- To enhance your psychic skills, brew some Psychic Tea.

- Familiarize yourself with the journey so that you can reproduce it silently for yourself; use a tape recorder or have a trusted individual serve as your guide.

MEETING YOUR ANIMAL ALLY: A GUIDED VISUALIZATION

You're leaving home. Watch yourself close the door. All your responsibilities are being cared for. You have no worries to concern you. You walk with purpose.

At first the landscape is familiar but eventually you arrive in a wide field full of grass and flowers. There is no clear path, yet you walk with assurance. Someone awaits you: you know where you're going. You walk through a fragrant field, until you arrive at a thick wood. It's darker under the canopy of trees but you look down and right in front of your feet is a clear white path. You proceed into the woods.

The fragrance of the trees is divine. Birds sing to you. It's dark but sunlight trickles through the branches and you can see your way clearly. Your feet know where to go. The path takes you deeper and deeper into the forest. You feel no fear, but peace and self-assurance. You walk and walk, deeper and deeper, until the path simply ends. You are still deep in the forest. You look down and see a square trap door. You reach down and pull it open: you see stairs descending. As you enter, you discover a torch and matches hanging on the wall, waiting for you. You light the torch, reach up and close the trap door and descend into Earth.

You walk and walk, it's cool and dry. Finally you reach the bottom. It's dark here, the only light is from your torch. A path guides you forward. In the distance, you can see a faint light and you walk toward it. Gradually it becomes brighter and you no longer need your torch. The path widens. Somehow you find yourself under open skies, approaching a small, pretty shore. Peaceful water plays gently on the ground. You take off your shoes and wet your toes. The water is just right. Gradually, you become aware that you are not alone. Someone has been patiently awaiting your arrival. When you're ready, look up and see who it is.

You can stay as long as you wish. You may communicate in any way with the one who waits for you or you may simply gaze and share the moment. However, when you feel that your visit is complete, ask your ally if there is a gift you may take back with you.

Reverse the process and return home. Put your shoes back on, light your torch, go back through the passageway, up the stairs, open the trap door, feel the fresh air and extinguish your torch, hanging it up with the matches so that they are waiting for you whenever you need them. Close the door, walk calmly and purposefully through the woods, through the lovely field, back through your neighborhood and enter your home.

• • •

Inevitably, some of our animal allies initially disappoint us. We long for wild, powerful, exotic creatures and when instead we discover our allies include such mundane animals as mice, spiders and ants, we feel let down, our egos deflated. Just as there are no *bad* colors, there are no bad or weak animals. No one can teach you better how to budget, how to make something from nothing, than Mouse. The animal most associated with dream skills is Lizard. Although we've developed negative associations with some animals, these aren't inherent.

If you are not pleased with your animal ally:

- Research: find out everything you can about your ally, no matter how mundane, about its personality and its life style. Look for traditional legends regarding your animal, not from only one but from many cultures. Negative associations tend to be culture-bound. Many Westerners, for instance, fear bats, yet in traditional Chinese folklore, bats are perhaps the luckiest creatures of all while amongst some Native American traditions bats are sacred. You may be surprised and pleased by what you learn. Allow yourself to learn what your ally feels you need to know.

- There's something to be said for allies who are common, everyday animals: they're around and available as an actual presence. A squirrel or a crow or a blue jay can actually interact with you in person, offering encouragement and positive reinforcement and supplying clues for your journey with some regularity. They're able to visit you and initiate contact.

> To attain needed skills and information, surround yourself with the appropriate images, concentrate and focus upon them, and then invite them into your dreams.

The difference between working with an animal spirit as a tool or as an ally is one of spectrum. There are animals to teach every skill. You may approach anyone for a brief lesson.

In the Spells part of this book, you'll find directions advising you of which animals to work with for love, money or other purposes. There are however some animals who very specifically teach us about magic, about finding and enhancing our psychic gifts. They will teach you to discover your own magical aptitude and help you learn how to work with animal powers.

Animal teachers of magic fall into two categories:

1.*Threshold animals* are among the few who comfortably frequent the borders between the wilderness and human habitation. They are not "tame" animals, although unlike many "wild" animals, they tend to be able to thrive despite our presence. These creatures travel the frontier between the human and animal realms, delivering important and special messages when they choose. Humans interest them. Unless taught otherwise, they are not afraid of us. An encounter with any of these creatures carries a powerful message from Earth. These animals guide you to discover your magical aptitude and the most positive direction for your magic. Threshold animals include mammals such as dolphins, coyotes and jackals, however, the animals most intrinsically linked to Earth's magic are snakes and the corvid cousins, raven and crow.

2. *Familiar animals* are literally that, they're "familiar" to us. These include what are known as "livestock" and "companion animals." Think of the stereotypical witches' familiars: usually frogs, cats, dogs, rabbits, lizards or birds, these remain popular companion animals. That's because the animals who have historically been most eager to work with humans moved in with us and evolved into what are now dubbed "domestic animals." Like our own powers, their spiritual gifts are often overlooked and taken for granted. Our own personal dissatisfaction and self-doubt is reflected in our general treatment of familiars. On the whole, humans have not reciprocated kindly for their gifts: breeding and "domestication" techniques have sapped these creatures, particularly cows and sheep, of their innate spiritual power. Pay attention to the animals with whom you have the most actual direct contact. Who knows? Your most magical partners may already live in your home. These animals nourish our psychic ability. Close positive physical proximity increases your own personal power. The most popular and powerful familiar animals are cats, dogs and horses.

Threshold Animals

RAVEN AND CROW

Raven is the primary magical ambassador from the animal kingdom. Raven and his cousin, Crow, are the shaman's allies. They teach and perform soul retrieval and transformation. Raven journeys back and forth between dimensions, the realms of life and death, spirit and flesh and can deliver and transmit messages. Raven gives magic lessons and teaches you how to hone your skills. Raven sparks the courage to face the unknown, to journey into unmarked territory. Raven teaches how to balance caution and courage, how to turn fear into a survival skill rather than a liability. Raven is a sponsor of healing emotion and teaches the futility of healing the body without also healing the spirit and emotions.

Crows and ravens are often referred to interchangeably although technically the raven is a larger, shaggier bird possessing slightly different habits. When mythology distinguishes between them, ravens are more associated with transformative magic, while crows are associated with healing. Neither will work with you before you are ready, although they may drop in from time to time with encouragement. If you're nearly there, you may receive company and assistance from their little blue cousin, the jay.

Ornithologists consider crows and ravens to be the geniuses of the bird kingdom. They are extremely intelligent, demonstrate a sense of humor, use tools and have a concept of counting. Crows mate for life and are faithful. Both parents care for the young who may live with them for several years. Crows alert each other to food and danger, take care of one another and provide for their injured as best as they are able. Young males wishing to gain entry to a community do so by ingratiating themselves to mature females with young, assisting them and bringing them extra food.

Science has demonstrated exactly how much crows have in common with humans, only confirming what folklore, mythology and religion has suggested for millennia. An amazingly broad spectrum of cultures, Earthwide, has considered ravens and crows sacred, recounting crow's lessons and legends as hero, trickster and sometimes as Earth's Supreme Creator. These include Celtic, Greek, Japanese, Jewish, Native American, Scandinavian, Vietnamese and especially the indigenous cultures of Siberia and Pacific Coastal North America. In all these cultures and legends, crows and ravens guide and serve humans.

According to one legend, Raven created the universe. Everything was
wonderful, perfect, peaceful. Raven was bored. So he scrapped that
world and formed another more interesting, flawed one, creating people
in his own image for his amusement.

Crows are not afraid of people. They are among the easiest animals to communicate with, because, like people, they enjoy communication for its own sake. They are humbling birds, one look in their eyes lets you know that, as with cats, they have no doubt which of you is more intelligent and it isn't you. Watch crows as they eat: one unselfishly posts as guard while the others indulge and then they'll take turns.

- To see a crow with food in its beak is a sign of tremendous good fortune, an assurance of future economic prosperity. If they pause to make eye contact with you, to thrust their beak in your direction, to make sure you've seen their sign, the message is even stronger.

SNAKE

Snake is the animal most associated with Earth's wisdom. As it lacks arms and legs, unless a snake is held captive, its entire body is in constant connection with Earth. Many ancient traditions believed that snakes could transmit Earth's secrets and knowledge to people, should they choose. The ancient Romans considered snakes to be particular allies of human women, healing and empowering them, encouraging proper functioning of both body and psychic aptitude.

Because the snake periodically sheds its skin, first appearing dull then emerging shiny and new, it is associated with rebirth and rejuvenation. Snake's power is particularly multifaceted. Snake is believed to be the official repository and guardian of Earth's secrets. In addition to magic lessons, Snake can assist you with all matters regarding health, fertility, knowledge and wealth. Snake can also be approached as a research tool and resource whenever you need to learn something. Snake can also be considered the animal equivalent of a white candle: if you don't know which animal to address, you can always approach Snake.

Snakes have an independent presence. Ultimately their loyalty is to Earth, not to humans. A snake is never "tame" although it may live among us. They rarely volunteer their wisdom, unlike Raven who on occasion demonstrates a protective and parental attitude toward humans. If you need information from Snake, assume that you will have to initiate contact.

Shed snakeskins or crow feathers are believed to be powerful and precious magical implements. The catch is: they must be given freely. If you find one, consider it a gift, perhaps acknowledgement that you've mastered a level of magical knowledge and skill. Harming any animal is believed to be unlucky but causing harm or discomfort to snakes, ravens or crows, or indeed to any of the threshold animals, is considered particularly inauspicious, really bad karma. Body parts taken by force may backfire upon you: crows, for one, are famous tricksters. If you want crow feathers, feed them, they tend to be generous with feathers as payment (remember, they won't come before you're ready) or request them from a crow-rehabilitation center. Many people keep snakes as companion animals, obtaining their skins as they shed. Likewise you can request shed skins at a rehabilitation center or zoo.

> *Of course, there's an exception to every rule. If Snake has made introductory overtures to you, this indicates that you possess innate healing skills and aptitude. Snake has appeared to encourage you to maximize your potential and to share its knowledge with you, so that you, too, will be a vehicle of healing energy.*

- Abandoned snakeskins are worn as belts and girdles to rejuvenate female fertility. Snakeskins are also sometimes wrapped around aching joints to provide relief.

- Abandoned crow feathers are used to focus magical concentration. Use it to waft incense smoke or the smoke from a dried herb bundle over your crystal ball. A crow feather under your pillow or placed whole inside a dream pillow assists with astral projection and lucid dreaming.

Familiar Animals

CAT

Anyone who has ever lived with a cat scoffs at the designation *domestic*. Cats will prove to you that animals choose us. Cats teach us how to joyfully access Earth's wisdom and bounty. You can't access Pure Magic if you're secretly afraid that taking pleasure from Earth or achieving success will endanger your soul. If you are uncomfortable reaping Earth's bounties, if you're not sure you deserve to be happy and successful, approach Cat for some lessons. Cats are among the most popular companion animals worldwide, however if sharing your life with an actual cat is not practicable for you, use imagery and visualizations to tap into the power. In this way, you can learn from Cat even if you or someone near you is allergic to their fur.

- If you're not sure you can trust Earth to be a place of goodness, if you doubt on any level that you deserve good fortune *and* you also don't like or are afraid of cats, Cat may be particularly important for you. Remember that you don't have to work with an actual living cat. Get some pictures or figurines and begin to untangle the mystery of your thoughts and fears. A statue of Bastet may be very beneficial.

> Egypt's cat goddess, Bastet, was no minor deity but the subject of great religious veneration for centuries. Depicted as a cat or as a woman with a cat's head, Bastet's domain includes all of Earth's sensual pleasures: love, sex, magic, music, food and perfume. Bastet embodies the gentle power of the sun that nourishes and stimulates pleasure and growth. (Her sister, lion-headed Sekhmet, serves as her alter ego, embodying destructive, scorching solar power.) Bastet was considered the special protector of women and children.

Cat's main domains of power are magic and fertility. Cats have traditionally been associated with female sensual power. When this power was held in high esteem, cats were associated with goddesses. When this power became feared and denigrated, cats bore the brunt. The earliest record that exists for the execution of cats in connection to magic dates from 962 in

France. Hundreds of thousands of cats would be killed in Europe until the last recorded execution in England, scant years before the American Revolution, in 1712.

- If you are afraid to express, contact, or enhance your innate magical or sensual powers, bring the image of Cat into your life as a healing force.

Maneki Neko. The Japanese Beckoning Cat Amulet.

Maneki Neko, the Japanese Beckoning Cat, brings good luck. Virtually unknown one hundred years ago, Maneki Neko has rapidly become one of the most popular amulets, not only in Japan but all over Earth. The typical image of "the beckoning cat" depicts a Japanese bobtail cat holding up one paw in invitation. This amulet may be familiar to you as it beckons from the windows of innumerable sushi bars and mall stores specializing in Japanese toys, attesting to the belief in Maneki Neko's power to provide prosperity.

Various legends attest to the roots of this image: in one, the cat saves a samurai's life, in another it brings prosperity to a monastery, in still another, it brings economic success to its namesake cathouse, a house of prostitution. Whichever legend you prefer, different types of Maneki Nekos exist to fill your needs. Maneki Neko should be placed near a door or window, looking out.

> Do you long for a powerful amulet but fear that they are rare and expensive, beyond your reach? Don't despair. An extremely popular, accessible and powerful amulet takes the form of a cat. If you can't find one at the mall—and it's quite possible that you can—you'll find Maneki Neko at stores specializing in items from Japan.

- A cat with a beckoning left hand invites business.

- A cat with a beckoning right hand invokes cash.

- Maneki Neko bells cleanse the aura while providing prosperity.

The cats are color coded for luck, too: a white cat brings good luck and happiness, a gold cat is best for attracting wealth and prosperity, a black cat brings spiritual protection while a rare red Maneki Neko attracts good health.

- A small Maneki Neko of any color worn around the waist protects against pain and illness.

- If the image is unavailable, even displaying the Japanese written symbol for *cat* is believed to bear some protective capacity.

DOG

Dogs came to live with us so long ago that the distinctions between dogs and their ancestor, the wolf, are largely based upon their relationships with humans. Some anthropologists believe that when humans began their initial migrations over Earth, they were already accompanied by dogs, who may or may not have been "tame." We didn't domesticate dogs as much as they chose us. Even cultures that didn't domesticate animals, such as those of North America prior to European contact, kept dogs.

Dogs are our most faithful companions and devoted protectors. They are our intrepid psychic guides. Dogs are the creatures who travel with greatest ease between the realms of the living and the dead. In many cultures, it was believed that without a dog as a guide, the human soul would never arrive at the next destination. Sometimes a favorite dog was buried with a person. Perhaps more kindly, in ancient Mexico, clay statues of dogs were placed in the grave instead. Dogs also patrol the border between life and death, determining who gains entry and in the case of shamans, who can leave. Greek myths recount tales of shamans bearing dog treats to guarantee their exit, as three-headed Cerberus was reputed to guard the gates of Hades, the underworld.

We still retain dogs for protection on the physical realm: whether for our families, homes, property or ourselves. Dogs will provide spiritual and psychic protection, too, if you let them. When embarking upon any psychic exploration, whether contacting unknown allies, expanding your magical faculties, practicing astral travel, divination or shamanism, encourage a canine presence to accompany you. This can be your own dog, who might enjoy stretching his magical powers alongside you, or if this isn't possible or comfortable for you, use canine imagery.

- Envision a companion canine guard. Because this dog will be a spiritual guardian and companion, not responsible for actually guarding your home, whatever breed makes you feel safest and most comfortable is best for you, whether it's a huge mastiff or a cute teacup poodle.

- Keep photographs, drawings, statues or toy dogs close to you while working magic. Tuck a small photo of a dog into a dream pillow for extra safety while you sleep.

- Roman gravestones utilized images of dogs to symbolize love and fidelity beyond the grave. If you are attempting to contact those no longer among the living, use dog power to facilitate and protect you. Keep a canine image near where you work, whether photograph, drawing or statue. A photograph of a beloved, trusted dog who has also passed over may be most effective.

Over the years, special dog amulets have evolved for the purpose of reaping the benefit of Dog's protective qualities without actually having a living dog. In some cases, these amulets are believed to maximize the dog's shamanic and protective power. The most readily available include:

- Traditional Mexican clay figures, based upon ancient Toltec images. Place them near where you practice divination or anywhere in your home that you perceive as spiritually vulnerable.

- Statuettes of Anubis, Egypt's black jackal-headed guide and guardian of the dead.

- Chinese Fu dogs. Fu means luck, and yes, they're actually is such a breed, considered to be the living link between Chinese wolves and other modern Chinese dog breeds. Believed exceptionally auspicious, stone and porcelain images of Fu dogs placed near doors serve as house amulets providing spiritual protection and good fortune.

HORSE

Horses are more than vehicles of transportation, they're vehicles of transformation. Horses entering a culture provide sweeping change. Horse power entering a life opens doors and possibilities. The general consensus among traditional philosophies is that horses contain more magical power and vitality than any other species. Merely being in their presence increases your own vitality, stamina and magical ability. The most common animal allies found in fairy tales are horses, who typically accompany and assist the hero, often able to speak, but only in the hero's presence. Horses enter our lives to help us achieve our destiny and to help make our dreams come true.

Riding a horse, at its finest expression, creates a fusion of human and animal, the two becoming as one. That physical expression may be the single finest example of human/animal energy transmission. If you do ride and have never yet considered magic, try it, you may be surprised at the reservoir of magical potential awaiting you. However, working with horse magic, absorbing its energy, is not limited to horseback riding, neither now nor historically. The magical relationship between horse and human is not limited to riding. Humans venerated horses long before they saddled them.

- Horse power increases the quantity of our magical ability. Being within their presence or surrounding yourself with their imagery increases the magical power you possess to draw upon. Horse images can be wonderfully specific. Toy stores sell collector's toys that reflect the wide variety of the breed. What's your fantasy horse? Do you long for a massive, stolid, dependable draft horse or is it a fast, flashy Arabian stallion that kindles your imagination? The type of horse you envision reveals something about the type of magic most important to you right now.

- Horses also provide stamina: if you find yourself always almost reaching your magical goals, consider keeping a horse charm or some equine image nearby to replenish your resources and provide help and encouragement.

- In addition to Pure Magic, horses also encourage the full expression of both male and female power. They also encourage both men and women to accept and appreciate each other's power. Women who wish to access and harmonize their full spiritual and sexual powers and men who have difficulty accepting women as equals or who are uncomfortable with expressions of female power might consider keeping horse imagery in close proximity.

While beneficial actions toward an animal individual or species engenders good will from its presiding spirit, any harm caused may likewise lead to unwillingness to provide you with assistance and power. Usually it's quite clear whether you've bestowed kindness or harm. Horses are a special case. You may be unaware of participating in any cruelty toward them, however, one of the most popular modern menopausal "remedies" is created from the urine of mares kept perpetually pregnant, their young taken away, the males usually sold as meat. By ingesting such a product, your ability to tap into horse power is limited or curtailed, ironically, as menopause is traditionally believed to herald great surges of extra magic power.

> If you have been involved in any action detrimental to an animal, horse or otherwise, you can remedy the situation by ceasing the harmful action, immediately participating in some positive act benefiting that animal and, perhaps, petitioning the presiding animal spirit for forgiveness. Continue with these acts until you receive a response.

SPIRIT LAND

Potentially the most powerful and exhilarating magic involves working with spirits, yet nothing else demonstrates how far removed we are from our Earthly origins. No culture lacks a history of spirit contact and assistance; for most of our history, it's been a common human experience. However, today, when the average human has little personal contact with our fellow mammals, let alone beings of other dimensions, what was once everyday reality can be challenging and frustrating.

The simplest definition is that these spirits are powerful, living entities who resist human efforts to define them. Frankly, *Bewitched*'s Samantha is far more credible as a spirit than as a witch. Witches are resolutely human. Burn them, they suffer and die. The English word "witch" comes from the same root as "wise." Wise humans recall the old Earth knowledge that leads to success; whatever extra **supernatural** power they may also possess typically comes courtesy of their spirit helpers.

Spirits can do the sort of magical tricks we long to do; our limitations don't exist for them. Many spirits are shape-shifters. They can appear in the image of a human, but that's merely a form for them; don't be fooled. Because people have always preferred to communicate with what looks like a person, they accommodate us. The most powerful among them can assume many forms. Although the general consensus is that spirits are not truly immortal, most have life spans so long that for all intents and purposes, they may as well be.

Whether you find spirit allies more or less challenging than animal allies depends upon your personal beliefs. On one hand, animals are clearly alive and present on Earth. On the other hand, spirits typically share our form and most have emotions, desires and communication skills similar to our own. For some people, spirits' very "other-worldly" quality creates an aura of sacredness and trust.

Many spirits are as attracted to humans as we are to them. Like Samantha, many masquerade as people, intermingle with us, even marry and settle down with us. Whatever they are, they apparently have the capacity to interbreed with us, like wolves with dogs. Unlike on television, the children are invariably human (sorry!) but often possess special protection and skills, courtesy of their spirit parent. Spirits and humans maintain relationships based on mutual attraction and mutual benefit.

For many, the initial and greatest obstacle to accessing these spirits is language. Seemingly simple words like *god, goddess* or *gods* are actually charged with highly personal meanings. We think we know what we mean by those words but they may mean very different things to different people. The spirits are not identical, their powers, interests and dispositions are far from identical, yet in English we have a very limited range of vocabulary words with which to discuss them.

There are spiritual entities who are Creator Spirits, who claim to have created existence as we know it. Different names may identify the same ones. It's hard to tell. There are also those whom we call gods or goddesses in English whose domains are much narrower, their own origins are described, they are not creator but creations like us, perhaps more akin to an angel or saint. The terms *god* or *goddess* unfortunately cause many to feel that they are threatening their initial religious teachings or being disloyal to their faith.

Every people on Earth had contact with spirit beings and developed their own vocabulary: angel, orisha, loa, djinn, daemon, mystère, you could fill a page. In English, we have but a blanket word, *spirit,* but other languages may have a variety of names to differentiate between these beings. Don't let words prevent you from accessing this power, your birthright. Choose the words that are comfortable for you. Remember, language doesn't exist independently of people. Other humans create language; adjust it so that it benefits you. If you need assistance, the Egyptian spiritual sponsor of both words and magic is Thoth.

The Yoruba Model for Practical Spiritual Interaction

The Yoruba people of West Africa use the word *orisha* to name these spirit powers. Anyone wishing to do extensive spirit work would do well to contemplate the structure of traditional Yoruba religion. The Yoruba are a monotheistic people; they have one supreme creator, Olodumare, who encompasses both male and female. Although Olodumare loves humans, we are not the center of the universe. Among Olodumare's other creations was the concept of delegating. Olodumare created assorted spirit beings, the orisha, each possessing its own department of interest, to assist in Earth's harmonious operation. Just as there are orishas whose function it is to encourage agriculture or wilderness, so there are orishas who facilitate every aspect of human existence. Any area or interest that can be envisioned possesses an orisha who serves in a supervisory capacity.

> *Whatever you perceive these spirits to be, it is crucial, if you intend to work with them, to see them as something alive and independent from you. The goddess within is fine for raising consciousness, self-esteem or a sense of the personal sacred but if you plan on actually asking for assistance, seeing them as part of you or a projection of yourself limits interaction and potentially causes problems. It becomes too easy to dismiss your experiences as not real.*

• Ogun, for instance, is the patron of metal. He takes care of those who are in close contact with that material: soldiers, jewelers, taxicab drivers. If you were worried about your son the soldier, you might direct your petition toward Ogun.

- Yemaya is matron of women. If your personal obstacles fall under the general heading of "women's troubles," you'd petition Yemaya instead.

The most conservative count of orishas is 401, although only about forty are actively involved with humans on any sort of consistent, regular basis. Each orisha has various forms that they consistently assume. Each also possesses various preferences in food, fragrance, colors and gifts. These preferences are used as vehicles of two-way communication. Yemaya's color is blue. To attract her notice, you might somehow prominently feature that color. She, in turn, might use the color to send a signal to you. It's an eminently practical system and in the case of the Yoruba, still a living, vital one. The Yoruba remain as living testimony to human/spirit interaction. There is no culture that didn't at one time possess some similar system. You can use Yoruba methods as a model for spirit interaction, regardless of your own ethnic origins or that of your spirit ally.

Why Do Spirits Help Us?

Spirits assist us for any number of reasons. Some do it because they like us. Some do it because, basically, it's their job. That's their function, their *raison d'être*. If you needed legal advice, you'd call a lawyer. If your child needs special spiritual protection, you might consider calling Bes or Kwan Yin.

Spirits assist humans for other reasons. Some do it as professional patronage. Hecate is matron of midwives. If you are a working midwife, you've earned the right to call upon her. Tanit sponsors astrologers. If you need help, in any department, her door is open for you. Coatlique may be fierce and forbidding to most but she has a soft spot for florists.

Some spirits feel ties of ethnic loyalty. Atargatis is especially fond of Syria. If that is your cultural origin or if you possess some other type of tie, consider that you have her private number. In African-influenced Brazil, Yemaya, Queen of the Sea is a national heroine: any African who survived the Middle Passage is believed to have done so via her grace. Any descendant of those individuals can feel that communication has already been established, the phone lines are open.

Some spirits love certain people because they recognize something of their essence within them. Anat suffers terribly from infertility; she has been known to heal human women who share her experience. Demeter suffered the trauma of a kidnapped child; if that's your personal pain, she shares it.

If a spirit resonates for you, odds are it's because they're already calling you, already lingering in the shadows. Should this ultimately not be a relationship you desire, respectfully decline. Take a moment to explain (English or other human language is just fine; they tend to understand us a lot better than we understand them), perhaps burn a little frankincense or something similar as a sign of respect but just say no, thank you. You don't have to accept anything that doesn't feel right to you, whether these are favors, gifts or advice.

Should you accept, however, or at least not clearly decline, the spirits do expect to get paid. These are mutually beneficial relationships: on some level, spirits benefit from us, too. They feed of our energy, our offerings, our attention. However, they are independent, they do not exist solely to serve us. Always assume that even the lowest level spirit being has powers greater than a human's, or at least possesses a few tricks up their sleeves. Frankly, the more powerful they are, the more generally benevolent they tend to be. It is best to be as specific as you can while working with spirits. Ask for the one you want by name, don't just put out a general call. Herein lies the danger of the Ouija board; spirits sitting around with nothing to do tend to be the ones no one else has called for and probably for good reason. Ouija boards are an excellent device should you have an appointment with a spiritual entity whom you already trust. However, haphazardly using one to call whoever is around is a little like opening your front door in a busy metropolis and allowing whoever is passing by with nothing better to do to enter your home.

> *Consider a one-time favor to be somewhat like a commission. Very specifically and explicitly tell them what you desire, what your method of payment will be and when to expect it.*

Be as specific and clear when communicating as possible. Let them know what you want, a relationship or a favor. Relationships are ongoing:

the spirit assists you, you're expected to demonstrate respect and appreciation periodically. The finest human/spirit relationships are filled with mutual love and respect.

APPROPRIATE PAYMENTS

- Artistic expression. Create a tribute to the spirit's power and generosity. Let inspiration and ability guide you as to whether poetry, painting, a Web site or other medium is most appropriate.

- Rituals honor the spirits and increase their power as well. Let circumstances and the spirits themselves guide you as to the nature and form of your ritual. Moroccan women offer henna parties in the name of their spirit helpers. Water spirits may appreciate a journey to the beach while fiery types may prefer some candles. Bursts of intuition are often messages from the spirit world: let them tell you what they want.

- Most spirits have animals and plant allies of whom they are very fond. These animals are their most frequent messengers, in dreams and elsewhere. Any good deed performed upon their behalf will be greatly appreciated by the spirit.

Altars as Vehicles of Communication

Altars are tableaux or arrangements of specific articles. The simplest altar consists of nothing more than a candle and a glass of water. The most lavish, complex Vodou altars are small rooms packed with lovingly, meticulously arranged treasures. Every item or article involved in the creation of an altar is carefully chosen. In addition to objects, candles, fragrance, food and drink may be included on an altar. Nothing is random.

ALTARS SERVE MANY PURPOSES

- They call in spiritual assistance. The components of the altar serve as signals to the spirit that their presence is desired. The components traditionally share in the essence of that spirit or else they are favored materials. The arrangement attracts the spirit's notice and welcomes them.

- Altars serve as a forum for communication. By adjusting the items upon your altar, you can demonstrate your needs using symbolic language. For instance, you might maintain a permanent altar to Oshun, a particularly versatile, powerful and gregarious spirit. However by varying the colors of the candles you signal what your immediate needs may be. Oshun's personal colors are yellow and orange: a yellow or orange candle is burned to signal that it is her presence, not another's, that you invite. In addition, you might also burn a blue candle for physical healing or emotional relief or a green one if your immediate crisis is cash.

- Altars serve as a focal point. You don't truly *need* an altar. You don't really need anything. Whatever communication transpires actually occurs on the mental or spiritual plane. Spirit magic is potentially the least expensive magic of all: all the items, all the fragrances or incense are merely vehicles, signals or tributes. All that you truly need is your ability to concentrate and create that mental connection with the spiritual entity. Once you're experienced, you'll recognize when the connection has been made; it's as if a switch has been turned on or a phone line is suddenly open. This can be done via visualization, dreams or pure focused thought. owever, as simple as that sounds, the reality is that for many people this process can be extremely challenging, especially in the beginning. The altar creates a point upon which to focus one's attention, making it easier to focus upon the spirit and intensify concentration and communication.

- Statues and images of spirits serve the same purpose. They serve to focus our inner vision. If they help you, the image can serve as the center of the altar, the eye upon which you focus. If you're uncomfortable with graven images, just don't use them. They're not for you. Don't confuse the image with the deity, who is a spirit being, although some sacredness will eventually attach to all components of an altar and many feel that once something has been included on an altar, it should then be reserved for sacred purposes.

- Images and altars create a comfortable home for the spirit, a preferred rest stop on their journeys, so to speak. If they're happy, they'll linger and potentially offer assistance without your having to ask or even be able to identify what it is you need help with. You provide spirits with a comfortable, clear way to communicate with you.

• Altars serve as tribute and thanks for favors and wisdom granted.

The most traditional altars are placed on tables. They may also be built outside. Place altars where the spirit is most likely to be happy. Water spirits enjoy the bathroom, fire spirits the hearth. Spirits of romance like to be in the bedroom; their invisible presence can add sparks to your love life.

Ancestors

The most accessible, responsive spirits of all may be your personal ancestral spirits. It is assumed in many cultures, that following death, some part of the individual stays behind to provide protection to descendants. The remaining family in return is expected to remember them, honor that memory, be a source of pride and perhaps offer gestures of respect on occasion.

Although you may always petition anyone with whom you feel kinship, by definition, ancestral spirits must be deceased blood relatives. It is not necessary for you to know who they actually were nor do you need to know their names, although any details you have strengthen the process. Which ancestors should you appeal to? Whichever ones you want. Your actual descent, your DNA if you will, goes back to the dawning of human time. If you're not comfortable with your immediate ancestors, go back further. Visualize them hovering over you, waiting to be honored and put to work.

Are you a messy eater? If food constantly falls off your fork, if it's always dropping onto your clothes, this may be your ancestors telling you they want a word with you. Set up some communication and see whether your table habits suddenly become neater.

To communicate, pay homage or ask for direction, erect a family altar. All that is required is a glass of pure springwater and a white candle. Burn candles for seven days, extinguishing the flames when not supervised. The spirits care about your safety. It's not necessary to change the water or add to it if it evaporates. If it pleases you, make a more elaborate altar. Put out photographs of relatives if you have them or display something that symbolizes those relations for you. If you think they'd really prefer a cup of coffee, a glass of wine or something stronger, place that out in addition. (The water is a requirement; it's more for purposes of attracting spiritual attention than for drinking.) Serve the ancestors food they would like, food representative of your ancestry and their time. If that isn't possible, offer them something special to you. Offer them what you would give them if they could visit and tell you of their and your history, offer you advice born of observation and wisdom.

Spirit Sponsors of Magic

Should a spirit answer your petition, they will want you to recognize their response. Spirits tend to have specific manifestations: specific shapes they can assume. They also possess what are called attributes: these are the symbols that communicate their power and presence. Neptune is rarely without a trident. The trident alone may signal his presence. Spirits most typically communicate with you via these symbols in your dreams or in what passes for coincidence in daily life. They want credit for favors granted. They want to communicate. They want you to recognize them and will do their best to make themselves recognizable.

A greater selection of spirit allies exist than plant, animal, metal or mineral allies. There are spirits for everything: fishing, specific career goals, artistic ambitions, marriage, animals, women, perfume, beer, pregnancy, you name it. There are even spirits like Hermes and Ellegua who provide increased access to other spirits: they are spiritual gatekeepers. Later as we explore different goals of magic, we'll examine some of the most helpful spirit allies, who they are, what they like and how best to communicate with them.

Some spirits, however, are specifically teachers and sponsors of Earth Magic. Emerging from many continents, they encourage human psychic ability, provide protection and guidance to the magical arts.

MINONA

Minona dwells deep in the forests of Benin, formerly the kingdom of Dahomey, ancestral home of the Fon people, birthplace of Vodou. Minona is famed as a protector of women. She imparts fertility to women and

Earth. When Minona's mother, First Woman, observed chaos on Earth, she charged Minona with the purpose of teaching women divination using palm kernels so that they could read Earth's omens, and balance could be established. She also creates, inspires and activates the Dahomean charms known as *gbo*; these are created from metals, herbs and other materials. Minona has no temples or public shrines. She lives quietly in the wilderness, teaching benevolent and protective magic to those women who value her knowledge. In return, women create altars in her honor within their homes, offering her fresh fruits.

Although media attention tends to target the destruction of South American rainforests, African rainforests are under siege, too. In addition to a personal altar, Minona would be pleased by gestures on behalf of her forest home and its indigenous flora and fauna.

BABA YAGA

Baba Yaga lives in a clearing within a deep Russian birch forest in a hut that stands and moves on giant chicken's feet surrounded by a fence made from human bones and skulls, remnants of visitors who disappointed her. Baba Yaga rides a mortar and pestle. She is a master herbalist and can cure any ailment. She has a slew of magic tricks up her sleeve. She is the protective mistress of the forest animals and loves the wilderness. Baba Yaga has iron teeth and is bone thin, although she has a voracious appetite and is somewhat of a gourmet to boot. She chews up those who displease her but will heal, instruct and reward those whom she finds deserving, albeit somewhat grudgingly and with attitude. Baba Yaga can reveal secrets and produce miracles, however she has a harsh personality. Don't expect a warm, cuddly *babushka*, even if she likes you. Baba Yaga rewards bravery, industry and creativity in men and women alike.

Baba Yaga has a soft spot for Virgos. She is affiliated with the fire and earth elements. Her planet is the sun. She loves all wild animals but her sacred animal is the horse.

KAPO

Kapo, the Red Eel Woman, was born in Tahiti but soon made her way to Hawaii. Wild and temperamental, like her famous younger sister, volcano goddess, Pele, Kapo was both feared and admired as the matron of powerful

Hawaiian sorcerers. Like Minona, Kapo teaches magic that can be used for either benevolent or malevolent purposes: what you do with your knowledge is purely your responsibility. Kapo can also be invoked to reverse any evil magic: to return any malevolent power that has been directed toward you. Like most Hawaiian deities, Kapo assumes many forms: plant, tree, human or animal. As a woman, she is consistently graceful (she is a master hula dancer), beautiful and seductive. In addition to her vast knowledge of Earth's magic powers, Kapo teaches methods of enhancing and controlling women's reproductive capacities.

Kapo loves wild, untamed places. Molokai, the island most associated with her, still remains the most unspoiled of the major Hawaiian islands. Her special plant is the pandanus. Contact her at night, out of doors, especially when it's windy or stormy. You can please her—and maintain access to her—through hula dancing and by working to preserve wilderness wherever you are, but most especially in Hawaii.

FREYA

Freya isn't interested in little huts in the forest. She lives in a splendid palace, where love songs play continuously. Freya is among the most versatile spirits, with dominion over beauty, romance, sex, fertility, childbirth, enchantment, magic, witchcraft, prosperity and war. Freya is the most beautiful Norse spirit and their original shaman. Her ancient priestesses, known as *volvas,* provided traveling shamanic services to their communities. Freya is rarely seen without her precious magical gold necklace, which she obtained at great cost. To get it, she had to sleep with the four dwarves who were its craftsmen.

Two very large gray cats named Bee-gold (Honey) and Tree-gold (Amber) draw her chariot. Freya also owns a falcon-feather cloak that enables her to transform into a falcon and fly. A master shape-shifter, she can take any shape she chooses. An excellent teacher, Freya provides instruction in magic as well as psychic and shamanic skills for men and women. She knows the secrets of the runes, will provide instruction and communicate with you through them.

Freya's sacred animal is the cat. Traditionally she showed favor to those who put out pans of milk for her beloved creatures; this became an old Norse country custom. European cats would eventually be slaughtered in the thousands specifically for their associations with Freya. Military veterans, jewelers and students of the magical arts may consider themselves under her protection.

HECATE

Hecate, the Queen of the Night, emerged in what is now modern Turkey. She is most famous as the companion of Demeter in her quest to find her kidnapped daughter, Persephone. Hecate is believed to be the unseen witness to every crime; she can be appealed to for justice, particularly when the crime is of a sexual nature against a woman or female child. Hecate would eventually serve as Persephone's handmaiden in her capacity as Queen of the Underworld. Freya and Hecate would serve as the models for European stereotypes of witches, Freya as the dangerously seductive witch, Hecate as the wizened crone.

Hecate holds dominion over life, death, regeneration and magic. She rules wisdom, choices, expiation, vengeance and travel. Hecate guards the frontier between life and death. She serves as intermediary between the spirit world and that of humans. Hecate holds the power to grant or deny any human's wish.

Hecate most typically manifests as a mature woman or as a black dog. Dogs are her sacred creatures. Cerberus, the three-headed hound who guarded the gates of the Greek underworld, may or may not be Hecate in disguise. Hecate has a particularly strong bond with her familiar animal; even when manifesting in human form, Hecate is rarely without canine companionship. On the rare occasion when she turns up alone, there will be some sort of dog reference so that you'll recognize her; she often circles in the manner of dogs. Her attributes include a toad, a pomegranate, a key, a cauldron, a broom, torch or knife.

Hecate is most powerful during the dark moon phase. She only accepts offerings and petitions after dark, the only acceptable illumination being candles or torches. The last day of each month is dedicated to her and is the best time to ask for favors, inspiration or instruction. In addition, Wiccans celebrate November 16th as Hecate Night. Midwives, herbalists and magical practitioners may consider themselves already among Hecate's initiates. Garlic, honey and lavender are favored offerings. Traditionally, offerings for Hecate are placed on a stone or small plate and left at a crossroads after dark. Do not return for the plate or any part but consider all of it part of the sacrifice. (In other words, if you don't want to lose a plate, use a paper one.)

Traditionally, Hecate's followers held dinners in her honor. Devotees feasted and shared their magical knowledge. Leftovers were placed outside the door or at a crossroads for Hecate and her hounds. Cynics scoff that these leftovers were actually consumed by feral dogs or homeless people without realizing that this was Hecate's intent, this is one way she accepts offerings. Her ancient devotees also stained their palms and soles with henna in her honor. She recognizes herself in this gesture. Any action on behalf of dogs, Hecate's sacred messengers, is probably the offering she appreciates most.

TLAZOLTEOTL

Tlazolteotl's image may be most familiar to modern movie viewers as the stolen idol at the beginning of *Raiders of the Lost Ark*. In that image, she is depicted naked and squatting, grimacing in childbirth. The Conquistadors were amazed and frightened when they encountered other images of this fierce Aztec deity. They thought they had left feminine images like this back home in Europe; riding naked on a broomstick, accompanied by an owl or a raven and wearing a peaked bark hat.

Tlazolteotl is a spirit of magic, witchcraft, healing, love, sex, desire and a protector of women. In her capacity as the Spirit of Garbage, Tlazolteotl cleanses Earth, removing spiritual waste. She cleanses humans as well and is credited with inventing the *temazcal*, the Aztec sweat bath.

Tlazolteotl offers special protection to midwives as well as female doctors and health practitioners. Her sacred creatures include bats, snakes, ravens and owls. Should she make a personal appearance, her face is often painted: white smeared in the upper regions, a black band around her mouth. Although she is fierce, she protects those she loves and possesses many magic secrets. Tlazolteotl wears a feather bracelet or a turquoise necklace with round gold bells.

ISIS

Isis, world-renowned as the "Mistress of Magic," is the most famous spiritual teacher of magic and bears a unique relationship with human beings. Among the most ancient and consistently worshipped of deities, her saga has been retold for at least five thousand years. At the peak of her fame, Isis was venerated from the depths of Africa, throughout Western Asia and Europe as far as England's Thames River.

Magic, both its gifts and its limitations, permeates Isis's myth. Magic enters Isis's life from her very first breath. Because her mother's pregnancy breaks a spiritual injunction, a curse is laid upon her so that she cannot give birth. Luckily, Lord Thoth, baboon-headed inventor of enchantment, secretly loves Isis's mother. Determined to provide assistance, he creates dice and gambles for high stakes with the moon god, controller of the calendar, and is thus able to magically rearrange the entire calendar year so that she can safely deliver her quadruplets. Thoth will also become something of a godfather to Isis, instructing and encouraging her until her magic outshines his.

Isis determines to become the most skilled magical practitioner of all time. She succeeds, until ultimately, the only magic that remains out of her grasp is that requiring knowledge of the Supreme Creator's hidden name of power. By creating a snake from earth and spit, she forces him to reveal that name, so that she emerges as the most powerful presence of all.

This is a good thing for Isis because the saga of her life story contains all the drama of a soap opera or a *telenovela*. As her story unfolds, she's rich, beautiful, talented and kind, happily married to her true love, her twin brother Osiris, with whom she fell in love in the womb. Unfortunately she also possesses a very dysfunctional family, leading to a terrible crime, resulting in her early widowhood.

Using her knowledge of magic, Isis manages to locate her beloved's body, not once but twice. The first time Isis located Osiris's corpse, all the way up the Mediterranean in Syria, it was still intact. She brought it home to Egypt, hoping to be able to resurrect him somehow.

Unfortunately, the murderer, their brother Seth, was also an esteemed magician. Determined to prevent this resurrection and possess Isis for himself, Seth, hot on her trail, locates the body as she searches for needed botanicals, chops Osiris into fourteen pieces and scatters them along the length of the Nile. Refusing to submit to despair, Isis assembles a coven of powerful friends and allies, searches out the pieces and manages to magically put them back together one by one, with the exception of one crucial piece, swallowed by a fish. Luckily, Isis's magical skills enable her to construct a functional gold penis. With the help of her allies, she's able to resurrect Osiris just long enough to conceive the son she's destined to bear.

Of course, there's always a catch: having conceived her son, she must protect him and herself long enough for him to grow up and avenge his father. In constant danger, with Seth's henchmen searching ceaselessly for her, Isis hides out in the Nile swamps, in something akin to a witness-protection program. Despite all her knowledge and ability, Isis is now unable to use her magic because, as in Disney's *Sleeping Beauty*, those are the clues that will betray her location and identity.

Although she can't practice magic, Isis's education continues. She learns the value of girlfriends. Her most powerful magic, the resurrection of Osiris, wasn't accomplished alone and her buddies continue to protect her ever after. The formerly pampered princess spends years hiding out in the Nile swamps, giving birth secretly in the bushes, begging for charity and subsistence, toiling as a laborer, afraid to use either her name, her skills or to access her waiting fortune.

Isis learns what it means to be human, the hard way. No television fantasies for her, à la *Bewitched*'s Samantha: Isis's biggest problem should only be a nosy neighbor and an embarrassed husband. No middle-class illusions for Isis about the charm of doing housework by hand; she knows that being human is likely to mean poverty and powerlessness. Isis knows the realities of single motherhood, about literally begging to provide food for a child, about humiliation, about giving birth in less than ideal circumstances, about depending upon neighbors you barely know to assist with the safety of your beloved child. Her human neighbors didn't fail her. Throughout her saga, Isis receives assistance from plants, spirits, crocodiles and scorpions but human power counts too and is given due credit. Isis learned to love and respect people and when it was finally safe to reassume her power, to provide for them.

Isis is considered the most benevolent of all spirits. She is particularly protective of women, children and single mothers. There is no area with which she will not provide assistance. There is nothing you cannot ask her. There is no secret that she does not know. There is no shame because Isis already knows the hidden secrets of your heart. She accepts any offering given with love and respect, although she is partial to the fragrance of myrrh. Her colors are usually given as black and blue. Her talismanic mineral is bloodstone. The herb vervain is believed to have sprung from her tears.

MINERALS AND METALS

Crystals

Rocks, crystals and gemstones are used for healing, to balance and enhance emotions and to stimulate specific skills. Magically, they are used for attraction and protection. The jewelry we crave may reveal important information about our spiritual and physical needs. If you only wear jewelry for adornment, you are settling for very little, as it can also serve as a shield against evil influences and a magnet to attract good fortune.

HOW DO YOU KNOW WHICH CRYSTAL IS FOR YOU?

Choose one whose attributes match your needs and desires. Allow your heart to choose. Which appeals to you, which calls to you? Which intrigues you? It will be a mutual agreement. The crystal chooses you as much as you choose it. If a stone doesn't wish to work with you, for whatever reason, perhaps because it's not beneficial for you, it won't stay. If you keep losing the same piece of jewelry or if a stone keeps popping out of a ring, perhaps it's best to retire it for a while or give it to someone else. Likewise, stones and metals that appear out of nowhere or are given to you as gifts deserve a second glance even if at first they weren't what you wished for.

Like other families of powers, minerals can be used as tools or as allies. They're fairly simple to use as tools, all you have to do is recognize them as helpful objects radiating various forces and influences and magnetically attracting others. In order to benefit from them, you need physical proximity.

- Crystals and gemstones are used as talismans, in mojo hands, as meditation tools, for healing and massage.

- Water can be infused with a crystal's energy for use in baths, potions and room sprays: place the crystal in pure springwater overnight under the moon. (Not all crystals can be placed in water without causing damange to them. Do your research first.)

- Placing crystals in your bath (larger ones that can't go down the drain) stimulates energy and spiritual cleansing. (As with the previous suggestions, make sure these are crystals that will not dissolve or be damaged if placed in water.)

- Crystals can be used to empower altars and candles.

Crystals and gemstones absorb and store energy: they may need to be cleansed periodically, fed and recharged. Various methods for cleaning exist. Choose what feels most appropriate for you.

- Bury the stone in Earth overnight or for up to seven days. This is strongest and most efficient if done outside, however, if you have little available access, a flowerpot filled with dirt works, too. If burying outside, make sure you mark the spot, unless you're considering returning the stone to Earth's womb.

- Place the crystal in direct sunlight or give alternating sun/moon baths.

- Pass the crystal through cleansing incense smoke. Copal, frankincense, mugwort or sage are particularly potent and effective.

- Clear crystals may benefit from saltwater; either collect ocean water or add sea salt to springwater. A splash of apple cider vinegar added to the water may be beneficial, too.

- Don't expose colored crystals to salt. It has a tendency to leach their color or to even damage the more fragile ones, like moldavite. Use sun/moon baths for delicate crystals. Alternately, add a few drops of Dr. Bach's Rescue Remedy or similar flower essence formula to pure springwater instead, particularly following any stressful or traumatic situation.

Crystals exert their power most forcefully if used as allies rather than tools. In order to do this, however, you must be able to acknowledge that they have "life" of some sort, even if not identical to what humans know as life. In order to communicate with them and receive information, you must be able to acknowl edge that minerals possess some type of consciousness.

Crystals do attempt to communicate with you, in their own way, as visually as they can. If kept in constant contact with the flesh, crystals and gemstones (the distinction having to do with scarcity and monetary worth) provide a running commentary on your state of being. Turquoise, for instance, loses its luster and may even crack, if you are ill or surrounded by toxins. Blue topaz provides a barometer of your sex life: it darkens and turns cloudy if your experiences are consistently miserable. Rubies grow pale if you have a blood dysfunction or if you are generally devitalized. In order to provide this information to you, the stones must actually touch your skin. Make sure your jewelry settings allow this. Clear quartz and amethyst serve as environmental cleansers. Lack of sparkle and a dull appearance indicate that they're full to the brim with toxic substances like a vacuum cleaner bag stuffed full. They need to be emptied and cleansed.

Crystals and gemstones exist in endless varieties. As with fragrance and herbs, more are readily available to us than ever before. As with spirits, there are crystals for virtually every purpose. However, there are some crystals that specifically boost our psychic abilities and enhance our magical power.

Lodestone: also know as magnetite, is magnetic iron ore and a powerful magical tool. Lodestones are used to draw whatever you need to you, whether it's enhanced personal power, gambling luck, money or true love. Wearing or carrying a lodestone is believed to enhance and protect your own personal power. Lodestones can also draw *out* toxic blocks and pain, emotional as well as physical. Place upon the appropriate spot during meditation, ritual or visualization.

Although lodestones are powerful, to be most effective their power must be consistently replenished.

- In Hoodoo tradition, lodestones are fed with magnetic sand (fine iron shot) or dressed with fragrance oils. Coordinate the oil to suit your magical purpose. Thus if you want the lodestone to draw prosperity, choose one of the money-drawing oils from the Spell section.

- In a Mexican tradition, lodestones are put to work during the week, worn on a chain around the neck or in a medicine pouch, but taken off on Friday night and given the weekend off. To replenish the stone's energy, it's placed in a glass of either water or wine overnight

and then fed iron filings on Saturday before being placed around
the neck once again on Sunday night or Monday morning.

Moldavite: enhances psychic ability and perceptions and can be a truly
intense ally. At its finest, moldavite provides a grounding, healing effect for
those who don't feel at home here on Earth, those who feel like strangers
and also for those who may need extra protection against environmental
toxins. If you discover yourself feeling disconnected or "spacey," minimize
contact with moldavite for a while. Some consider it safer not to wear or
carry it while driving or reserve it only for ritual use. It is a particularly
fragile stone; don't cleanse with salt.

> Use moonstone to contact others. Cuprite, a deep red stone with a high
> copper content, helps access information regarding your own past lives.
> It also helps to heal and forge relationships with fathers, both earthly and
> spiritual.

Moonstone: is known as the "Earth Mother Stone" and is considered a
prime psychic stimulant. Its energy is powerfully aligned with the moon.
Women who are already very psychic or lunar-influenced might want to
avoid close proximity to moonstone during their own moontime because
it may stimulate psychic imbalance and hypersensitivity.

You can replenish your stone's power by placing it in moonlight overnight. Another old nickname for this stone is "Wolf's Eye," indicating that
the stone can be used to sharpen your perception of spirits and ghosts.

Quartz: looks like beautiful ice. Among the most beneficial and versatile
of magical tools, clear quartz crystals are made into magical knives and
incorporated into magic wands. Used to activate, cleanse and stimulate
powers, yours or any other, quartz protects your vitality. Place quartz
crystals near botanicals to encourage growth and enhance power. Pack a
crystal in with Tarot cards or any other divination or magic tool. Quartz
provides guidance and protection for spiritual quests.

Smoky Quartz: is a protective ally during magic or any psychic journeys.
It promotes knowledge, security and creativity. Smoky quartz is particularly beneficial for contacting ancestral spirits: place it on an altar, inside a
dream pillow or gaze within the stone.

Sodalite: helps develop magical ability and endurance. Place it on the Third Eye chakra, just slightly above the space between your brows, to stimulate psychic perceptive capacity.

Topaz: is traditionally used to contact spirit allies and offers a window into other dimensions. It helps maintain emotional balance while expanding one's magic skills. It helps overcome fear of the unknown and to develop trust in Earth. Topaz provides a calming effect. Topaz comes in various shades. Use the color that evokes the deepest sense of peace and serenity for you.

CRYSTAL GAZING

Crystals open windows to the future and past and help us cope with the present. A round, clear quartz ball is the most traditional material for crystal gazing, however, different types and shapes of crystal can be used as well. Aquamarine lends itself very well to the art while a smoky quartz ball is considered especially beneficial for communicating with spirits and ghosts. Smooth obsidian mirrors are a traditional Mexican divination tool. Any crystal can be used, however. You can crystal-gaze with an uncut or unshaped crystal as successfully as with a ball.

The key ingredient to success is your attitude. You must recognize that crystal gazing is an interactive process that enables your crystal to most fully serve as your ally, providing you with knowledge, information and inspiration. It isn't something that you can demand from a crystal: Information is given cooperatively with an attitude of love and respect.

How Do I Crystal-Gaze?

- First sit down with your crystal as you would with a treasured friend. Make sure you have a comfortable area and privacy.

- You might want to burn some incense to cleanse and enhance the atmosphere, your receptivity, and your crystal's clarity and ability. Mugwort loosens restrictions on your psychic power. White sage blocks the entry of negative spiritual entities. Smoke from copal, Dittany of Crete, frankincense and/or wormwood signals an invitation to the spirits.

- When you're ready, gaze into your crystal. The trick, which takes a little practice, is finding the correct balance between relaxation and a fixed stare. You want to gaze intently but also allow your gaze to be loose, a little out of focus. Let your eyes wander and explore the depths of your crystal. Don't allow any distractions. When you see shadows form within the crystal, follow them.

- When you have completed your journey, burn incense, take a magic or protective bath or in some way provide a conclusion for your ritual.

Crystal Bead Bracelet

These are among the most popular modern amulets. At best, they're extremely effective as the stones are in constant contact with the skin, right at the wrist pulse. (You can also adapt these instructions to make necklaces or anklets: just vary the length of cord and the quantity of beads.) Unfortunately, may of the bracelets on the market are made from plastic beads and hold no power. Choose your own beads for your own purpose. Using one type of crystal gemstone bead intensifies the effect; you can also mix and match beads, however. Once you've gathered your materials, you can custom-make a bracelet in less than ten minutes.

Crystal beads

One Crimp Bead

Elastic Cord

The quantity of beads required is dependent upon the size of the beads and the size of the wearer's wrist. String the beads onto the desired length of cord, leaving an inch of empty space on either end of the beads. String a crimp bead onto one end of the cord. Bring the loose end around to form a circle. Fit this loose end through the opposite end of the crimp bead. Pull both ends tight and press down on the crimp bead (you may need crimping pliers). Tie both ends of the cord into a knot and trim.

Metals

Although the magic power of crystals is widely recognized, the influence radiated by metal is often ignored. This is unfortunate, as most of us come into daily contact with metal, particularly in terms of jewelry. Metal, too, radiates a powerful influence. In Chinese philosophy, metal is considered so essential and powerful that it is classified as one of the elements, right alongside fire, water, air and earth.

IRON

The metal most associated with magic is iron. Although not shiny or beautiful like silver or gold, at times iron's value was perceived as superior. The invading Spaniards, for instance, noted that Aztec priests prized their iron ritual knives above their golden ones. Throughout the traditional cultures of Africa and Western Asia, ironworkers were and still are considered master magical practitioners, simultaneously respected and feared. Known as Masters of Fire, they are believed to have access to the secrets of Earth's womb. Because extraction of metals and precious substances from Earth was considered safe only if one possessed alliances with powerful spirits, the ironworker's skill and well-being laid testament to his personal magical prowess. Ironworkers often double as herbal physicians and amulet carvers.

> Because iron is not found in its pure state except as a meteorite, it was known as the "Metal of Heaven." Iron's celestial origins were recognized early in human history and meteorites were perceived as supreme conduits to the spirit realm. The Temple of Artemis at Ephesus was one of the ancient world's Seven Wonders: the original statue housed inside was carved from a meteorite. Likewise, the most sacred representation of the great goddess Cybele was an uncut meteor.

- Iron is prized for its protective and healing capacities. Iron boxes safeguard magical treasures and keep their powers intact. An iron bed protects you from spiritual dangers, enhances the dream process and promotes physical healing.

- As iron is also associated with virility and fertility, an iron bed is also considered conducive for romance and conception. A necklace of round iron beads serves as a fertility talisman.

- Iron is associated with the well-being of children. In India and throughout Europe, iron amulets are placed near cradles to provide protection for newborns and children. In Africa, iron anklets are believed to hold a child to Earth; in China, small iron locks worn around the neck serve the same function.

- Bend a horseshoe nail into a ring for good health and fortune.

Associated Planet: Mars

Associated Spirit: Ogun

• • •

Although there are various types of metal, copper, gold and silver are most commonly worn as jewelry. It's worthwhile to consider what sort of power radiates from each.

COPPER

Copper is a purely positive metal. Considered to hold sacred properties by various cultures in North America and India, copper stimulates healing and romance.

- Copper's healing powers are especially prized for counteracting joint or nerve pain. The copper bracelet is well-known, however there are other ways to access copper's healing capacities. During the Middle Ages, Europeans commonly wrapped pure copper wire around their waist to relieve rheumatism. In India, rings and earrings are fashioned from copper to ward off the Sciatica Spirit.

- Copper jewelry is worn as a talisman to attract and maintain romance.

Associated Planet: Venus

Associated Deities: Aphrodite, Oshun

SILVER

Silver, like copper, is considered a purely positive metal. No ill effects can come from wearing it, nor is any quantity considered unhealthy. Silver is considered clean and incorruptible. Silver is believed to provide a spiritually protective influence and is among the most popular materials for amulets.

- Silver bells maintain the safety of one's aura and immediate area. Ring them if you feel spiritually endangered. Keep one close to your bed if you suffer from nightmares to dispel any lingering bad dreams.

- Silver is believed to regenerate fertility. Fertility charms are most potent if carved from this metal.

Associated Planet: Moon

Associated Deities: Artemis, Diana

Wear copper jewelry to attract love. Switch to silver if you wish to start a family.

GOLD

Gold, although universally desired, is considered with ambivalence. Although beautiful and precious, it is feared as a corrupting influence and as an addictive substance, potentially as dangerous and destructive as any narcotic. In fairy tales, dangerous rings that appear enticing but really guarantee disaster for the wearer are inevitably formed from gold. Gold is considered safest when worn by spiritually mature and grounded healers and teachers.

- Chinese tradition values gold for maintaining personal vitality. Wear small amounts, balanced with healing, protective metals and stones.

- Ancient Scandinavians treasured small gold amulets carried as magnets for attracting prosperity.

Associated Planet: Sun

Associated Spirit: Freya

Gold Fever Do you have gold fever? You do if you suffer from a hunger for acquisitiveness, if you are driven by an urge to possess, if what you already have is never sufficient to satisfy your cravings. Wearing great quantities of gold on a daily basis is likely to contribute to, or create this imbalance, however there are individuals who are particularly vulnerable to even small amounts of gold. There is a ritual remedy. You and your jewelry both need to be cleansed:

1. At the full moon, remove all the gold that you wear, including a wedding ring.

2. Cleanse the metal by passing it through sage or juniper smoke. (If your fever is bad, don't pass it too quickly. Let the metal linger in the smoke.)

3. Place the metal to rest, exposed to the moonlight, on a white linen or cotton cloth.

4. You will need two baths, a cleansing bath at night, followed by a protective bath the following morning. Choose those that appeal to you from the Spell section.

5. Do not replace any jewelry until the second bath is completed. After your protective bath, select one piece of jewelry to return to your body. Wrap other pieces safely and securely, ideally in a magic box, enhanced with iron or protective crystals or herbs.

6. Select one additional piece of gold to wear each morning, paying attention to whether your sense of balance is maintained. As soon as you feel that balance tip, you've reached your limit.

7. Remove the last piece and make a mental tally: You can determine what quantity of gold is not detrimental by either the number of pieces or by accumulated mass. Do not exceed that quantity, although you may vary the pieces. Whenever you feel a relapse, repeat the process. Bolster with cleansing baths as needed.

BOTANICALS

Botanicals are ironically both the most challenging and most prevalent allies. Perhaps their very commonality creates the challenge: because plants are all around us, it's easy to underestimate their power. To some extent, you can choose whether to work with crystals, metals, spirits or animal allies. It is very difficult to perform any sort of magic without the aid of botanicals. There are very few spells that do not somehow involve botanicals. Botanicals are used in many forms: as plants (either the living whole plant or fresh or dried plant parts) and as plant-derived materials, especially essential oils and flower essences.

Just as with animal allies, each plant has a presiding spirit, and it is actually this entity with whom you form your alliance. The entity may appear in the form of the plant, an animal or in human form, in dreams and in visions.

If working with animal allies, spirits, minerals or metals, magic can remain purely on the spiritual plain. Working with plants adds a new dimension. Herbalism is the most ancient medical system and plants remain the basis for most modern medications. Herbalism is a holistic medical system: interaction with botanicals affects humans on the physical, emotional and spiritual planes simultaneously. With the sole exception of flower essences, *there is always a physical interaction,* although some plants are very gentle and others have a reasonably neutral effect for most. You need to know what effect they will have upon your body, not only when taking herbs internally as tea or as food but also when using them in baths, incense or oils.

Every effort has been made to feature only herbs that are generally safe and to note any exceptions. However, if you possess any physical vulnerability, whether high or low blood pressure, a seizure disorder or suppressed immune system, you need to research the potential effect of any plants that you come into contact with. Many botanicals are not safe for use during pregnancy or nursing, nor should herbs ever be administered to young children without expert supervision.

How did humans learn about the individual properties of plants? Scientific wisdom considers that it came about through an extended period of trial and error. Shamanic wisdom considers that the plants and their presiding spirits actually communicated their properties directly, usually through song and vision and by serving as allies to chosen individuals who then shared their acquired knowledge with others. The intelligence and consciousness of plants is subject to both scientific and occult study. There are many individuals who claim to have direct, ongoing communication with plants and their presiding spirits.

True Oils

For as long as can be recalled, oils have been perceived as precious and sacred. Many traditions have their own holy oils and unguents. In the Mediterranean region, it's olive, whereas in the tropics it may be coconut or palm. Oils serve as your vehicle for introducing herbal and aromatic substances into your body, whether via massage, bath oils or food.

In general, true oils, known as base or fixed oils, are extracted from seeds or fruits of plants, where their primary function is energy storage. Each oil has its own nature and possesses its own healing properties.

- Camellia seed oil is a Japanese beauty secret for fine skin.

- Castor oil has traditionally been used to stimulate hair growth.

> *Different plants share many colloquial names, for instance if you request "birthroot" or "graveyard dust," you may receive any one of a number of plants. Each Latin classification, however, names one and only one species. A reputable vendor always supplies the Latin name so that you can be sure of what you are obtaining. For the sake of power and safety, rely upon these classifications. Latin classifications for the botanicals cited in this book may be found in the appendix on page 281.*

- Jojoba oil, technically not an oil but a plant wax, tones the bust.

- Rosehip seed oil reduces scars.

Cold-pressed oils are preferable; they retain as much of their own power as possible. If the label doesn't specify cold-pressed, then the oils have been extracted using heat or chemical solvents (this may be the only way to extract certain oils). At best, some of the healing, magical properties have been lost. At worst, you are applying toxins to your skin.

Essential Oils

Essential oils are not true oils. They are volatile liquids extracted by various methods from fragrant botanical materials. Modern aromatherapy is the manipulation of essential oils for therapeutic and cosmetic purposes. Its roots stretch back to ancient China, Egypt, Mesopotamia and the Middle East. Essential oils are perhaps the purest, most potent expression of a plant's power and play a profound role in rituals, potions and spells.

> *Avoid mineral oils, including what is commonly known as "baby oil." These are derived from petroleum products and have no beneficial magical properties.*

Essential oils are highly concentrated substances with profound physical impact. Never take them internally without expert supervision. Even externally, they are to be used sparingly, drop by drop. This is one case where more is rarely better. When creating an enchanted bath or oil, essential oils are usually the last ingredient added so as to maximize the intensity of fragrance.

> *Many essential oils antidote homeopathics. Do not combine use; do not store them together.*

Every essential oil has its own distinct personality and various therapeutic and ritual uses. A good aromatherapy encyclopedia will give you a sense of the scope of this healing art. A few oils, however, are especially beneficial for the art of Earth magic.

- **Patchouli** and **Vetiver** are both natives of Asia. Although they smell nothing alike, both are deep strong fragrances that evoke the scent of Earth. In their dried plant form, they are a component of many spells. Natural allies, they are often used together. As essential oils, both are unusual: brown, viscous, even *oily*, rather than the typical clear, watery fluid.

- Farther west, the scent of **Myrrh** was believed to embody the essence of the Earth Mother. Myrrh is a resin that seeps from thorny desert trees native to Ethiopia, Oman, Somalia and Yemen. It has a subtle, mysterious fragrance, quite unlike patchouli and vetiver. In addition to the essential oil, myrrh resin may be burned as incense.

Use any of these fragrances to align your energy with Earth's and provide a grounding influence for you. Choose whichever appeals to you most; vetiver and patchouli can also be harmonized and used together. Wear a drop as perfume (all have reputations as aphrodisiacs, although patchouli tends to evoke a love/hate response) or merely inhale the scent.

If you'd prefer to serve as the magical canvas yourself, add one or two drops of the essential oil to one teaspoon of sweet almond, apricot kernel or grapeseed oil. Gently massage onto your cleansed face before bedtime. In addition to aligning your energy with Earth's and influencing your dreams, each of the oils has a reputation for improving skin tone and quality. Patchouli has even been reputed to decrease or halt the spread of wrinkles. (See! You can learn to love the fragrance.)

Pure Magic Fragrance Ritual

1. Cut a thin strip from a paper coffee filter.

2. Add 1 drop of either myrrh, vetiver, or patchouli oil to the paper and inhale the fragrance at 5-minute intervals.

3. Observe the changes in mood and pace that the oil draws from you.

- Physical Restrictions: Vetiver and myrrh should be avoided during pregnancy while patchouli is not beneficial for those with a history of eating disorders.

Flower Essences

Witches, alchemists and all those steeped in Earth wisdom have always treasured dew, rain and moisture gathered from plants. Infused with the specific power belonging to the plant, the tiny particles of liquid were also perceived as containing the perfect balance of the four elements: not only the power of water but also that of Earth, as radiated through the plant, the surrounding air and fire from the shining sun.

The ancients were limited to the plants growing on their doorsteps. You are not. The modern science of flower essences brings the power of plants from all over Earth directly to you.

Fragrance Oils

Aromatherapy's increasing popularity ensures that the rarest and most exotic blossoms are consistently available for our spells. However, certain fragrances are rarely found among essential oils, either because an essential oil cannot be produced or, more likely, because the cost is prohibitive. Instead synthetic reproductions, known as fragrance oils exist. (Also sometimes called "perfume oils." Some perfume oils, however, are made from genuine material: ask before you buy.) Some are dead ringers for the original fragrance. Because no actual plant

> *material is involved, the oil lacks the plant's true power. However, fine*
> *fragrance oils do have uses: aroma alone may serve to evoke a response*
> *from your brain. In general, fragrance oils are fine for dressing candles,*
> *but not for body or bath.*

The direct descendant of these botanical potions, the flower essences were first prepared in their modern form in Great Britain in the 1930s by Dr. Edward Bach, a prominent Harley Street physician and homeopath. Dr. Bach came to the conclusion that true complete healing was not possible if approached solely from the physical plane. Emotional and spiritual imbalances were the root of illness and dysfunction, and therefore true healing must be accessed through soul and emotion. He devoted the rest of his life, at great personal sacrifice, to developing the original flower essence remedies. Dr. Bach reported that the plants communicated directly with him, sharing their secrets with him.

Dr. Bach's original thirty-eight remedies were almost entirely derived from British flora. Emerging during the Great Depression, the bulk of the remedies served especially to relieve confusion, despair, depression and fear. Since that time, many other flower essence practitioners have followed in Dr. Bach's pioneering footsteps so that there is now greater access to a wider variety of botanical powers than ever before. The availability of flower essences range as far afield as the Australian Bush, the Sonora Desert, the Alaskan wilderness, Hawaii, California and the rainforests of Peru. As befitting true New Age substances, many were created specifically to facilitate metaphysical and spiritual goals. There are specific essences for strengthening and accessing your magical skills, also for healing divisions between the genders and building bridges to other spiritual realms.

HOW TO USE FLOWER ESSENCES

- The most common method of use is internal. Flower essences are usually sold as concentrated stock bottles and must be further diluted in pure springwater. The general dosage is four drops four times a day, however instructions are available on the bottles or from the manufacturers.

- Flower essences can also be applied topically, rubbed gently onto the body. A few drops on the soles of the feet or on the thin skin between thumb and forefinger before bedtime are especially beneficial. Flower essences can also be added to massage oil or bath.

- A room spray or atmospheric cleanser can be created by adding flower essences to a spray bottle of springwater.

- Flower essences can be used to enhance and heal the power of crystals, plants and amulets. Apply a few drops as needed.

Although flower essences and essential oils have confusingly similar names and are sold in very similar packages (tiny glass vials), they are by no means identical or interchangeable. Essential oils are actually plant extracts, with extremely potent and scientifically documented physical effects. All essential oils, for instance, are antiseptic, to varying degrees. How flower essences work remains the subject of debate, the general consensus being that they are a form of vibrational healing. Flower essences are pure water infused and charged with the plant's energy and vibration. There is no need to kill the plant to create the essence; typically only carefully selected leaves and blossoms are used. The essences are designed to provide a bridge between the plant's healing aura and your own. There is no direct physical effect; instead their profound effect is felt upon the emotional and spiritual plane. They are safe for everyone's use, children and animals included. Flower essence remedies can also be used to benefit plants and crystals.

Flower essences are created for every situation and emotional state. Good source books will bestow a sense of their scope. The following flower essences are especially beneficial for enhancing your magical aptitude. Descriptions of the essences are followed by the name of their manufacturer. Flower essences are available directly from the manufacturer (listed in the appendix on page 281) and also from many health food stores and alternatively oriented pharmacies.

- **Angelica** (*Angelica arcangelica*): enhances the ability to perceive and recognize protection and guidance from spirit beings, especially angels. It is indicated for those who feel bereft of spiritual

guidance and protection and can be especially beneficial during
threshold experiences. (FES)

- **Angel's Trumpet** (*Datura candida*): provides assistance for those
  who would like to do psychic work but can't quite accept the reality
  of psychic forces and energies. (FES)

- **Green Bells of Ireland** (*Molucella laevis*): recommended for those
  who feel ungrounded, those who lack a conscious heart connection
  to the natural world and also for those who feel unaware of, or
  unable to access, the light and intelligence present in nature. This
  remedy is intended to strengthen the connection between Earth
  and one's body. (Alaskan Flower Essence Project, Pegasus)

- **Mugwort** (*Artemisia vulgaris*): the single most profound essence
  for evoking psychic skill and perceptions, it promotes alignment
  with the moon, corrects imbalances in the feminine cycle and
  promotes greater awareness of dreams and psychic ability. (FES,
  Pegasus)

- **Saguaro** (*Cereus giganteus*): Because balance is crucial, with all this
  talk of Earth Mother energy, this essence enhances appreciation of
  the male energy that serves as protector, provider and true partner
  to Earth's feminine energy. For men, saguaro can help forge a path;
  for women, it helps heal losses. For both, it provides inspiration
  and healing. Saguaro eases a sense of alienation from one's own
  parentage and spiritual traditions. Saguaro reinforces an awareness
  of the ancient and sacred. It provides a sense of lineage, a linking of
  oneself to Earth's holy traditions. (Desert Alchemy, FES, Pegasus)

- **Saint John's Wort** (*Hypericum perforatum*): increases spiritual
  awareness and consciousness. It also has a protective capacity. As
  your psychic work and ability increases, as you become increasingly
  aware of other powers, feelings of vulnerability may arise. Saint
  John's Wort provides a psychic shield, soothes fears, provides
  courage and security and calms the effects of disturbing dreams.
  (Desert Alchemy, FES, Pegasus)

- **Star Tulip** (*Calochorus tolmiei*): creates an aura of receptivity and
  enables one to tune into other energies, particularly in dreams and

meditation. Star tulip is indicated for those who feel hard and rittle, cut off from Earth and other living beings, especially for those who are unable to meditate or pray but yet feel the need. Star tulip stimulates psychic awakening and receptivity to one's inner voices. (FES)

- **Yarrow** (*Achillea millefolium*): strengthens and cleanses the personal aura and provides a profound psychic shield. It is indicated for those who feel drained by exposure to toxic forces, whether physical, spiritual or human. (Alaskan Flower Essence Project, Desert Alchemy, FES, Pegasus)

Incense

Every culture and people on Earth has a link to incense, the process of using scented smoke to permeate the air for spiritual purposes. Incense is the easiest method of expressing gratitude to Earth and your spirit allies for favors granted. Real incense cleanses, protects, serves as a vehicle for prayer and petition and invites the presence of spirit allies.

Once upon a time, incense existed as mass national industries. Frankincense and myrrh were Earth's most expensive items, mainly because of their value as burnt offerings. Entering an urban area, you would be met with clouds of sacred smoke and its evocative fragrance. In a sense, industrialized nations still create incense: Today smokestacks spew foul smelling toxins and pollutants into the atmosphere. Who do we try to attract or propitiate?

Incense can be stationary. It may be used indoors or outdoors. In Japan, incense remains a spiritual art. Japanese incense is increasingly available outside its homeland. If you wish to purchase ready-made incense, it is among the purest and finest.

Incense is the most ancient fragrance art. Remains have been found in Paleolithic caves. If cave people had the technology to make incense, so do you. Incense does not have to come in cone or stick form, it can also be loose. For the most basic incense, pulverize dried plant material (leaves, bark, blossoms, resin), place on a small lit charcoal and allow the fragrance to permeate an area. Trust your nose: the incense should smell good. Incense is easiest left loose, but if you prefer little cones, you can easily make your own without resorting to the artificial substances contained in most commercial incense.

Incense Cones

Dissolve gum arabic in water (1 part powder to 2 parts water). Gum arabic is available from incense supply houses but it's probably less expensive to purchase it from an Indian grocery store. Allow it to soak for about three hours.

In the meantime, pulverize your herbal material until it is powdered. Mix the incense powder into the liquid until you can shape it into small cones with your hands. Allow the cones to dry in a warm area.

Dried Herb Bundles

Juniper, Lavender, Rosemary and/or Sage

Thin cotton thread

Use one of the above herbs or any combination. Other herbs may also be used but the ones above are strong spiritual cleansers and are easily and quickly dried. When the herbs are completely dried, bind them together, all facing the same direction with thin cotton thread to form a six- to eight-inch wand. Light the tip and direct the smoke with your hand, a fan, or a feather toward whatever needs cleansing.

Potpourri

Commonly disguised as room freshener and typically made from synthetic substances, colors, and even fragrance, potpourri's origins lie in ancient botanical magic. Essentially incense that won't be burnt, fragrant plant materials were carefully combined. Rather than placed in open bowls, they were closed within airtight boxes. When a hit of fragrance was desired, a blast of power or intensity, the box would be opened and the fragrance inhaled. Different potpourris were created to invoke different effects: individual formulas are listed among the spells. Potpourri can also be simmered on the stove, allowing the fragrance to waft throughout the surrounding area. This method harnesses the power of all four elements: air, earth, fire and water. Fine simmering potpourri can be very simple: a few cinnamon sticks and a handful of whole cloves, for example.

> *Herbs may be purchased already dried. Sources are listed in the appendix. However, it's very simple to dry fresh herbs. Hang them upside down in small bunches, so that they are not too crowded. Use professional herb dryers that look like horizontal ladders, or attach the bunches to a wire hanger. Let them hang, out of direct sunlight, in a well-ventilated area until dry.*

Whole Plants

Essential oils and flower essences bestow a concentrated dose of plant energy. In many cases, however, you may want to work with the whole plant. You may find that if you wish to work with a particular plant, you're obligated to grow it yourself. This may be for a variety of reasons.

- Some plants are rare to an area. You may need to nurture some indoors or order from a specialist nursery.

- What you desire may not be marketable: the alchemists treasured fresh morning dew caught upon the leaves of lady's mantle. They called it "water from heaven" and prized it as an ingredient in many enchanted potions. If you want some (and you very well might; it's reputed to provide a beautiful complexion!), you'll have to grow it and gather it yourself.

- In some cases, it's best to have your own fresh stock of plants, to save on expense and safety. Your own roses are not only more powerful than the florists, but you'll save a small fortune and, as you place the petals in your bath, you also have the assurance of knowing no toxic pesticides and preservatives taint them and potentially you.

- In the case of root charms, often the only way to guarantee that you have the genuine article is to actually start with the whole plant. Too many commercial preparations purporting to include items like High John the Conqueror or Adam and Eve Root contain only petroleum products.

- Unfortunately, in a growing number of cases, the only way to access a power may be to grow your own, because there isn't any other source.

The decimation of the animal kingdom is well-known and well publicized, but humans have done no less damage to plants. A 1998 international study conducted by sixteen organizations, including the Smithsonian Institute, indicates that at least one out of every eight known plant species on Earth is now either threatened with extinction or nearly extinct.

When you harvest plants, whether they are those you have nurtured or otherwise, it is customary to leave a token of your gratitude. Consider it payment for services rendered or a gesture of alliance: no healthy relationship is one-sided. At the very least, consider it demonstrating good manners. The traditional Native American offering is a pinch of tobacco. Other cultures suggest a little honey. English folk custom recommends oatmeal, while the ancient Romans offered bread and wine. A libation of pure water is always appropriate.

Solomon's Seal was once a very prominent magical plant, a favorite of ancient spell books and grimoires. No spells in which it features prominently are included here because there's no point. It's unlikely that you'll ever see it. Beth Root derives from another very endangered plant. Native to North America, indigenous Americans prized it as a love potion. The root was boiled and then dropped into the desired man's food; upon consumption, he should have eyes only for his enchantress. Beth Root was heartily adopted into African-American occult traditions, where it went under the name Low John the Conqueror. Only a few decades ago, Low

John was a common Hoodoo charm, used for preserving family peace and encouraging economic prosperity. You'll rarely find it marketed, because it can't be found in the wild anymore. If you want it, you'll have to grow it. The magic that you perform together can be especially potent because the very existence of your ally indicates to Earth your willingness to provide healing for her as well as to provide for your own desires. The best way to gain an ally is to be an ally.

In the past, wildcrafting, the process of collecting wild plants, has been the preferred method. Common metaphysical wisdom held that wild plants were considered to be at the peak of their powers. With the wilderness under siege and quickly disappearing, this is no longer true. Wildcrafting, with few exceptions, has become the equivalent of poaching. It is unethical to remove wild plants; from a magical perspective whatever power they possess may backfire on you. The best way to generate your personal power is to replenish Earth and nature, not continue to deplete it. The strongest, most powerful plant allies will be the ones you nourish and nurture. They will become familiar with you, your family, your needs and desires at the same time that you are providing for theirs. If you are unable to do so, try to find a nursery that will grow them for you.

The Magic Garden

A magic garden transforms a portion of Earth into a living altar. Rather than landscaping based solely on superficial appearance or ease of availability (for instance, going to the nursery and seeing what's on sale) plants are carefully selected based upon the power that they radiate. Everyone's magic garden is unique because the botanical power is combined with your own. There are no limitations based upon the size of your garden. You may have acres or a tiny space. You may choose to convert your whole backyard or reserve a tiny corner for ritual use. Apartment dwellers can create their magic gardens in pots, on windowsills, ledges or fire escapes. You can purchase whole plants or receive cuttings from others. However, the single most basic and primal magic exercise is growing plants from seeds. Just as salt and honey are camouflaged as everyday ingredients, so sprouting seeds is too often relegated to a child's kindergarten project. Historically, cultivation has been an act fraught with magic, ritual and power.

A magical garden is a collaboration between nature and yourself; not merely the imposition of your will. Your garden needs to be tended enough to keep the plants healthy, but not so much that the plants are deprived of their power. Give them some free reign. Chamomile is the plant doctor. Place it near plants that are ailing. If you see chamomile start to creep, watch where it goes. It may be paying a house call. Likewise, round circles of tree seedlings, especially ash seedlings, mark a fairy dance ground. If you let it remain, so will the fairies.

Magic gardens can be created to serve various purposes: to attract money, love or protection, to honor a spirit or animal ally. Plant allies can be gathered around you for any purpose, not least being pleasure. We'll examine different sample gardens in the Spell section, but for now, let your imagination flow freely. Visualize your magic garden as a living altar: add statues, crystals and fragrance however you are inspired.

Every culture, every spiritual school has its own sacred plants. These can be gathered together to create a place of Earthly power and a bower to replenish your own energy.

Druid Herb Garden

Queen of the Meadow

Primroses

Vervain

Water mint

These were among the Druids' most cherished plants. Water mint thrives in a somewhat damp climate. Substitute another mint to suit your climate.

Fragrant Night Garden

If you need encouragement to go outside and moongaze, or if you wish to create an enchanted setting for a little night magic, consider a selection of the following flowers. They may look innocuous enough during the daytime, but at night watch beautiful luminous white flowers emerge. Not that you need to use your eyes: these flowers fill the night with their powerful, seductive fragrance: **Angel's Trumpet, Evening Primrose, Moon Flower, Night Jasmine, Night Scented Stock, Ornamental Tobacco, Spider Flower.**

Just as some animals and humans have more magic power than others, so some plants are considered particularly highly charged, especially where enchantments are concerned.

VERVAIN

Vervain, known as the Enchanter's Herb, is believed to be the plant most fond and protective of humans. Unlike herbs that thrive best in the wilderness, vervain prefers to grow near people. According to legend, this herb sprang from the tears of Isis. Vervain bears the gifts of romance and protection.

- The Greeks and Romans tied it into bundles and used it to sweep their holy altars and sacred spaces.

- Vervain is an aphrodisiac, used to entice a lover. It's a traditional component of love spells from Africa to Europe and is still in heavy rotation in New Orleans and the American South.

- Bathing in vervain-infused waters or even rubbing any part of the plant against any part of you is said to grant prophetic power, cause your deepest wishes to be fulfilled, make your worst enemies become your friends and protect against disease and malicious enchantment.

YARROW

Yarrow's Latin name, *Achillea millefolium,* commemorates the Greek warrior, Achilles, son of a sea spirit, invincible but for his heel. He carried yarrow to staunch the blood of his troops. A bandage soaked in an herbal infusion, or one or two drops of essential oil, will halt bleeding as if by magic. Yarrow's English name is thought to derive from the Greek *hieros*: sacred. The plant was preserved in Mediterranean temples and used in European love charms.

- The Chinese oracle, the *I-Ching*, now involves throwing coins for divination. Originally, the system utilized stalks of yarrow.

- Leaves and roots are used as talismans against evil and as conductors of loving, benevolent energy. Create amulets or carry in a medicine pouch.

- Boughs of yarrow hung over the conjugal bed stimulate joy and romance.

- Hung in the house on Midsummer's Eve, yarrow helps guard the family against illness in the coming year.

MISTLETOE

Mistletoe's poisonous berries look like tiny full moons but with age they assume a golden hue. Native to a region stretching from Northern Europe to Northwest Africa and east all the way to Japan, mistletoe is considered holy and magical by virtually every culture that has encountered it. Mistletoe is prized material for magic wands and amulets of all kinds. It is the plant most associated today with Druid magic.

> *Caution: Mistletoe is poisonous enough to be fatal. Never leave mistletoe where children or animals have access to the leaves or berries. Definitely not for internal consumption.*

Mistletoe doesn't even grow in Earth but is a parasite that attaches itself to trees. The Druids believed that it was unfortunate for mistletoe to ever touch Earth and created an elaborate system for plucking it from the tree, using a golden sickle, with nets to catch it before it landed. (They harvested vervain, on the other hand, with an iron sickle.) To actually see mistletoe plummet to Earth is a warning of ensuing trouble and a spiritual recommendation to seek protection.

Mistletoe isn't only for kissing at Christmas. Mistletoe can be beneficial all year long and not just for couples, either.

- A sprig hung over the bed brings sweet dreams.

- Hung up over doors, windows or in barns, mistletoe creates a protective shield.

- A piece of mistletoe in a charm bag brings protection from disease and enchantments.

- Fertility amulets are created by setting pearls into carved pieces of mistletoe to wear as a brooch.

• • •

Henna and **mugwort** may be the two most magically power-packed plants of all. Certainly, they are the plants most beneficial for increasing your personal enchanted potential. Henna magnetically draws Earth's most positive magical good fortune toward you while mugwort helps you discover and unearth the magic hidden within yourself.

HENNA

Henna, a flowering shrub found throughout Asia and along Africa's Mediterranean coast, has provided humans with healing, romance, enchantment and beauty for thousands of years. In the West, henna is most famous as body ornamentation, an alternative to tattooing and in fact, henna does have much to recommend itself in this area. It is painless and temporary, with no risk of infection. Henna's dried, powdered leaves are cooked up into a paste, creating the enchanting dye.

Traces of henna have been found on the hands of Egyptian mummies as far back as five thousand years ago. From that time until the present, henna has been used to transform the body into a living amulet. Henna provides protection, prosperity, fertility, good health, romance and joy. It brings you into immediate contact with the sacred. If you have had henna painted on you and you did not receive an immediate surge of spiritual uplift, then something was not right, either with the henna or with the ritual.

A fine henna artisan knows more than just how to mix up a good batch of henna and how to draw a pretty picture. She knows which designs to draw where so as to produce desired results. On the subcontinent, brides are adorned with peacocks and ripe mangoes, simultaneously celebrating and stimulating their unleashed sensuality. The married woman wishing to proclaim her love for her husband has dots and waves painted upon her palms: dots representing the rain of love that she longs to shower over him, waves for the passion she can barely control. A married woman with worries needs other designs. In Morocco, an eye inside a heart drawn upon one's palm safeguards one's lover from the covetous glances of others. The design of a horse will stimulate her partner to his utmost virility. To honor a young girl's first menstruation, a deer may be painted upon her soles. To heal and assuage fears of infertility, a date palm is applied to the thighs.

Although henna is popular, powerful and beneficial, much of what you'll find available commercially is poor quality. Henna paste only lasts for a few days; premixed henna in tubes may have been sitting like that for years. Exactly what's in the tube may also be a mystery; premixed henna tends to come from countries whose ingredient labeling requirements are less than stringent. Either hire a reputable henna artist or mix up the stuff yourself.

Cooking up henna is not the hard part. Depending upon what you envision your design to look like and the extent of your artistic talent, drawing may or may not be difficult. The hardest part of henna for most Westerners is the time and stillness involved. Henna cannot be hurried. It is a sensuous, leisurely ritual. The *Kama Sutra* lists henna as one of the erotic arts required for women to know, but henna teaches other arts as well. Given the opportunity, henna will teach you to become the master of your time rather than the slave of your clock.

The Henna Ritual

Although you may paint henna anywhere you prefer, it works best on hands and feet. Whatever area you plan to henna must be free from all lotions and creams and then the skin must be exfoliated: a loofa or ayaté works well. Something is then placed upon the skin as a primer: if your skin is not sensitive, a drop of essential oil of eucalyptus is best. If you are sensitive, rub half a lemon over the area.

Henna paste can now be applied to your skin. In order to get a good color with staying power, it must remain on your skin for hours. Overnight is best. The paste goes on black. When it begins to dry and turn matte, a lemon/sugar mixture is applied for fixing and enhancement. This can be reapplied until a glaze forms. Henna craves heat, especially dry heat. Traditional rural henna artisans kept heated coals or stones for their clients to rest their hands and feet near. A hot cup of tea will work for you although you will not actually be able to touch it, only allow the heat to radiate toward your design. If you have had both palms done, you will not be able to drink the tea either, unless someone lifts it to your lips.

You really can't do anything while henna is applied. Henna laughs in the face of multitasking. You can talk. You could listen to music or watch a movie. Of course, if you've had both palms done, someone else will have to handle the remote. You could read if one hand is reasonably free or some-one turns your pages. If you've had one sole done, you'll have to hop. If you've had both painted, you will be unable to walk without wrecking your design. Ideally, you will have someone with you to pamper you and take care of you. If you don't have such a person, do your henna in segments, one foot or one hand at a time and save the rest for the next day.

Henna sets best while you sleep. One of the advantages of doing henna at home is that you can time its application for right before bed-time. Once the lemon and sugar is done, wrap your design carefully and gently in toilet paper, mummy style. Leave it on for six to eight hours, the longer you can, the better your color will be. Eventually, the paste will come off by itself. Once it starts to peel off, crumble it off or scrape it off. Remove the last bits with some olive oil on a cotton ball. Avoid exposing it to water for the first twenty-four hours. You will have an orange-col-ored design, which will take a further twenty-four to forty-eight hours to evolve into its final shade.

Henna is a living being. You cannot control nor completely predict exactly what shade will result nor how long the henna will remain. Henna's palate ranges from red to brick to brown.

> There is no such thing as "black henna"; anything marketed as such contains other substances, some of which are harmful enough to send you to the hospital with burns.

A henna stain should last a minimum of two weeks. It may last as long as twelve. To some extent, this is dependent upon the quality of the henna and the care and talent of the artisan, but there is also a personal, chemical interaction involved. Henna loves some people; they never receive a weak shade. Others have to work and experiment to achieve the color they want. The color ultimately received is always an eagerly awaited mystery.

Henna Flowers and Fragrance: In India, henna plants are grown in the backyard as hedges and for personal use. It's not likely that most of us will be able to grow enough to produce sufficient powder but there are other reasons to grow a henna plant. The dye comes from the leaves. The flowers have their own power. Blossoms packed into woolens repel moths. Spiritual protection is provided and your clothes retain the fragrance.

Henna's fragrance is legendary. An old saying in India states that when henna is in bloom, snakes and men draw near. Arabic tradition says just breathing the fragrance of the blossoms restores fertility and rejuvenates virility. An essential oil is produced, although it is rare and expensive. The paste, too, has its aroma which lingers on the flesh as long as the design does. In Asia and Africa, the aroma of henna is believed to reduce men to putty in a woman's hand. Henna has a distinctive aroma: earthy, primal and green. It evokes strong reactions. Should someone dislike the fragrance, you can add rosewater or orange blossom water to the paste.

> In some traditions, the depth of henna's hue is believed to reflect the depth of a woman's love. In other traditions, the depth of color reflects the love a mother-in-law bears for her son's wife: the richer the shade, the deeper and more genuine the love.

There are thousands of recipes for henna paste and thousands more for the lemon/sugar aftermath. Recipes are hoarded and treasured and kept as family secrets. A very basic recipe follows: feel free to improvise. Some substitute a shot of espresso for the tea. Others add assorted spices, like cardamom, cloves or fenugreek. Saffron is an expensive but seductive addition. Pink or red rose petals can be added, too. Okra is sometimes used to thicken the paste. Strain all solids from the liquid before adding henna. Have fun!

Henna Pasté

½ cup loose black tea

½ cup henna powder

4 cups water

1 fresh lemon or lime

1 teaspoon essential oil of eucalyptus

Any color enhancers you wish to add such as spices, rose petals or sliced, dried limes

1. Your henna powder should be green and fragrant. It must be sifted. Put it through a very fine mesh strainer. You can stretch panty hose over a bowl and push the powder through.

2. Boil the tea leaves in 4 cups of water until the water has been reduced by about half.

3. Add whatever additional ingredients you would like.

4. Let the brew simmer for approximately one hour.

5. Allow the brew to cool on the stove, preferably overnight, without removing any of the solid ingredients yet.

6. Strain and discard the solids, reserving the liquid.

7. Add the juice of 1 lemon or lime (only the juice, no pulp or seeds) to the brew.

8. Warm the brew gently but do not boil.

9. Begin to add your henna powder, spoonful by spoonful, stirring all the while. I'm not giving you precise amounts because you need to achieve a consistency and your eyes and hands will help you do this better than numbers. The henna should ultimately be the consistency of cake batter Stick a spoon into the mixture and see how the paste drips off.

If it runs off quickly and easily, it's too thin; add more powder. If it clumps and doesn't flow at all, add more liquid, a bit at a time.

10. Once the correct consistency is achieved, add the teaspoon of eucalyptus oil.

11. Put a little paste on your skin for fifteen minutes. Although the henna isn't full strength yet, it should leave a faint orange mark. Testing is a good idea because a lot of time and effort will be invested after this point. Who wants to painstakingly draw a design and wait eight hours just to find out that the henna didn't take?

12. Let the finished paste rest for about six hours, covered in a warm place. You're ready!

Lemon and Sugar

Juice 2 lemons using a strainer so that the juice separates from the pulp and seeds, which can be discarded. Add about 2 teaspoons of sugar for each lemon. Stir to dissolve the sugar completely.

• • •

There are all sorts of methods for applying henna, ranging from pastry-baglike plastic cones to plastic squeeze bottles to plain old sticks. There is no right or wrong way, only what works for you.

Henna fades away completely on human skin, nails, hair and horse's manes, too. Everywhere else, consider it a permanent dye. Be careful where you prepare and apply it. Cover the area with newspapers or plastic. You will never get it out of a carpet. Of course, sometimes this is an attribute. Henna can be used to paint enchanting designs on magical articles. Henna can be used to create a beautiful and protective finishing touch for a small chest to safeguard your treasures.

Henna Treasure Chest

Henna paste

An unfinished wooden box

The henna will not take if the box is coated with any lacquer, varnish or similar substance. To test, apply a small amount of henna paste in a manner that can be incorporated into the eventual design. Leave on for fifteen minutes and then scrape off. A pale orange stain should remain. If it doesn't, some sort of finish is on the wood, which must be removed.

Begin your design in the center. Then work from the edges inward. Take your time and work in stages. Henna's colors evolve with time. The color as it first appears is not the finished shade. Eventually, the colors will be consistent.

MUGWORT

The single most important and versatile plant used for magic and for stimulating psychic skills is mugwort. Consider her the plant kingdom's magical ambassador. Mugwort, *Artemisia vulgaris*, also known as the Mother Herb, holds the key to the realm of dreams and clairvoyance. If you think you don't dream, if you're not sure you possess a psychic bone, mugwort will show you different. Not only that, while you're trying out your psychic and magical wings, mugwort offers spiritual protection.

Mugwort's uses in psychic work are innumerable. Fortune-tellers sip mugwort tea to strengthen their vision. Crystal balls can be cleansed in mugwort-infused waters. The herb is one of the primary tools for attempting astral projection, controlled out-of-body experiences. Mugwort provides psychic freedom but keeps the bonds to Earth tight, allowing the soul to journey with confidence. Most of the commercial formulas that you will find promoting their ability to enhance your psychic skills contain mugwort as a primary ingredient.

Mugwort also has talismanic uses. Mugwort placed at the entrance of a home blocks the entry of infection. Worn or carried, mugwort becomes a charm against disease, evil spirits and fatigue. It is a traditional traveler's talisman carried to ward off all danger and evil.

There is also Native American mugwort. What is usually described as desert sage, traditionally used by Southwestern Indians as a spiritual cleanser, is actually Artemisia tridentata, mugwort's cousin. Burn it as psychic–inducing incense.

Midsummer's Night brings mugwort to the height of her powers. French tradition recommends that garlands of mugwort be woven and wrapped around the head or waist while dancing around the Midsummer's bonfires. Afterwards, the garlands are thrown into the fire to protect their wearer from bad luck, disease and any malevolent magic that might be directed toward them.

Mugwort has an independent nature. Although she is an ally to humans, she's not overly sociable, no rose-preening for admirers. Mugwort prefers what humans term wasteland: she grows rampant on stony ground, among ruins and beside roadways. Mugwort, unlike so many other plants, is not overly endangered. Naturalized in North America, mugwort now grows rampant through the midwestern United States and parts of Canada.

You can buy dried mugwort easily and inexpensively. Good luck trying to buy a living mugwort plant at your local nursery. Many might prefer that it be endangered, considering it a weed.

Mugwort is a perennial herb that can reach heights of over seven feet during summer. It is best propagated by cuttings or root divisions in the fall. It is not easily cultivated although some have success growing the plant indoors or in the garden. If you can induce mugwort to grow, she is an invaluable plant ally, traditionally very willing, even eager, to impart her secrets to humans, especially women.

Mugwort is not a gentle herb. Its actions are typically not gradual but abrupt. Depending upon your purpose, when using mugwort, you will likely see results within days rather than weeks. *It is not safe for use during pregnancy. It is too powerful for children.* Mugwort is available in various forms, which, even more than with many plants, are not interchangeable.

> *It's not that mugwort bestows psychic capacity; instead, her primary gift is to unearth the power locked within you, liberate, enhance and guide it.*

- The **herb** is safe to use for most people with the exception of children and pregnant and nursing women. It may be prepared as an infusion for tea or bath. An infused oil can be created from mugwort's blossoms. Mugwort eases menstrual cramps and stimulates a sluggish cycle. It can also be used to align one's menstrual cycle with the moon. A cup of mugwort tea enhances psychic ability and vision.

- The **flower essence remedy** is the gentlest form of mugwort and is the most profound remedy for psychic or magical work. It can be added to massage oil or bathwater in addition to internal administration. Add one drop to mugwort or other herbal tea.

- **Essential oil** *of mugwort is not safe and must never be used unless under expert professional guidance.* Beware of anything marketed as either Mugwort, Artemisia or Armoise Oil (mugwort's French name). Mugwort's toxic, dangerous potential is concentrated in her essential oil. Many members of the Artemisia family, including mugwort, contain thujone, a neurotoxin.

DREAMS

Before we begin serious spellcraft, let's linger a little in dreamland.

Dreams allow us to receive and transmit magical communiqués although we may not remember them upon awakening nor do we always understand them. Sleep and the dream state are where healing and rhythmic readjustments most frequently occur.

Although some use the phrase "just a dream" to indicate a hopeless cause or a figment of the imagination, there are many who believe that we each possess a special dream soul that actually journeys while we sleep. The experiences we have in dreams are genuine, just operating on a different plane of existence. We can meet the ones we love, have adventures, journey to spiritual realms and seek crucial information.

Ancient temples of healing, the first hospitals, offered herbal therapies, hydrotherapy, aromatic essences and cleansing smoke, but also invited the ailing and infertile to sleep and dream on the sacred premises. It was believed that divine spirits would communicate remedies through dreams and perform miracle cures.

The caduceus, the modern emblem of the medical profession, a staff encircled by two entwined snakes, recalls the wise, healing serpents that inhabited those early hospitals.

Although states of tension and fatigue can occasionally stimulate an energy surge effective for emergency enchantment, unless you are sufficiently rested you can't consistently access your true magical potential.

How much sleep do you need? Enough to wake up feeling refreshed and enough to dream. Some believe that the true purpose of sleep is to provide access to the dream state. Our souls need these opportunities to visit other realms and other powers, to replenish our own forces and solve personal mysteries. The malady known as sleep deprivation may actually be dream deprivation.

There are of course always exceptions. People suffering severe disharmony, on any level, physical, spiritual, emotional, are often unable to sleep. Some have dreams too intense to handle. Others are petrified of communication with the Other Side; they cannot believe that Earth and her universe mean them any good.

Whether you recall your dreams or not, you do dream. Some people dream in color, others solely in black-and-white. People typically have five dreams every night, each successively longer than the last. The longest, most significant dream is usually the last one, the one that occurs on the threshold between sleep and waking.

You can train yourself to remember your dreams. You can, if you wish, develop the technique of lucid dreaming whereby you retain consciousness and awareness during your dreams. Using this technique you can actively participate in your dreams, ask the questions you want, have the adventures you want versus just having your dreams happen *to you*. You can induce the dreams you wish or need to have.

Active dreaming is a process that requires patience and focus. Many of these skills can be acquired on your own: In the following pages we'll explore some magical tools that will assist you. Although most see results quickly and dramatically, true mastery of the dream state takes time. If the topic intrigues you, there are entire books devoted to lucid dreaming as well as dream laboratories, societies and workshops that can encourage and assist you to take control of your dreams.

> *If a dream holds a special message for you and you don't understand it as it was intended, the dream will likely repeat itself until you do.*

There are people who make dates with others to meet in dreams. When they awake, both can recall the shared dream. Twins, in particular, are believed to have an aptitude for this art. Lovers, separated by distance, have trained themselves to meet in the dreamland, where they can enjoy the romance denied them during the day.

You are most likely to receive communication from other life forces during your dreams. If you request information or assistance from any spiritual entity, you will likely receive the answer in your dreams, perhaps immediately but also perhaps days or weeks later. Sometimes the information you receive is intended for someone else. A friend once had a dream about me that was so intensely vivid that she tracked me down while I was on vacation to describe it. Unknowingly, she was reporting the response to my secret petition. She didn't understand the details of what she was telling me, but I did. When others turn up in your dreams, share the information and request that others share with you.

Remembering Your Dreams

The second you move abruptly or even sit up, you begin to lose fragments of your dreams. That's why noisy, ringing alarm clocks that make you jump are so destructive to dreams. If you need an alarm consistently to wake you, try to set the volume as low as possible or better yet, wake up to music that will transition you awake rather than jolting you up.

> *A trick to remembering your dreams: keep a glass of water or mugwort tea by your bed. Take a sip before you go to sleep, telling yourself, "When I awake, I will have another sip and recall my dreams." This isn't an instantaneous process: gradually you will*

remember more of your dreams. If you're aware that you dream but the dreams remain elusive, just out of reach, rub warmed hazelnut oil into the soles of your feet at bedtime. Add a drop of mugwort flower essence to the warmed oil for intensification, sort of like fine-tuning a television to improve focus.

Keep a pad and paper near where you sleep. Think of the dream state and the waking state as ends of a spectrum, rather than rigidly divided. You need to be awake enough to write but asleep enough to recall your dream accurately, one foot in both worlds, as it were. As soon as you transition out of a dream, write down everything you remember, every tiny detail, with minimal movement and minimal light. Don't go back to sleep, intending to write down the dream later, assuming that because it was intense or significant it will be remembered. Try this experiment: write down a dream immediately and then later when fully awake, before you read what you've written, try to reproduce the dream. You will be amazed at how many details have already dissipated into air. Write down all your dreams, even the ones you think are boring and insignificant now. Months later, go back and read your journal. You will begin to discover your personal vocabulary, the symbols that pop up over and over. Write down the dates of your dreams and keep a daily journal as well. You may discover you have prophetic abilities you've never recognized.

Having the Dreams You Desire

Dream Pillows

To incubate special dreams and provide healing sound sleep, make a dream pillow. Yes, there are commercially available ones out there but by making your own, you can control the contents and receive the dreams that you desire.

No need to be a skillful sewer. You're making this for yourself. No one will inspect how even the stitches are. If you really hate to sew, wrap the herbs up in a white handkerchief and tie with a red, blue or silver bow. It won't be as comfortable as a little pillow and the herbs do have a tendency to spill out but it will be effective. Drawstring bags work, too. If you want a shortcut or if you've found a really great-looking commercial dream pillow, gently remove the stitches from one end and either replace the herbs or dress them with a little fragrance oil.

A basic pillow is made by cutting two pieces of muslin or some soft, plain material. Natural fabrics breathe better than synthetics and allow you better access to the herb's fragrance.

The standard size is 12 inches by 8 inches but you can adjust this to your own liking. Personally, I prefer small ones half that size. Stitch three sides of the two cloths together so that one end is left open. Turn the little bag inside out so that the seams and knots are now on the inside. The goal is to make everything as smooth as possible, so like "The Princess and the Pea," there is nothing to disturb your slumber. This is the inner bag in which you will place your dream herbs. Following the insertion of the herbs, sew the last seam shut.

For some this is sufficient. Others like to add another bag as a cover. It should be only slightly larger so that the first bag fits inside. It should also be made from a natural fabric that allows access to the herbal aroma. Silk is popular, as is cotton or linen. Flax calls in Hulda, another Germanic Queen of Witches, a staunch provider of dreams, wealth and health. You can decorate this bag, just be careful to leave it as smooth as possible. You can also add fasteners, just make sure they're smooth and situated where they won't stick you. This bag may be washed. The pillow that contains the herbs may only be washed if you remove the herbs.

The simplest dream pillow of all is filled with mugwort alone.

- Mugwort intensifies dreams, making them linger so that you're more likely to remember them.

- Mugwort encourages clairvoyance and is an invaluable tool if you're trying to contact the spirit realm.

- Mugwort provides spiritual protection while you sleep. You can take some chances in your dream life with the knowledge that mugwort provides a shield against any psychic dangers.

- If you really want confidence, place mugwort directly upon your chest as you sleep, either by laying the pillow there or by placing either a sprig of the herb or a small flannel bag containing dried mugwort. A wormwood twig or root works, too.

• • •

There are many herbs and fragrances that are beneficial for dreaming. You're not restricted to only one dream pillow. The only stipulations are that you don't want an aroma so stimulating that it keeps you awake. Also make sure you like the smell. It doesn't matter what it's supposed to do if the smell irritates you and keeps you restless and awake. You also don't want any sharp edges in your pillows. All materials should be considered from that standpoint. Rose petals are thus better than rosebuds, which can be hard and pointy. Grind dried herbs in your mortar and pestle to make them softer and powdery.

Combine the herbs as you wish. You can use one or many. You may want to balance herbs that promote restful sleep with those that promote active dreaming. Some recipes follow (see page 127): use these as guidelines to proportion rather than as a rigid amount. A standard-size dream pillow takes about 8 to 10 ounces of dried herbs, but everything depends upon the actual size of your pillow and whether the intensity of the fragrance pleases you. Don't stuff the pillow too full: you want it to remain loose and flat, so that it's comfortable under your head, not lumpy and hard.

- Because crystals need to be cleansed frequently, they are better kept out of dream pillows, but dream roots may be added, such as High John the Conqueror or wormwood. Use only a small piece and bury it in the center of your pillow, covering it with softer herbs.

Mix your herbs in a container. If you're adding fragrance oils, add only a very few drops of liquid. Mix with a wooden chopstick or twig. Allow the mixture to dry completely before stuffing your pillow. If the smell isn't strong enough, add the liquid in batches, drop by drop, allowing the herbs to completely dry out before adding more, although be aware that fragrances tend to seem stronger in the dark when there is less outside stimulation. If the herbs get too wet, they may rot or smell acrid and are more likely to produce disturbing dreams than beautiful ones.

A Selection of Dream Herbs

- **Alecost:** facilitates contact with the Earth Mother.

- **Angelica:** provides prophetic dreams, visions and protection.

- **Anise:** repels nightmares—use only a smidgen of the seed, as many find the fragrance of anise to be stimulating. A little should stimulate pleasant, romantic, sexy dreams. Anise may also increase psychic potential.

> Cover your mattress with whole dried bay leaves and then cover with a clean white sheet to attract good fortune and sweet dreams.

- **Bay Laurel:** provides prophetic dreams and creative inspiration, gives spiritual protection and inspires self-confidence. Crumble the dried leaves, as whole bay leaves can be very sharp. The tips can stick you right through the fabric.

- **Bee Balm:** provides restful sleep.

- **Black Mustard Seeds:** repel night demons and malevolent forces.

- **Calendula Blossoms:** promote sound, peaceful sleep and physical healing, soothes nerves.

- **Catnip:** promotes romantic dreams and restful, sound sleep providing you don't have a cat who will claw you in an attempt to reach your pillow.

- **Chamomile Blossoms:** provide romantic and financially inspirational dreams, spiritual protection and sound restful sleep.

- **Cloves:** initial scent is stimulating, but for most, continuous inhalation produces relaxation and deep, restful sleep. It promotes psychic and erotic dreams. Cloves also provide spiritual protection. Grind the cloves (smash them in your mortar and pestle) so that they'll be more comfortable.

- **Henna:** brings good fortune, protection, fertility, romantic and erotic dreams. Henna produces a grounding effect, provides links to the Earth Mother and the Fire Angels.

- **Hops:** provides peaceful, healing, very sound sleep.

- **Lavender Blossoms:** promote peaceful sleep and sweet dreams. Lavender's fragrance is reputed to allow you to see ghosts.

- **Lilac Blossoms:** provide access to past life memories and heal broken hearts.

- **Linden Blossoms:** promote inspirational dreams, sound restful sleep.

- **Mullein:** protects against nightmares.

- **Peppermint:** encourages visions of one's future.

- **Purslane:** protects the sleeper from spiritual dangers.

- **Rose:** brings romantic, erotic and psychic dreams. Rose eases grief and provides protection; promotes intense healing while one sleeps. Rose is beneficial for threshold states including premarital, premenstrual and premenopausal.

- **Rosemary:** some find rosemary's scent too stimulating to permit sleep, so experiment with only a little bit at first. Dried blossoms may be preferable to the leaves. Rosemary provides mental stimulation while one sleeps and is excellent for students. It promotes romantic dreams and provides psychic protection.

- **Saint John's Wort:** promotes psychic healing and soothes stress. Saint John's Wort strengthens resolve and is beneficial for those battling addictions, it also stimulates psychic power and provides spiritual protection.

- **Spruce Needles:** pulverize them into powder. A Shoshone charm to prevent illness, spruce needles will also provide deep, peaceful sleep.

- **Vanilla Bean:** promotes romantic and erotic dreams.

- **Vervain:** provides protection and sound sleep, financial inspiration and romantic dreams. A Pawnee recommendation for pleasant dreams.

- **Wormwood (root):** provides protection, romance, psychic enhancement, encourages communication with the spirits.

Although dream pillows can be created to stimulate whatever dreams you desire, some specifically promote sleep, encourage the dream process and facilitate your psychic capacity and skills.

Insomnia Pillow

You'd love to dream, if only you could get to sleep. . . . Hops provide sound slumber.

4 ounces dried hops

2 ounces dried rose petals

2 ounces either calendula, cowslip or lavender blossoms

Prophetic Dreams Pillow

When you need to know what happens next.

4 ounces dried peppermint leaves

4 ounces dried rose petals

A few drops essential oil of sandalwood

Fly Me To The Moon: An Astral Projection Pillow

Artemis is the Greek goddess of the moon and magic. If you're trying to fly, sample Artemis's two favorite herbs.

4 ounces dried mugwort

4 ounces dried Dittany of Crete

To provide a grounding effect beneficial for safe astral projection, place individual jasper crystals over each of the seven chakra points.

DREAM OILS

Only a very little is needed at a time, so use these drop by drop, in combination with dream pillows or independently.

- Place a drop on your sheets or pillow or rub one drop onto your forehead at bedtime.

- For a luxurious and relaxing bedtime ritual, warm up a little walnut or hazelnut oil.

- Add a few drops of the dream oil of your choice and massage into your feet and ankles.

- If you share a bed, massage each other and make a date to rendezvous in dreamland.

You're not limited to oil. Sprigs of any of these plants on your pillow or a potted plant placed near your bed—so that its scent wafts over you— can be effective, too.

Dream Plants

- **Bergamot:** soothes nerves, aids peaceful sleep.

- **Coconut:** provides spiritual protection, promotes romantic dreams.

- **Frankincense:** encourages deep, rhythmic breathing, soothes worries and stress, provides spiritual protection, calls in powerful spirits.

- **Gardenia:** brings romantic and erotic dreams, provides psychic protection.

- **Heliotrope:** promotes healing, prophetic dreams and financial inspiration.

- **Hibiscus:** promotes erotic dreams and prophetic dreams.

- **Honeysuckle:** promotes erotic dreams, psychic dreams, used to access buried memories. Honeysuckle will also help you forget a lost love and lessen destructive nostalgia.

- **Hyacinth:** provides spiritual protection, soothes disturbing dreams.

- **Jasmine:** promotes romantic and sensual dreams, invigorates the libido and provides spiritual healing.

- **Juniper:** provides protection, assists in accessing buried memories, promotes healing on all planes.

- **Lavender:** promotes sound sleep, peaceful and romantic dreams.

- **Mimosa:** promotes prophetic dreams, provides a shield for those who are psychically and emotionally vulnerable.

- **Mugwort Infused Oil:** intensifies the entire dreaming process. Use only a tiny bit at a time, as mugwort tends to provide exciting, adventurous dreaming. Some enjoy it but others find the dreams too intense and wild and wake up more tired than rested.

- **Myrrh:** promotes erotic dreams, offers spiritual protection and has a soothing, healing effect.

- **Neroli:** provides peaceful sleep, protection and eases stress.

> *Orange blossoms were traditionally placed upon a bride's pillow to arouse erotic interest while assuaging her fears. Essential oil of Neroli is extracted from orange blossoms and is among the most expensive oils. Petitgrain, extracted from the twigs and unripe fruits of the orange and comparatively inexpensive, is more than adequately substituted. Petitgrain's ability to induce sound sleep may be even more potent.*

- **Rose:** relieves stress and tension, allays grief, heals a broken heart, provides romantic dreams.

- **Tagetes:** stimulates erotic dreams and encourages communication with those who've passed from this existence, whether to receive or transmit a message.

A warm bath before bedtime soothes the spirit and relaxes the body. Add a fragrance that elicits dreams. Some of the most powerful psychic fragrances, gardenia and heliotrope for instance, are rarely available as essential oils, although, in theory, they exist. Because producing an essential oil from these flowers is so labor intensive, or yields such tiny quantities, what is commercially available is almost inevitably a synthetic reproduction. Some smell so similar that they may stimulate your psychic imagination anyway and may be effective; however they do lack the physical properties and power of the true plant. Make infused waters from fresh blossoms. Add these to bathwater, place in a spray bottle and spritz the bedroom or sheets, or use as a facial toner before bed.

Sweet Dreams Bath

Bay leaves

Lilac blossoms

Yellow rose petals

Make an infusion with a fistful of each of the dried botanicals and add to your bath. If you have fresh flowers, just let them drift in the tub. (Don't clean up the residue left in the tub until after you wake up; the effort will awaken you.)

There are other ways to use plants to promote dreaming. Try placing one of these under your pillow:

Ash leaf promotes prophetic dreams.

Bay leaf keeps the tone of your dreams pleasant. Placed under your pillow on Valentine's Day, a bay leaf helps you dream up your true love.

Calendula blossoms provide prophetic dreams and help you to identify a thief.

Cinquefoil normally has five points. A rare seven-pointed specimen under your pillow will help you call up the image of your true love.

Daisy roots bring dreams of absent or long-lost lovers.

Eucalyptus Seedpods guard against colds and infections and help build up physical immunity while you sleep.

Four Leaf Clovers bring dreams of love and help you to visualize your true love.

Remember Your Dreams Bath

4 drops essential oil of juniper

4 drops essential oil of lavender

4 drops essential oil of mimosa

Draw a warm bath and then add the essential oils. Swirl them around and enter the tub.

And if cost is no object . . .

Luxurious Remember Your Dreams Bath

4 drops essential oil of jasmine

4 drops essential oil of lavender

2 drops honeysuckle absolute

2 drops essential oil of neroli

Draw a warm bath and add the essential oils just prior to entering the water.

• • •

Herbs can also be burned in the bedroom to provide restful sleep and stimulate dreams and psychic protection. The incense is prepared and burned *before* you sleep.

1. Close the doors and windows.

2. Walk through the room with your incense, fanning the fragrance into all corners and especially around the bed.

3. Allow the incense to burn out naturally and dispose of it safely.

4. When you're ready to sleep, open doors and windows as desired.

Dream Incense

Chopped or powdered bay leaves

Cedarwood shavings

Lavender blossoms

Pulverize equal parts and then burn. This incense should stimulate more vivid dreams and help you to remember them better.

Sweet Dreams Anti-Insomnia Incense

Frankincense resin

Storax resin

Rose blossoms

This incense promotes deep sleep while stimulating sweet dreams. Storax has served as a remedy for insomnia since ancient Mesopotamia. Pound the two resins together in your mortar and pestle, then add the rose blossoms and burn.

Calea zacatechichi, *a native of the Mexican rainforest also known as Dream Herb, is treasured for its ability to facilitate reception of spiritual advice and information in dreams. Traditional method of use is tea, however, newcomers beware: it doesn't taste very good. Unlike mugwort, which can be doctored with a little peppermint and lemon balm, there's not too much you can do to improve the flavor of zacatechichi. Try burning it as incense before you sleep; the effects*

remain profound. No need to venture into the rainforest to gather
zacatechichi; it grows easily from seed indoors. Burn it alone or
partnered with dried sage.

STONES AND CRYSTALS

- Stones and crystals can also facilitate dreaming and protect slumber.

- An amethyst under your pillow encourages sound sleep and promotes prophetic dreams.

- A garnet under your pillow keeps nightmares away.

- Citrine serves to stimulate dreams.

- Red coral attached to a bedpost dispels nightmares and protects against any spiritual dangers.

- A moonstone worn upon the body while you sleep performs the same functions as red coral.

- A precious gemstone isn't necessarily your most powerful tool. Finding a plain old pebble with a natural hole in it is a gift from the Earth Mother, to foster communication and enable you to receive healing dreams. Run a cord through the pebble and attach to your bed or yourself.

• • •

And finally, are you having too many dreams? Do you need a break? Hang a sprig of lemon verbena around your neck at bedtime as a temporary cease and desist.

PART THREE

Spells

The desires that spark enchantments are universal. As unique as each individual may be, as a species, we have a lot in common. The most common magical goals, from every tradition and from every corner of Earth, are safety, prosperity, health, good looks, love, sex and fertility, the last three in various combinations and not necessarily together.

There are two categories of spells in this book:

1. Spells to enhance and refine your psychic potential and maximize your magical power.

2. Spells to further your goals and attain your desires.

   - Because everyone is an individual and because there are so many styles and traditions of Pure Magic, you've been offered a wide variety of spells in each category. Which one is the most powerful? The one that resonates most for you. Read through them and see which ones call to you.

   - Many magical ingredients are quite familiar from the supermarket and garden. Others like "devil's shoestrings" or "tonka beans" may seem mysterious to you. All the ingredients in this book are available, if not from your local market, then by mail order or through the Internet. Look at the appendix in the back of the book for sources.

Although many of the spells in this book include precise measurements, you'll notice that many do not. No, this isn't just to confuse you. When precise measurements have not been given, this means that you should follow your nose and instincts to determine what proportion feels correct to you.

The Magic Calendar

Any day and every day are good days for magic, but each day's power is not identical.

- When you wish to *increase* something, a fortune or love, let's say, harmonize your magic with the waxing moon: initiate your spell or ritual at the new moon.

- When you wish to *decrease* something, weight or animosity, for example, harmonize your magic with the waning moon: initiate your spell or ritual at the full moon.

The sun's power on Earth is measured by the solstices and equinoxes. These are potent times to assert your power. The solstices are particularly powerful times for candle magic or any spells using fire.

Not all days of power are measured by the sun's rays. During the period beginning on the first Friday in October until the second day of November, the veils separating spiritual realms are extremely sheer: this may be the easiest time to summon the spirits or contact your ancestors.

May 1st and St. John's Eve, the night of June 24th, are charged with extra magical power, especially for enchantment involving love, protection and fertility. These days are extremely beneficial for any botanical or nature magic. May 1st is the ideal day for contacting the fairies.

You have your own individual days of power. Astrologers can reveal these to you. Your birthday is your own personal New Year, a time for any new beginnings you desire. New Year's day is a great time to initiate any new spell.

Luckily, you don't have to wait for your birthday or January 1st for a cause to celebrate. Some forty calendars are currently in use on Earth and someone is celebrating a New Year virtually every month. Feel free to begin a New Year as frequently as necessary; take advantage of these opportunities to initiate new magic and new goals or regenerate old ones that have stalled.

- Ethiopian and Jewish New Year's coincide with the new moon near the autumn equinox.

- Persian New Year coincides with the vernal equinox, the first day of Aries.

- Chinese and Vietnamese mark the New Year at the second new moon following the winter solstice with Tibetan New Year following shortly after.

- Halloween marks what was once the start of the Celtic New Year.

Where to Practice Magic

Any place you feel comfortable expressing your power is the best place to practice magic. Ultimately, magic is the expression of your power, so wherever that power shines brightest is the right place for you. Some places, however, contribute some extra power of their own. Outside, look for threshold areas.

- The seashore, where ocean meets land.

- Beside a natural source of water, a river, spring or lake, provided the area is not too "tame," provided you can perceive some wild, natural power.

- Within a circle of trees. (Count how many trees are in your circle and study the mystical significance of the number.)

- On a mountain or in the desert.

- In your own magic garden.

The potential for power is always greater outside if you stand with your bare feet on Earth or in natural living water. Be respectful and walk gently upon Earth.

There are places of power inside your home, too. A lot of your magic may be brewed up in your kitchen. Arrange botanicals and crystals so that they empower and cleanse the atmosphere, providing you with some extra surges of power. Check under the Protection Spells section on page 154 for some hints.

THE BATHROOM: YOUR PERSONAL SHRINE

Submerging oneself in water is among Earth's oldest magical rituals. Once upon a time, people regularly journeyed to sacred springs, rivers, lakes and oceans. Some still do, for spiritual ritual or health. Modern technology has provided you with your own sacred water shrine: your bathroom. You have your own source of water, although it is up to you to boost its healing powers via herbs and oils. It is also one of the few places that modern people are usually granted a modicum of privacy, the privacy sometimes necessary to maintain magical focus. Your bathroom is easily converted into a magic laboratory and shrine. This can be discreetly and quickly done, even if you share one bathroom with a large household. A bathtub is preferable for enchantments, as it encourages you to linger and allows you to submerge, but with a little imagination, a shower stall can be adapted as well.

Some spirits actually prefer that their altars be placed in bathrooms. Any spirit that is associated with the water element will be happy ensconced in the most watery room of your house. These spirits of water tend to be purveyors of romance, sensuality and women's good health. Enjoy a long, soothing soak and listen to their advice.

- Decorate a small area with shells, images of fish and mermaids, anything marine oriented.

- Bring candles, crystals or incense into the bathroom, too.

- Place beach sand in glass containers so that you can run your fingers through it whenever you need to feel the Earth Mother's presence.

Words of Power

"Star light, star bright, first star I see tonight..."

For many people, magic doesn't feel *real* or complete unless there is a verbal accompaniment, a little rhyme perhaps or some mysterious phrase. In some traditions every spell has a verbal component. In fantasy magic, cartoons or fiction, magic spells may consist of words alone: *hocus pocus* or *abracadabra*.

Words, however, can be very tricky. Just look at *abracadabra* Its origins lie in ancient Hebrew word amulets. For some, it remains a genuine word of power but for many others, it's a joke. Because words are so personal, I haven't assigned any specific words or rhymes for spells, although some come with suggestions. Words are supposed to increase the power of your magic; if anything makes you feel silly, foolish or self-conscious, then it's having the opposite effect. My recommendation is to make up your own.

- Say what you feel as simply, clearly and concisely as you can. Consider the implications of all that you say and make sure that what you are expressing is what you truly mean.

- Rhymes are useful, if only because they're easy to remember if you need to repeat them.

- Positive affirmations are great, too. Always speak in the present tense because speaking in the future, "I will be happy" versus "I am happy" keeps your destiny always out of reach.

Low-level malevolent spirits have been known to lurk in bathrooms near the toilet. Chinese tradition has protective Spirits of the Lavatory to deal with them, but essential oil of cajuput can also do the trick. Just sprinkle a drop or two near the toilet bowl periodically, particularly if someone is ill.

Let's Get Real: Realistic Expectations of Magic

Magical powers are natural powers. Magic is part of real life. Magic is not an excuse to assume that Earthly laws, the rules of nature, will somehow be suspended, that exceptions will be made for you. Magic just reminds us that Earth's laws are a little more complex than we often care to remember.

Remember, thinking symbolically means that things operate on multiple levels simultaneously. Yes, that big, strange, stray dog may be your response to a petition from Hecate but no, that doesn't necessarily mean that you should approach and pet it. Seeing a coyote in your neighborhood is powerful good luck but not if you leave your little Dandie Dinmont terrier in the backyard unattended. Magic isn't license to abandon common sense. Ideally, they enhance each other.

Magic doesn't supersede the laws of nature: it *is* a law of nature. Magic works best in conjunction with other efforts on other planes, as mutual reinforcement. You can do all the fertility spells you like; if you're not having sex, too, or at least in vitro, they can't work. Even Isis, who can revive the dead, at least momentarily, needed that golden penis. No matter how many professional success candles you light, if you don't show up for the job interview, you're wasting the wax. There are contraceptive spells. These aren't intended to allow you to forget biological cycles: they work hand-in-hand reinforcing each other. Don't use magic as a challenge to Earth, unless you don't care who wins.

What does it mean when, despite your best efforts, your spell just doesn't work, when, as Muddy Waters sings, "I've got my mojo working but it just don't work on you"? When a medication doesn't help, we don't throw out the whole pharmacy, yet so many of us are willing to throw in the towel on magic, to refute its existence, when a spell doesn't work for us.

Maybe something in the preparation of the spell wasn't completely correct. Maybe the most beneficial time or day wasn't chosen. Maybe the energy wasn't right. Sometimes the spell bears repeating or sometimes, it just isn't the right spell for you. You may need to substitute another. Sometimes magic just doesn't operate on the schedule we desire and all that's called for is a little patience.

Sometimes, when a spell doesn't work, it's a message from the Earth Mother to reassess your situation and alternatives. Once in a while, we ask for things that we sincerely believe at that time to be in our best interest but the Earth Mother thinks different. Sometimes the powers that be don't grant our wishes or they put obstacles in the way of our magic for our own protection. How many of us, years later, have looked back wonderingly at narrow escapes, grateful we didn't receive what we requested at the time? When a charm consistently fails, consider whether this is your scenario: Are you really asking for what's best for you?

Magic involves energy adjustments. With a little experience, you will feel something, I can only describe it as being like a "click," that indicates that your spell is complete and likely to be successful. It's like a key in a lock, you can play and play with it, but when it actually turns and opens, you're aware, you feel it as it's opening the door. You'll also feel right away if the spell doesn't work. No need to wait for weeks; you'll know pretty immediately if you need to find an alternative. This awareness comes with experience and experience can only follow practice.

AURA-CLEANSING SPELLS

What do you do if you're feeling a little grubby? Take a bath, take a shower? Aura cleansing, also known as purification, removes psychic debris or vibrations that cling to you. Purification baths and incense cleanse and bolster your aura; many also replenish lost psychic energy. They are a good first step before any ritual.

- Some magical practitioners incorporate aura cleansing into their regular schedules as a kind of "magical maintenance," once a week or monthly, whenever feels right, either to remove accumulated negative energy or as a formality before magic, sort of like cleaning the house before company comes.

- If any sort of negative experience or encounter, nonmagical as well as enchanted, leaves you feeling a little "tainted" or out-of-balance, turn to an aura-cleansing spell or ritual for relief.

- Although aura cleansing is a perfunctory component of magic for many, it also serves another crucial purpose. If you have suffered trauma or humiliation, violence or rape, anything that leaves you feeling "defiled" or "unclean," purification spells and rituals can have a profoundly healing impact. Use them as needed; use as many as necessary to initiate and maintain the healing process. Special aura-cleansing animal and spirit allies provide assistance, as well.

In order for these spells and rituals to be effective, they must result in your feeling psychically cleansed. Because different people have different needs, many different types of purification rituals exist, some quite sensuous and pleasurable, others focused and intense. Some utilize the power of water, others depend on fire or crystals. Choose whatever resonates loudest for you. Read through the spells and see what calls to you.

Quick Fix Aura-Cleansing Bath

The simplest aura-cleansing bath of all.

> 1 cup salt
>
> 1 cup vinegar, preferably lemon vinegar but rice or apple cider vinegar is fine, too.

Toss the ingredients into a tub of water. Completely effective as is, but feel free to add essential oils or herbs of your choice.

Purification Bath

> 2 tablespoons anise seeds
>
> 9 bay leaves

Create a strong water infusion. Do not strain but add the herbs to your bath with the infused waters. Relax in the bath until you feel cleansed.

Seven Roses Aura-Cleansing Bath

7 red roses

Handful of salt

Splash of vinegar

Splash of lemon juice

Splash of pure springwater and/or holy water

1. Fill your tub with water.

2. Remove the roses from the stems. Watch out for any thorns.

3. Throw all the ingredients into the tub.

4. Spend seven minutes in your bath, rubbing yourself with the roses, submerging yourself periodically and focusing upon your goals.

5. Dry off with a clean towel, white or unbleached cotton if possible, and put on fresh clothes.

Aura-cleansing spells can be combined for intensification purposes. Burn purification incense in the bathroom prior to taking your aura-cleansing bath.

Now, here's the hard part: walk out of the room without looking back. The roses have a tendency to come apart in the tub. This is one of the messier spells. Depending upon how important tidiness is to you, you may be tempted to stop and clean your tub. Don't. It's vital for the success of this spell that you put some time in between taking the bath and cleaning up the residue. If at all possible, get someone else to clean the tub for you. If not possible, walk out of the room and do something positive or enjoyable that lifts your spirits. After at least an hour, when you feel calm, strong and distanced from any negative feelings that may have caused you to take this bath, you may clean the tub.

Sandalwood Spirit-Cleansing Face Mask

Sandalwood's use as the primary agent of ancient spiritual purification rites only slightly trails that of frankincense and myrrh. Sandalwood incense may be burned to purify the atmosphere; a few drops of the essential oil added to a full tub of warm water creates an instant and luxuriously scented purification bath. It can also be used in a face mask that cleanses the aura and creates a protective barrier against spiritual harm, while improving skin tone (in particular for dry, dehydrated or aging skin).

> 1 tablespoon sandalwood powder (available from Indian grocery
> or supply stores)
>
> Springwater

1. Place the sandalwood powder in your cupped palm or use a seashell for mixing.

2. Add warm water drop by drop until a thin paste is formed.

3. Spread the paste onto your face.

4. Wait about 10 minutes or until it stiffens and then rinse off.

Cleansing crystals include amethyst, clear quartz and malachite

- Wear or carry small ones for a cleansing effect between rituals.

- Place larger crystals in the bath to intensify any purification bath.

- Large crystals arranged in your home or work area can serve as psychic vacuum cleaners.

- Remember to clean and recharge frequently. Go back to the crystal pages, if you've forgotten how.

Florida Water

For centuries, explorers, adventurers and spiritual seekers searched Earth for miraculous healing waters: the water of life, the Fountain of Youth, holy water that would cleanse you of your sins. Ponce de Leon scoured what is now Florida searching for the Fountain of Youth. He never found it but one of the most popular modern purification formulas is known as Florida Water.

Florida Water has a lovely, fresh, citrus-floral aroma. It's suitable for use purely as a refreshing bath, cologne or facial toner but in the Afro-Caribbean traditions, Florida Water is much more. It's believed to have great spiritual significance and is an old standby for spirit cleansing and protection.

- Put some in a spray bottle to sprinkle over an area or person.

- Keep a spray bottle in the refrigerator to revive your energy.

- Blend some with pure glycerin soap and pour into a mold to make soap bars.

- Add an equal amount of Florida Water to unscented liquid soap for a cleansing, foaming bath.

Animal Allies for Aura Cleansing
Deer • Dove • Vulture

Keep an image or figure of one or more of these creatures near you as you perform your purification ritual. If you are recovering from trauma and feel the need for intensive aura cleansing, keep an image close to your body: wear or carry a charm. Learn all that you can about these animals' lives and habits, meditate upon their images and wait for healing advice.

There are as many recipes for Florida Water as there are practitioners. Here are two.

Florida Water Formula #1

2 cups vodka or other alcohol*

2 tablespoons rose water

16 drops essential oil of bergamot

12 drops essential oil of lavender

6 drops essential oil of lemon

2 drops essential oil of jasmine

2 drops rose attar

Florida Water Formula #2

2 cups vodka or other alcohol*

2 tablespoons orange flower water

1 tablespoon turmeric

16 drops essential oil of bergamot

12 drops essential oil of lavender

6 drops essential oil of lemon

2 drops rose attar

2 drops essential oil of neroli

Silver is the metal that promotes purification and provides protection.

Combine all the ingredients in a bottle. If using Formula #2, shake vigorously to distribute the turmeric.

---

* Alcohol must be minimum 60 proof. Vodka is preferable only because it has no fragrance. Florida Water is for reitual use, not for drinking.

Candomblé Cleansing Incense

This formula is popular in the African-Brazilian spiritual tradition of Candomblé.

Frankincense resin

Myrrh resin

Powdered thyme

1. Use equal proportions or allow your nose to guide you.

2. Grind the resins together, then add the powdered thyme and burn.

Aura-Cleansing Incense

The following formula is called for whenever any enchantment results in uneasiness, also known as "look what the Ouija board dragged in."

Agrimony

Mugwort

Sage

Burn equal parts of the dried herbs.

Spirit Ally: Tlazolteotl

Tlazolteotl is the Aztec Spirit of Garbage. She cleanses Earth of psychic and physical waste. Decorate her altar with obsidian, smoky quartz and/or turquoise and images of her favorite animals: bats, owls and ravens. Tlazolteotl invented the temazcal sweat bath to assist humans with purification. They are once again popular in Mexico; perhaps a visit is called for. If this is not possible, try a steam bath instead.

Coconut Cleansing Candle

White or brown pour-and-melt wax*

Pure coconut extract

Container (ideally half a coconut shell or a terra-cotta pot)

Candle wick

This candle's fragrance will perfume and cleanse the room where it's placed even when not burning.

1. Melt the wax according to package directions.

2. Stir in the coconut extract. The quantity depends upon your taste for the fragrance: you need enough for the aroma to be clear and distinct.

> *Sage planted around your house constantly purifies the atmosphere.*
> *Different species bear different types of flowers, in varying shades.*
> *Experiment and see which pleases you most.*

3. Pour the melted, scented wax into a terra-cotta pot, half a coconut shell or any other safe container.

4. Make sure that the wick is attached safely, either by holding it in place until the wax hardens or by attaching it to a pencil laid over the top of the container.

5. Allow the wax to harden.

---

*   Available from craft stores as well as candle supply stores.

For heavy-duty cleansing, burn some incense in the bathroom as you draw the bath, strategically arrange some amethyst clusters and light some white, yellow or brown candles. A coconut-scented candle is ideal as that fragrance is reputed to send most malevolent entities running for the hills. To be effective, though, it has to be real coconut, not artificial. If you can't find one, make one yourself.

Obeah-Style Coconut Cleansing Candle

Based upon formulas deriving from Jamaican spiritual traditions, this potent candle is housed in a coconut but impregnated with other tropical fragrances.

White or brown pour-and-melt wax*

Half a coconut shell

Essential oils of ginger, jasmine, lemon, myrrh, patchouli

Candle wick

1. Melt the wax according to package directions

2. Before pouring, but after removing from the heat source, stir in the essential oils.

3. Add the wax to the shell, making sure that the wick is attached safely as above.

---

* Available from craft stores as well as candle supply stores.

• • •

You may also feel the need to spiritually cleanse an area. There are a number of tried-and-true easy methods of banishing any "bad vibrations." Many magical practitioners also feel that prior to any serious magic, for best success, the aura of the room should be as thoroughly cleansed and prepared as your own.

Vinegar Room Cleanser

One cup of vinegar in a bowl placed within a room purifies the atmosphere. Essential oils may be added as wished, with sandalwood and/or frankincense particularly effective.

> *A new home should always be cleansed if only to imprint your own personal, positive energy and begin with a fresh, clean slate. Don't bring your old broom to your new home, with the remnants of any spiritual garbage clinging to it. (This doesn't include brooms used solely for ritual purposes.) If the old residents have left you their broom, don't use that one either.*

Egg Bedroom Cleanser

Eggs are believed capable of absorbing negativity and psychic toxins. Consider them spiritual vacuum cleaners. Put one or two eggs* under the bed in a bowl of pure water to cleanse the atmosphere. Replace the eggs after a

---

* The number of eggs under the bed is based on the number of people regularly sleeping in it. If you have a family bed, add more as needed.

week. Should an egg develop a foul smell before the week is up, it's essentially indicating that the vacuum bag is full: replace immediately.

Discard the old ones, don't eat them.

Flower essences that promote a sense of spiritual cleanliness include Chaparral (FES, Pegasus), Crab Apple (Bach, Green Hope, Healing Herbs, Pegasus) and Pine (Bach, Healing Herbs).

Egg Domestic Dispute Disposal

Has a domestic dispute left you feeling shaken? (Not afraid—if that's the case, check the following protection spells.) Has the tense atmosphere failed to dissipate? To clear up these bad feelings, place one unbroken, uncooked egg in each corner of a room. Leave them there until the dark cloud lifts or for up to seven days. (If things aren't better within seven days, eggs alone won't do the trick!)

• • •

Eggs do have the disadvantage of being breakable. If you have kids, pets or you really need a big clean-up job, try onions instead. (This spell is also very good for cleansing the atmosphere when there's one room that just never feels *right* in your new home.)

Onion Bad-Vibe Removal

Chop one onion into quarters and place one piece in each corner of the room. Do not peel the onion. Allow the onion to remain overnight. Gather the pieces up the next day and, wearing rubber gloves, chop them (by hand, please! No food processors for this spell) and bury the small pieces outside. Repeat this process for five nights.

Hawaiian Aura Cleanser

Traditional Hawaiians used turmeric to cleanse an area or an individual in much the same way that Native North Americans might use sage, sweetgrass or cedar. Turmeric also produces a potent—and permanent—bright yellow dye. Watch out for fabrics and carpets.

Powdered turmeric (you may also use grated fresh turmeric rhizome, if available)

Water

1. Add the turmeric to the water.

2. Using a large leaf or feather, (a ti leaf was traditional) sprinkle the mixture wherever you perceive cleansing is needed.

3. This is a general purification formula, suitable for people, pets, crystals as well as rooms and areas.

Angelica Floor Wash

To cleanse a bad atmosphere from a room and provide spiritual protection.

1. Make a strong infusion from dried angelica.

2. Strain out the herbs.

3. Add the infusion with some white vinegar to a bucket of water to cleanse floors and surfaces.

Aura-cleansing essential oils include frankincense, manuka (New Zealand tea tree), myrrh, pine and rosemary. Essential oil of thyme can also be very effective, however, it's not safe for frequent use and not at all during pregnancy. Look for lemon thyme or thyme linalool, the gentlest types.

Banish Bad Vibes Floor Wash

Agrimony

Peppermint

1. Make a strong herbal infusion from the dried herbs.

2. Strain out the solids and add to a bucket of water with some white vinegar to cleanse floors and surfaces.

New Home Floor Wash

Basil: prosperity

Hyssop: cleansing and protection

Pine needles: new beginnings

1. Make a strong infusion from the dried botanicals (see page 16).

2. Strain out the solids.

3. Add to a bucket of water with some white vinegar and wash those floors!

> *To cleanse and renew defiled or tainted magical tools, bathe them in an agrimony and/or mugwort infusion. Alternatively, pass them through myrrh smoke.*

PROTECTION SPELLS

The primary purpose of protection spells is psychic self-defense: The removal and repelling of any malevolent energy attached to you or directed toward you. If you're afraid, if you possess that uneasy feeling that something is just not right, a protection spell can help rebuild confidence while providing a psychic shield.

Sometimes there's a fine line between aura-cleansing/purification spells and protection spells. A few of the strongest powers, rosemary or salt, for instance, may provide both effects. How will you know which spell you need? In general, cleansing spells provide internal psychic repairs and replenishment while protection spells create a spiritual shield that deflects danger from external sources.

For example:

- You've just witnessed a car accident and you are unnerved. Your protective aura may have been breached: draw a purification bath.

- You're terribly afraid you'll have a car crash, you possess a great sense of foreboding: take protective measures instead, or in addition to a purification ritual.

Many psychic practitioners perceive protection and purification spells to be two sides of a coin, both necessary steps to hone and enhance your personal power to the utmost degree.

A Magic Garden of Protection

Angelica, Clover, Dill, Flax, Gardenia, Garlic, Holly, Juniper, Oleander, Oregano, Rose, Rosemary, St. John's Wort, Vervain. For real feelings of security, try to include all of these plants. Use garlic to line the borders.

- While very lovely, oleander is also very poisonous. If children and pets will frequent your garden, then consider whether or not this is a safe addition.

Your own personal allies are always your greatest protectors, whether animal allies, guardian angels or others. They may be appealed to for any sort of assistance you may need. If you don't know who to turn to, appeals may always be sent to the Archangel Michael, humanity's defender. The most loyal, trustworthy and protective animal ally is Dog. Check back to the section on animal powers for more information on working with this power.

Sun and Moon Psychic Bodyguard Dream Pillow Stuffing

This pillow provides the equivalent of a wonderful fairy-tale brother and sister to watch over you while you sleep.

4 ounces dried mugwort

4 ounces dried Saint John's Wort

Tiny piece of real silver

• • •

Your heroic protectors await you in the kitchen: chiles, garlic, rosemary and salt. Garlic, rosemary and chiles provide protection by virtue of their mere presence. Hang near doors and windows. Salt is used more actively. Sprinkled on the ground, salt provides barriers to assorted negative entities and dangers. A Gullah tradition from the South Carolina islands suggests sprinkling salt around the bed to defy evil spirits and their bad intentions.

- Powdered angelica root sprinkled around your home provides a psychic barrier to evil.

Anti-Evil Eye Crystals

Carnelian, malachite and jet carved into the shape of a hand.

Special Cases:

Tiger's eye protects against accidents. Keep one in the glove compartment or around the rear-view mirror for safety in the automobile.

Divers traditionally wear or carry pearls for protection against sharks.

Don't Cross My Path

Garlic cloves, peeled

Handful of coarse sea salt

Generous handful of fresh rosemary

1. Grind together in a food processor or mash up with your mortar and pestle.

2. Sprinkle on the ground wherever you feel in need of psychic protection. Reputed to stop ghosts cold.

• • •

Salt is the most universal and most ancient agent of protection. Not only does it possess antiseptic properties to cleanse and protect the body, it also provides spiritual protection and cleansing. A handful of salt in the bath or rubbed against your skin quickly removes the day's ill vibrations. Making magic bath salts and salt scrubs is child's play, easy, quick, fun and cheap, plus the very action of mixing them up automatically puts the protection process in motion. Embellish with fragrance and herbs to further any magical goals.

Basic Bath Salts

½ cup baking soda

2 cups sea salt

Mix together and add to your bath. Add essential oils as desired or mix with very finely powdered herbs. (The advantage of essential oils is no clean up; residue from the herbs may remain in your tub or clog your drain.) The sea salt is the key ingredient: you may omit the baking soda if you choose or if you're feeling achy, substitute Epsom salts. Salt, like olive oil, wine, honey and essential oils, is always slightly different depending upon which corner of Earth it originates from. Experiment.

Extra Protection Bath Salts

4 drops essential oil of peppermint

4 drops essential oil of vetiver

2 drops essential oil of cinnamon

2 drops essential oil of ginger

1 cup of sea salt

Add the essential oils to the salt, stir and mix. These salts may make you tingle: not recommended for those with sensitive skin. In addition to adding to your bath, you can also use Extra Protection Salts as a protective floor sprinkle.

• • •

One of the most effective protective cleansers may also be the most luxurious. A simple mixture of salt and oil is transformed into a sensuous medium. Even if you harbor magical doubts, rest assured that, at the very least, this formula will leave your skin feeling renewed and refreshed. Rub the salt into your skin with gentle circular motions; visualize your goals, chant your affirmations.

Salt Scrubs

1 cup of salt

½ cup of oil

Pour the salt into an airtight jar (Mason jars are great). Add 1/2 cup of good quality oil. Safflower oil is reputed to lend the best consistency but I've also found success with sweet almond oil. Mix the oil into the salt until you achieve the consistency you desire. The wetter and looser the texture, the gentler it will be, although the dryer scrubs truly exfoliate and leave you feeling completely cleansed, spiritually and otherwise. If you prefer your scrub less dry than the basic formula, just keep adding extra oil in small increments until you are satisfied.

For purposes of purification and protection, the scrub is now complete. Add a handful to a tub of water or use it as a scrub to cleanse your body in either bath or shower. (Be careful! It's slippery.)

For intensification or additional magical goals, add essential oils to suit your purpose. Wait until you've achieved the desired consistency, then add essential oils, drop by drop, mixing thoroughly so that they're well distributed. For multiple desires, just combine different essential oils with the proviso that no more than 10 to 12 drops of essential oil per 1 cup of salt is necessary or advisable. Alternately, add 1 tablespoon of infused oil to 1 cup of salt.

> *Essential oils providing spiritual protection include cinnamon leaf,[*]*
> *frankincense, juniper, pine, rose, rosemary and sandalwood.*

---

[*]   A skin irritant; wear a drop on your hair rather than on your skin.

Protective Botanicals

- **Basil:** increases finances, helps to mend a lover's quarrel or attract luck to a new enterprise or home.

- **Bergamot:** attracts good fortune, increases finances.

- **Frankincense:** for courage, spiritual protection and to help cut the chains of negative relationships.

Protective Trees

Ash, Bay Laurel, Birch, Cedar, Dogwood, Hawthorn, Juniper, Oak, Olive, Rowan.

For utmost security, arrange the trees in a circle.

- **Gardenia:** for protection, to prevent others from causing strife in your life. (This is the mother-in-law fragrance.)

- **Geranium:** lifts spirits, breaks hexes.

- **Jasmine:** promotes romance, fertility and better sex.

- **Rose:** increases self-esteem, teaches you to love yourself.

- **Rosemary:** provides protection, protection and more protection!

- **Sandalwood:** provides spiritual protection

- **Ylang Ylang:** encourages others to speak freely with you.

St. John's Wort flower essence promotes feelings of spiritual safety.

The desire for protection was the impetus for the first amulets. It remains the primary desire and there are more types of protective amulets than any other kind. There are general protection amulets and there are also protective amulets that serve specific functions. There are special amulets to protect children, animals and the home.

- **Mirrors** make simple amulets. They reflect the Evil Eye right back where it came from and are also believed to confuse low-level malevolent spirit entities. (Painting your ceiling blue confuses them as to exactly where they are, inside or out, and sends them packing, too!)

- In China, **Feng Shui** has evolved into a science that analyzes where and how things should be arranged for protection, advancement and good fortune. When an area or arrangement is perceived as potentially unfortunate, mirrors are a frequent remedy. Mirrors are hung over the front door to return any potential "poison arrows." Inside, mirrors are placed carefully, not only considering what should be reflected, but what should not. General **Feng Shui** wisdom recommends against reflecting the main door, the master bedroom bed or toilets.

> In order for crystals to care for you at full capacity, you must care for them as well. If your protective crystal is seeing active duty, make sure that you cleanse and recharge it regularly.

- The color **black** provides psychic protection. Any black crystal can be used for personal protection, however **black tourmalines** are usually considered most powerful. While other black crystals absorb harmful energy, black tourmaline behaves like a shield and deflects it.

> Iron and silver are the metals that provide psychic protection.

The Body

Although we commonly look to sources outside ourselves to provide personal protection, traditionally some of the most powerful protection derives from images of the human body.

EYES

Nothing else defeats the Evil Eye like another eye. Another eye draws the Evil Eye toward it so that it is unable to glance elsewhere, then boomerangs the evil glance right back, behaving as a shield. Sometimes the eye image may be implied: a diamond, almond-shape or triangle is used, flanked by images of eyebrows. The eyebrows alone may be enough to convey the threat and send that Evil Eye packing. Small blue glass eyes from Greece and Turkey are hung from necklaces, on walls and on rearview mirrors. Traditionally, they are believed to work best if received as a gift.

• • •

The *Ojo de Dios* (Eye of God) is an ancient Huichol Indian amulet that is increasingly popular and widespread. Interestingly, just as in North Africa, a diamond shape is used to symbolize an eye. (The innermost diamond represents the eye's pupil.) The color of the yarn indicates what type of protection and power is needed. These amulets are also used to request prosperity and male children. Small ones are carried as personal amulets but larger ones adorn homes. Although the directions for this amulet involve many steps, it's actually an easy and relaxing one to create.

Ojo de Dios

wooden dowels

Knife, glue, scissors

Yarn in 2 or 3 colors

1. Mark the center of each dowel and make a notch with the knife.

2. Glue the dowels together to form a cross, fitting the notches together. It is as if there are four spokes of a wheel or four arms of a cross.

3. Choose one color of yarn to serve as the eye's pupil; loop the yarn several times around the center until it is completely covered.

4. Begin to wrap the yarn around the dowels. Start at the 1st dowel and move clockwise, like the sun, over and around the 2nd arm and up and over the 3rd. Wind the yarn around the 3rd and bring it to the 4th, wrap it around and come back to the 1st. (Keep the yarn tight but not pulled too hard.) Continue winding until you have a small diamond.

5. When you are ready, when the pupil diamond is complete, return to the 1st dowel (first spoke of the wheel), knot the yarn and cut it, leaving about a 1-inch tail.

6. Add the second color: this is the iris. Position it close to the inner diamond. Add a dab of glue (not completely authentic, but it will stay on better).

7. Wind always in the same clockwise pattern. When your new diamond is complete, return to the 1st dowel and knot and snip the yarn.

8. Affix a third color yarn or return to the first and proceed to make at least one more diamond. (You may make as many as you wish.)

9. Finish your *ojo* by winding the yarn around the 1st dowel until it is completely covered. Cut off any excess yarn. Wrap, knot or glue the end securely.

10. Repeat around the other three arms until they, too, are completely covered. Yarn tassels added to the ends of the dowels and a pom-pom on top add extra blessings.

HANDS

If you'd like to provide a protective amulet for yourself, grab a hand! Again, blue is the favored color—if you'd like to continue an ancient tradition, have children daub their hands in blue paint and then press them against your walls. The Hand of Power is one of the most ancient symbols of all, its use as a protective amulet going back to Paleolithic times. This image of the protective hand is worn literally all over Earth, from the Middle East and Native America to the Himalayas and all the way through Africa. Hands provide healing and offer blessings. The Moroccan saying "five in your eye" plunges the fingers defensively into the Evil Eye. An amulet may show a literal hand or five dots, lozenges or squares may also be used to transmit the message. Because five is the number of the fingers and insinuates the power of the hand, it is the number most featured in protective spells.

...

The following amulet originated in pre-Christian Scandinavia but remains popular today. The shape of the cross indicates that protection radiates out in all directions. Once you have the materials, it can be constructed in minutes.

Scandinavian House Protection Amulet

1. Form a cross with two birch twigs.

2. Bind them together with red thread and hang in your house.

3. For extra power and enhancement, attach crystals or roots, particularly angelica root, where the twigs meet.

PRIVATE PARTS

Along with human hands and eyes, genital imagery is believed to have protective qualities. These images are not necessarily considered erotic nor are they designed to titillate. Instead, they represent the power of the ancestors watching over us. Sometimes the image is reasonably literal and graphic: at one time, winged phalluses were a popular protective image. However, usually a symbolic geometry is utilized. The downward facing triangle represents the female genitalia. The upward facing triangle represents the male. When you overlap them together, well. (Those of a metaphysical or poetic bent like to say the overlapped triangles indicate the union of fire and water.)

The downward facing triangle is ubiquitous in African and West Asian amulets, representing that the protective quality of a woman's love is considered to be perhaps the most powerful force on Earth. Triangles provide a focus for protection deriving from generations of maternal concern, while their sharp sides slash at the Evil Eye.

• • •

According to Gullah tradition, basil leaves in the bath remove curses. For a simple and quick hex-removing bath, throw a handful of salt into the water with a splash of vinegar and a few fresh basil leaves. Basil-infused vinegar allows you access to this bath easily at any time. (Also good in salad dressings, but save some for the bath!)

Basil Vinegar

2 ½ cups white wine vinegar

6 tablespoons chopped fresh basil

5 garlic cloves, mashed

1. Boil the vinegar in a saucepan and pour it over the basil and garlic.

2. Cover and infuse for three days at room temperature.

3. Strain and pour the liquid into a sterilized bottle.

4. Add whole cloves of garlic and/or basil leaves for decoration and enhancement if you like. Add a splash to your bath, whenever you feel in need of a psychic shield.

Protéction Formula

4 drops essential oil of frankincense

4 drops essential oil of lavender

2 drops essential oil of rosemary

Blend the oils together and add to your bath water or mix with a cup of sweet almond oil for a protective massage.

• • •

Have you been hoodooed? You don't have to stay that way!

Curse Removal Bath

Angelica

Agrimony (breaks hexes! Also sends them back.)

Chamomile

Hydrangea flowers

Lovage

1. Use at least three of the above dried botanicals.

2. Take about a handful of each, place in a metal bowl and make a strong infusion (see page 16).

3. Strain and add to the bath or if you feel really in need of extra magic energy, add the plant material to your bath, too. Rub your body with the plants while in the tub. When the water has drained out and you're dressed, gather up the remaining plants from the tub and dispose of them outside, not inside your home.

Hexbreaker Bath

1 cup of coconut oil

Handful of salt

Lavender, lemon, patchouli, peppermint, lemon verbena

1. If the coconut oil has solidified, warm it gently over the stove until it liquefies, not allowing it to scorch or get too hot.

2. Add the salt and stir.

3. Now add the fragrances: you can use either finely powdered herbs
(a pinch) or essential oils (2 drops each) or a combination. You can
substitute a squeeze of lemon juice for the essential oil of lemon. Add
lemon zest, too, if you like.

- Most effective if timed to coincide with the full moon.

FEET

While images of the hands, eyes and genitals all avert the Evil Eye, feet
(real ones, not just images) are downright vulnerable. A human's psychic
Achilles heel is actually located a little lower on the soles of the feet. Feet
are not usually considered among the orifices, but feet, unless very cal-
lused, actually provide an excellent form of entry into the body for either
healing or malevolent forces. Absorption through the soles of the feet is a
favored method of administering poisons in the tropics; on the positive
side, footbaths are considered particularly fine venues of healing for aromatherapy or other herbal therapies.

> *Try this out for yourself: rub a cut clove of garlic against the soles of
> your feet and see how long it takes to taste the garlic in your mouth.
> Unless your feet are very callused, it shouldn't take too long.*

Poison doesn't have to be literal. The feet are considered vulnerable to
any malevolent energy circulating around, too, hence the saying "stepping
into the wrong territory." Protective rituals involving the feet actually provide all-around protection.

- First and foremost, **henna** painted upon the soles ornaments,
beautifies, disinfects, prevents athlete's foot and last, but not least,
seals in spiritual protection. If you lack the time or ability to create
a more elaborate design, emulate Bedouin women who simply
dip their entire sole into the henna paste, creating a solid block of
protection.

- Alternatively, if you fear you've been stepping into the wrong
territory, or have approached some unholy ground, you may find
the next ritual to be beneficial.

Foot Protéction Ritual

Dried mugwort

Dried peppermint

Dried rosemary

1 cup light vegetable oil, safflower or similar

½ cup of salt, plus 1 handful

¼ cup of hazelnut or walnut oil

4 drops essential oils of myrrh, vetiver or patchouli

1. Prepare a strong herbal infusion (see page 16) of equal parts mugwort, peppermint and rosemary.

2. Blend the salt and vegetable oil to create a salt scrub.

3. Fill a bucket with water as hot as you can stand for a footbath.

4. Add the infusion and a large handful of sea salt.

5. Moisten your feet slightly and apply the salt scrub to your feet, concentrating on the soles but going up as high as your ankles.

6. Soak your feet for 15 minutes in the bucket.

7. The ritual is sealed with a foot massage: warm a small amount, less than ¼ cup of walnut or hazelnut oil. (If you're on a budget, sunflower oil will work, too.)

8. Add 4 drops of myrrh, patchouli or vetiver to the oil. Massage into your feet, again beginning with the soles but moving up to the ankles.

9. This ritual is most effective performed right before bedtime. As soon as the ritual is done, get into bed (or better yet, perform the massage part in bed; your feet will be slippery) and try not to walk for several hours.

Devil's Shoestrings Ankle Bracelet

This lucky charm provides protection from the ground up. Devil's Shoe-strings are the colloquial name for the roots of plants belonging to the *Viburnum* family. They look like long strings. The name derives not from any inclination to evil, but because they're used to conceptually tie the devil's shoes together, tripping him up and preventing bad luck and malicious magic from following you. The trick is you need nine roots of equal length for this little amulet and they cannot be cut to size. Choose your roots carefully.

9 Devil's Shoestrings roots, equal lengths

Small piece of silver

1. Braid, weave or knot the roots together to form an ankle bracelet suitable in size for your ankle.

2. Attach the tiny piece of silver; this may be a bead or a lucky charm. You may also use a silver coin, but make sure it's genuine silver, not just silver colored.

3. Wear the anklet for good fortune and protection from harm.

• • •

Stereotypical images of Voodoo usually involve a little doll stuck with pins. Dolls are among the most common magical devices the world over and are used to provide romance, fertility or healing. Occasionally, though, dolls are used for malevolent enchantments, although that sort of destructive stick-pins-where-you-want-it-to-hurt magic actually derives from the British Isles and Northern Europe and usually utilizes a wax poppet. Dolls are not only used for inflicting damage, however, they can also be used to remove it.

Return to Sender Doll Ritual

2 pieces of red flannel

Stinging nettles

White paper and pen

Needle, thread, pins and scissors

1. Pin one piece of cloth directly on top of the other.

2. Draw a simple outline of a human body on the top piece as a pattern.

3. Cut the cloth to make two figures.

4. Sew the two pieces of flannel together, leaving a small opening at the head (or wherever you prefer). Don't add features or personalize it too much. You're not trying to hex anyone, just return something back from whence it came. Keep your little poppet nondescript. Save your creativity for elsewhere; there should be nothing that visually associates the doll with you.

5. Stuff the opening with the nettles (you may want to wear gloves; they really do sting) and sew up the hole.

6. Write "Return to Sender" on a small piece of white paper and pin it to the poppet.

7. Look the doll in the face and tell it what needs banishing.

8. Bring it to a garbage can at a distance from your home via a circuitous route and throw it away. Or leave it in the center of a four-way crossroads not too near your home.

(This spell is ideally performed in conjunction with a full moon.)

Personal Jinx Removal Ritual

Once released from mouth, words take on a life and power of their own. The child who is told that he will never amount to anything has been cursed as surely as if the most ancient metaphysical secret words had been used. "You're just like your father," "you'll never quit drinking," "no one will love you," the list of curses is endless.

Well, poisons have their antidotes and so do curses. If you feel that you, too, have been cursed in this fashion, whether it was this morning or long ago, here is a remedy:

1. Write the curse on a piece of paper exactly as you remember it, in detail, no matter how shameful.

2. When you're done, write CANCEL or VOID across it in big, bold letters. If it makes you feel better, scribble over all the old garbage.

3. When you feel ready, choose your element of destruction, whichever gives you the greatest sense of security and permanence: fire or water.

   - If you choose **water**: rip the paper into little bits and flush it down the toilet. Plain paper has a tendency to float up. Stand there and wait until you are sure that every last tiny scrap has disappeared down the drain, even if this means flushing repeatedly. Follow with steps to cleanse the toilet of negative energy plus some aura cleansing for you, too.

     Garlands of ginger flowers provide beauty, draw romance and give extra spiritual protection.

   - If you choose **fire**: burn the paper until not one letter can be identified. If the ashes are small enough, they can be washed down the drain; if not, scatter them in the wind. Do not bury in Earth.

• • •

Sometimes you scare yourself. The following bath is for when your own rage overwhelms you and you fear what you may do or say.

Overwhelming Anger Bath

Chamomile

Catnip

Lavender

4 drops cherry plum flower essence (Bach, Healing Herbs, Pegasus)

You may use either herbs or essential oils for this bath, whatever you have at hand or whichever you find more soothing.

- If you are using herbs, make a quick infusion using a fistful of each herb and add to a bath.

- Alternatively, especially if you're too overwhelmed to fuss in the kitchen, add 3 drops of each essential oil to your bath. An essential oil of catnip does exist; however, it's usually marketed under a more tasteful name: catmint, nepeta, mountain balm or even French marjoram. In any case, it can be difficult to find and shouldn't be used during pregnancy. If you don't have it, just leave it out, increasing the dosage of the other oils to 5 drops each.

- Place the cherry plum drops under your tongue or rub them into your forehead.

- If anger management is an issue for you, add the formula (cherry plum flower essence with either an herbal infusion or essential oils) to spring water, place it in a spray bottle and keep it on hand to cool yourself off.

PSYCHIC ENHANCEMENT SPELLS

There are powers and tools to provide every goal but there are also powers and tools to draw out and enhance your inherent psychic potential. The previous sections have examined in detail psychic-enhancing animal and spirit allies, crystals, metals and plants. Here are some potions, spells and rituals to further enhance your own personal power.

Psychic Stimulation Tea

1 tablespoon dried mugwort

1 teaspoon dried lemon balm

1 teaspoon dried peppermint leaves

1 teaspoon dried yarrow

¼ teaspoon coarsely ground cinnamon

Grind ingredients in mortar and pestle and place in a teapot. Pour boiling water over them and allow to brew for ten minutes. Strain and drink.

Psychic Enhancement Spice Necklace

Angelica root*

Cloves

Juniper berries

Nutmeg**

Star anise

sewing needles

---

*   Angelica root may also be found under its Chinese name, dong quai root.
**   A small power drill may be necessary to drill holes into nutmeg, although some claim that they are able to puncture the hard shell with a needle. If you're having trouble, just omit this one ingredient.

Approximately 36 inches of strong thread, dental floss or monofilament (fishline)

These spices enhance psychic ability, and the cloves and angelica also offer spiritual protection as you delve into the depths.

1. Soak the roots and spices overnight to soften them.

2. Cut the angelica root into the desired size.

3. Thread each end of the cord through one needle.

4. Add spices in the design of your choice, creating a symmetric pattern by using first one side of the thread, then the other. Arrange the smooth, round juniper berries so they will rest against your neck.

5. Focus on your goals and desires as you pierce and string the beads.

6. When each side measures 14 inches to the center, tie the ends of the thread, knot firmly and hang to air-dry.

7. Once dried, if cared for gently, your necklace will last for years.

- Wear this necklace during enchantments or divination.

- Store it together with your magical tools, Tarot cards or crystals to enhance and empower them and to harmonize your energy with theirs.

Spirit Ally

Dionysus, youngest of the Olympian Spirits, was forced to hide anonymously, vulnerable until he reached psychic and physical maturity. Only when, as the Greeks put it, he had "come into his power" could he openly take his place among the other gods, demonstrate his potency and fulfill his destiny. Dionysus recalls the frustration of being on the cusp of power and responds to pleas for assistance. His sacred attributes are grapes, wine, pines, leopards and donkeys.

Psychic Power Incense

To stimulate psychic perceptions and aptitude.

Celery seed

Powdered orrisroot

Keep the proportions equal. Use a pinch of both botanicals, if lighting on a small charcoal. Use 1 teaspoon each, if you have a larger censer.

Isis Oil

This oil, for bath or massage, imparts a little of Isis's psychic power and perceptions and petitions her for protection.

Tiny bloodstone crystal (even a chip!)

2 drops essential oil of ambrette seed

2 drops essential oil of jasmine

5 drops essential oil of myrrh

2 tablespoons sweet almond oil

A garland of mugwort worn around the waist stimulates psychic capacity.

Put the bloodstone inside a vial or container that can be shut tight. (The size of your container is dependant on the bloodstone: the tinier the better.) Add the essential oils to the almond oil and pour into your container. Close the container tight and roll it gently to distribute the oils. Use 1 drop at a time to anoint your third eye (on your lower forehead; centered just slightly above the bridge of your nose).

• • •

Water is the element most associated with psychic capacity and reception. Individuals born with water signs (Cancer, Scorpio, Pisces) prominent in their natal charts usually find that they have ready access to their psychic gifts. The following potion harnesses water power to increase your own. It's named for Marie Laveau, the first celebrity Voodoo practitioner. Born a free woman of color in New Orleans in 1792, she worked as a hairdresser, had fifteen children, none of whom succumbed to the dread Yellow Fever epidemics, and was renowned for her power and good deeds.

In German tradition, a piece of mistletoe carried into your new dwelling allows you to see any ghosts and communicate with them (i.e. find out why they're there and if they're friendly).

Marie Laveau Water

1 cup springwater

1 cup rainwater

1 cup rose water

1 cup holy water (check back at the entry for "water" in the Glossary to refresh your memory)

20 drops essential oil of lavender

Combine all the ingredients in an airtight bottle and shake vigorously. Add to your bath or use as inspired for psychic enhancement, aura cleansing and protection.

New Orleans Style Psychic Enhancement Bath

6 drops essential oil of rose geranium

6 drops essential oil of lavender

1. Draw a full bath of comfortably warm water.

2. Add the essential oils just prior to entering the water.

Moon Bath Salts

1 cup sea salts

½ cup baking soda

¼ cup powdered orrisroot

¼ cup dried vervain

5 drops essential oil of cypress

To enhance psychic receptivity and improve your intuition.

1. Combine the salt, baking soda and dried herbs.

2. Add to the bath as the water is running.

3. Add the cypress oil just as you enter the bath.

• • •

This next bath increases psychic inspiration while simultaneously cleansing the aura.

- Bay leaves, the crucial ingredient, are profound oracular substances. They are also the herb most connected with dolphin energy and this bath is particularly effective if you're trying to spiritually connect with that sea mammal.

- This bath has also been found to be particularly beneficial when you can't quite determine what gave you the creeps or when you can feel someone has directed malevolent energy toward you, but you can't quite figure out who.

Five Fingers Protection Bath

5 handfuls salt

5 dried or fresh bay leaves

5 lemons, cut in half

Splash of vinegar, lemon vinegar if possible

Glass of springwater

Glass of rose and/or holy water

1. Begin to draw a warm bath.

2. Add the salt and bay leaves to the bath first.

3. Squeeze each lemon half into the water, tossing the fruit in as well.

4. Add the other ingredients.

5. Enter the water. During the bath, submerge yourself completely five times, if possible. Stay in as long as you like. Rub your body with the lemons. If you need added inspiration, chew on the bay leaves a bit (but don't really eat them).

6. Stay in the tub while the water drains and let yourself air-dry alongside the leftover leaves and lemons.

Rosemary cleanses, protects but also reinvigorates psychic power. A cup of rosemary tea nourishes you following extensive magic or divination.

(Add some peppermint and lemon balm to improve the taste!) A rosemary bath patches up any worn spots in your aura.

• • •

Hardworking psychic practitioners sometimes experience a condition known as "psychic torpor." A little too much psychic work and not only is your physical energy depleted but you feel spacey, unbalanced and ungrounded. (And let's not forget the physical fatigue either! Psychic work is akin to athletics, although different muscles are used. As with any athletic activity, you will improve with practice, should always do warm-ups and may find yourself very hungry afterwards. There's a reason many psychics and witches battle weight problems. Concerned practitioners should stock up on celery sticks before starting their magic.)

Psychic Replenishing Bath

Basil

Lemon balm

Rosemary

You can use either dried or fresh herbs. Take a good fistful of each of the herbs and place in a bowl. Pour boiling water over them. Allow them to steep for 15 minutes. Strain and add the infusion to your bath water.

• • •

The following bath is beneficial for grounding if you've been doing lots of magic-questing and feel that oncoming psychic torpor. If you're drained but still find yourself stumped for a magical solution, add some whole bay leaves to the bath.

Don't Overwhelm Me Psychic Bath

4 drops essential oil of bay laurel*

2 drops essential oil of celery seed*

2 drops essential oil of Roman chamomile

4 drops essential oil of rosemary

Draw a full bath with a comfortable temperature. Enter the bath, sit down and add the essential oils, swirling them around in the water.

Magical Exercises

Allow Earth to replenish and recharge your psychic skills. The best way to add to your energy is to go outside:

- Stand on Earth barefoot, close your eyes and visualize her healing, powerful energy flowing into you through the soles of your feet. Standing barefoot in living water—a lake or the ocean—also charges your magical batteries.

- Be aware of the phases of the moon. Go outside or glance out your window every evening: is it full, a crescent, waxing, waning? Women: which moon period coincides with your menstrual period? Everyone: what moon period were you born under? As the moon returns to that point, watch your emotional and psychic reactions.

- If you are close to the ocean, pay attention to tidal rhythms, which reflect lunar influence on Earth. Observe any parallels to your own power.

As you attune your body to Earth's rhythms, your personal psychic energy will be liberated to surge and soar.

---

* Celery seed and bay laurel oils are contraindicated during pregnancy; omit and double the quantity of the chamomile oil. Even if you're not pregnant, bay oil is only safely used sporadically. If you find yourself taking this bath more than once a week, omit the bay and double the celery seed and chamomile.

SPIRIT SUMMONING

The Spirit Who Guards the Door Ellegba, or as he is sometimes affectionately known, **Papa Legba**, is the Yoruba guardian of doors, roads and paths. Papa Legba decides who will enter which door and who must remain outside. In some traditions, you must appeal to Papa Legba to open the spiritual gateway before any other spirits are able to enter. If your spirit communications are not proceeding as smoothly as you like, appeal to Papa Legba for assistance. You may also appeal to him to keep bad news from your door. His sacred day is Monday. Bring him gifts of fine rum, sweets or coins (always in odd numbers: for instance, you might give him five or seven pennies or candies but not six). He likes a good cigar now and then as well, particularly when he's done you a favor.

Animal Allies
Horse • Raven • Snake

A Magic Garden to Welcome Kind Spirits: Choose all or a selection of these plants to provide a psychic welcome mat to your home: **Amaranth, Angelica, Carnation, Dandelion, Dittany of Crete, Gardenia, Mugwort, Poppy, Rose, Saint John's Wort, Vervain, Wormwood**

A Fairy Flower Garden: Although most people are familiar with fairies from Celtic tales, fairies are familiar creatures all over Earth, from the Slavic countries to Southeast Asia to the deserts of Arabia. The following are some of their favorites. Grow as many as you can, reasonably near to each other, to create a fairy bower that will welcome the wee folk and make them feel at home—**Berry bushes, chamomile, Corsican mint, forget-me-nots, foxglove, hibiscus, hollyhocks, honeysuckle, lavender, lilac, milkweed, morning glories, pansies, peonies, primroses, rosemary, thyme, vincas, violets.**

According to Romany legend, wherever stinging nettles proliferate,
they're guarding entrances to Fairy Land's subterranean passageways.
Grow some and find out.

- Fairies like deep tangles of berries, herbs and flowers.

- Any place where ash, hawthorn and oak trees grow close together is reputedly guaranteed to house a fairy domain.

- A source of water is always attractive and helpful to them. A pond or small waterfall is best but a birdbath works, too.

- Statues, witch balls, lanterns and birdhouses provide interior decoration.

Crystals attract fairies and stimulate plant growth, too. Make circles of clear quartz or strategically arrange larger crystal clusters near favorite plants or sources of water. Burn some fairy incense as a welcoming signal: equal parts dried hollyhock and rosemary.

A piece of iron, even a small bead, wards off any malevolent entities you may inadvertently summon.

8pirit 8ummoning Oil

2 drops essential oil of lavender

2 drops essential oil of sandalwood

- Blend the oils together. Anoint yourself behind the ears or dab on your wrists as perfume.

- Place in an aroma diffuser and allow the smell to fill the room.

- Dilute in 1 tablespoon of grapeseed oil and use during massage or bath. (You can increase the quantity if needed, just be sure to maintain the proportions of essential oil to base oil.)

- Dilute the lavender oil alone within a spoonful of sandalwood paste (available where goods from India are sold) and rub into your hair or skin.

Incense is a traditional and powerful vehicle for summoning spirits.

Awaken the Spirits Incense

Dried carnation blossoms

Dittany of Crete

Gardenia petals

Dried mugwort

Frankincense resin

Pulverize equal parts of the substances. If the finished product is dry, leave it loose. If it's sticky and pasty, roll it into pea-size balls. Burn.

Divine spiritual entities are usually friendlier and more receptive to petitions than the spirits of dearly departed humans, with the exception of personal ancestors. You can call your immediate family any time, but it's generally considered more favorable to allow the spirits to approach first or at least to wait for times when they are likely to be receptive, especially the period beginning from the first Friday in October until November 2nd, the Day of the Dead. Waking up a spirit is a little like waking a very sound sleeper. Spirits have been known to be grouchy when disturbed. If you really need communication, keep a dish of honey on hand to soothe any bad moods.

Séance Incense

Frankincense resin

Sandalwood powder

A traditional fragrance favored by Spiritualists; mash the two components together in a mortar and pestle and burn.

Calling Up the Dead Incense

Traditionally, this incense is burned in the cemetery to request a visitation.

Dried amaranth flowers

Dittany of Crete

Wormwood

Burn equal parts of the dried herbs. Dittany of Crete may also be used alone: the image of the deceased is reputed to appear in the smoke just above the flame. Keep an eye out for it.

> *A circular bay leaf wreath attracts positive spirits and wards off malicious ones. Bunches of bay leaves hung up around the house are rumored to pacify poltergeists!*

Personal Oracle Bath Ritual

Once upon a time, people traveled to remote mountain and jungle shrines to request aid from gifted oracles and prophets. Perhaps you wish you could do this today; perhaps you have a dilemma that demands a psychic solution. Venture into your bathroom and discover the prophet within yourself. This ritual has two components: the first involves incense, the burning of herbs, while the second calls for a scented bath.

> Dried white sage*
>
> Dried yerba santa**
>
> Dried oracle sage***
>
> 1 tablespoon gardenia-infused water or oil
>
> 1 teaspoon pure vanilla extract

1. Grind equal parts of the dried herbs in a mortar and pestle or crumble them between your palms. (The quantity depends upon the size of your bathroom: you need just enough to get the room a little smoky; any more than that is unnecessary. Unless your bathroom is huge, no more than 1 teaspoon of each herb should be used.)

2. Burn them in a closed bathroom (closed doors and windows). Fill the room with smoke before taking your bath.

3. When the incense has almost burned down, run the bath and add the vanilla extract and gardenia infusion.

4. Ventilate the room prior to entering the bath.

5. Enter the water, relax, luxuriate, breathe deeply and focus upon what you need to know.

---

* White sage is a rare and endangered plant. It grows rapidly from seed, however, you may be able to supply your own needs. (Check the appendix for sources.) If not available, you may substitute garden or Mexican sage. No substitutes are possible for the other herbs, as their properties are unique.

** Yerba Santa provides spiritual protection and oracle sage, as its name suggests, is a divination tool. Some ethnobotanists believe that it is the legendary vision-inducing smoke used by the Aztecs. It is certainly used in that fashion by modern Mazatec Indians of Oaxaca.

*** In certain quantities and within certain rituals, oracle sage, locally known as Santa Maria for its associations with the protective mother, produces mild psychotropic effects. Burned respectfully as incense, it opens your mind to psychic inspiration.

DIVINATION SPELLS

Apollo is most renowned today as the classical Greek deity of music and the sun. A very complex spirit, with a temperament blending both violence and beauty, many of his other functions are often overlooked: He also served as Guardian of Grain, for instance, often in the guise of one of his animal allies, a mouse. Another of his allies, the crow, demonstrates that Apollo's other gifts to humans included therapeutic healing and psychic prophecy. Apollo came to Greece from the North bearing shamanic skills and oracles. Delphi, the most prominent oracle of its time, was originally an Earth oracle, guarded by a serpent of wisdom. Apollo slew the sacred guardian and violently settled himself in charge, where he consistently displayed his impeccably accurate prophetic ability.

According to ancient Chaldean wisdom, beautiful, pleasing fragrances consistently call in benevolent and generous spirits. Foul odors invite the presence of malevolent powers instead.

Apollo had various oracles, and this one, which prophesizes through grain, is easily reproduced in your kitchen.

Apollo's Balls of Fortune

1 cup flour

¼ cup water

1 egg

Paper

This quick spell is for when you need to make a decision, are beset by choices and you can't tell which to choose.

1. Write each alternative on a tiny slip of paper or color-code each one. Mix the flour and water to form a paste.

2. The egg serves as your binding agent, add a little bit at a time, you probably won't need the entire egg.

3. When the dough holds together, roll into small balls, one for each of your choices. They should look reasonably identical. Slip a piece of paper into each ball.

4. Put a little extra flour on some wax paper and roll the balls around, so that they're not so slippery and they get mixed up.

5. When you're ready, ask Apollo to direct your hand and pick your fortune.

   - In Apollo's ancient shrines, small baked balls containing answers and fortunes might be purchased. If you prefer, bake the balls until a toothpick inserted comes clean, allow them to cool and then choose your fortune.

   - But if you're really rushed and need to make a fast choice, balls of rolled aluminum foil may be substituted instead.

Daphnomancy

Among the prophetic materials used at the Oracle at Delphi were bay leaves, which were burned together with other botanicals to stimulate the residing prophetess's visions. A system of household divination involves bay alone. (And yes, *daphnomancy* is a real word simply meaning divination through bay leaves. The word honors Daphne, a nymph, who according to Greek myth, while fleeing from Apollo's advances was turned into the first bay laurel tree.)

> *Armadillo is the patron of those who delve extensively into psychic realms, providing defense, boundaries and bravery.*

Concentrate on a question while holding bay leaves in your hand. Either place a bay leaf onto a lit charcoal in an incense burner or seashell, or throw a few leaves into an open fire.

   - If the leaves crackle loudly and burn brightly, you've received a good sign, proceed. (Actual flames shooting up from the bay leaves are extra auspicious!)

- If the leaves sputter and refuse to burn or if the flame goes out, postpone your plans or change them.

Fortune-Telling Trees

Ash and elder tree branches are prized magic wand material, while having your own bay laurel tree keeps your stock of bay leaves always freshly at hand.

State of the Relationship Divination Oracle

Place two fresh bay leaves side by side on a burning charcoal.

- If they burn quickly to ashes, your relationship is harmonious and should be long-lasting.

- If they crackle while they burn, the relationship should last but may be studded with arguments.

- If they crackle fiercely and jump apart, look for another partner!

• • •

An English folk custom reveals your future lover.

ABC Love Oracle

Lavender blossoms

Pink rose petals

Violets

Cardboard

1. Make an infusion from the botanicals. Strain and reserve the water.

2. Write each letter of the alphabet on small individual squares of cardboard, each of equal size and thickness.

3. Place them facedown in a pan and pour the infusion over them (perhaps reserving some to bathe in or at least wash your face in; the fragrance should be very pretty). Let it stand overnight.

4. The following morning, see which letters have turned face up in the water to give you some clues as to your future beloved's name.

Ozark Love Oracle: The Sacrificial Mullein

Another romantic divination system comes from America's Ozark Mountains and was traditionally used by men wishing to clear up any doubts regarding their honey's fidelity.

1. First you need to locate a living mullein plant. This may be easier in the Ozarks than elsewhere but there is much to be said for some mullein in the backyard. Known as "witch's tapers" because once upon a time, they were dipped in wax or tallow, set alight and carried as torches, mullein is usually the primary ingredient in herbal eardrops and is also used to remedy some respiratory conditions.

2. Bend and point the mullein stalk in the direction of your love's home.

   • If his or her love is true, the mullein will grow upright again.

   • If this love is not meant to be, the mullein will die.

(Either way, give the mullein a few days to decide which way the wind is blowing.)

Avian Oracle

Birds are believed to serve as messengers between humans and the Spirit Realm. Let them help you out with perplexing decisions. All you need is some birdseed or some stale bread or cookies. This oracle is based on the ancient Roman tradition of augury (literally, divination through birds).

1. Scatter the birdseed or bread and watch the birds partake. Concentrate on your question.

2. If the birds fly off to your right, the answer is affirmative.

3. If they fly off to your left, the answer is negative.

4. If they scatter and fly in all directions, you do not have enough information to make your decision yet; it's more complex than it seems.

5. If the birds refuse to partake, take this matter seriously, your query may have more significance than it originally seems. Consider all the possible consequences and rethink your solutions.

LUCKY WISH SPELLS

Included here you will find spells for increasing general good fortune and good luck, as well as a few spells for the fulfillment of some specific desires:

- **The Spirit of Good Luck:** *Fortuna,* also known as Lady Luck, comes from Italy, where once upon a time, she was an extremely prominent deity possessing large temples and shrines. Fortuna provides blessings of good fortune for all and especially protection for women and children. (She held an ancient reputation for being especially responsive to pleas from women wishing to retain their husband's sexual interest!) Build Fortuna an altar containing her attributes: a wheel, a rudder and a cornucopia from which she will dispense bounteous good fortune.

- **Lucky Charm:** *Jade* attracts good friends and good fortune, promotes safety, material success, health and happiness.

> *Some animal allies are especially tied to the notion of good luck: Bat, Cat, Elephant, Horse, Rabbit are all considered especially fortuitous creatures. Concentrate upon them and perhaps their luck will rub off on you.*

Lucky Dream Pillow

For happy dreams, sound inspiration and good fortune.

Chopped bay laurel leaves

Chamomile blossoms

Lavender blossoms

Pine needles

Essential oil of patchouli

1. Pulverize equal proportions of the herbs.

2. Sprinkle with a few drops of patchouli, basing the quantity on how much you like the fragrance.

3. Mix and allow to dry before stuffing your pillow.

Lucky Spice Necklace

Allspice

Cloves

Ginseng root

Nutmeg*

Tonka beans

2 sewing needles

36 inches of strong thread, dental floss or monofilament (fishline)

This necklace attracts luck and good fortune. Tonka beans are related to vanilla beans; however they should not be eaten, as they contain substances that may not be beneficial for the human body. They have a lovely fragrance, attract love and money, bolster courage and self-confidence and are traditionally used to make wishes come true.

1. Soak the roots and spices overnight to soften them.

2. Once softened, you may cut the ginseng root to the size and shape you desire.

3. Thread each end of the cord through a needle.

4. Add spices and roots as you will, creating a symmetric pattern by using first one side of the thread, then the other.

5. Concentrate on your desire while you pierce and string the beads. Remain focused.

> Meditate on the Tarot image, *The Wheel of Fortune*, to start your own wheel turning in a positive direction!

6. Arrange the allspice berries so that they lie against your neck as they are round and smooth and shouldn't irritate your skin.

7. When each side measures 14 inches to the center, tie the ends of the thread, knot firmly and hang the necklace to air-dry. Once dried, your necklace should last for years.

---

* Once softened, the other ingredients may be pierced with a needle as you string them. Nutmeg's shell is so hard, it may require a small power drill. If this is a problem, just omit this ingredient.

Van Van Oil

This classic formula is used to turn bad luck into the best luck and open the road to success.

½ tablespoon castor oil

½ tablespoon jojoba oil

12 drops essential oil of lemongrass

1 drop essential oil of vetiver

Blend the castor and jojoba oils together first in a small glass bottle, then add the essential oils. Shake vigorously. Use Van Van oil to dress candles and charms. A single drop of Van Van oil recharges and energizes amulets. (This is a very concentrated oil: If you wish to use this formula in the bath or on your body, decrease the quantity of lemongrass by at least half or if you have sensitive skin, by even more.)

Uncrossing Oil

Are you beset with bad luck? Does nothing ever go right for you, seemingly without rhyme or reason? Perhaps psychic obstacles litter your path. This oil should remove them. The first four ingredients are crucial; the remainder are optional. You may include any of the optional ingredients or all of them.

1 tablespoon castor oil

1 teaspoon jojoba oil

Glass vial or small jar large enough to contain the items that you've included

6 to 10 drops essential oil of hyssop

A few grains of sea salt

Sprinkling fresh ground pepper

Tiny pinch cayenne pepper

Tiny pinch rue

Teeny sliver fresh garlic

Section of broken chain, as from a necklace

1. Blend the castor and jojoba oils together in the glass container.

2. Add the hyssop oil, salt and any other ingredients. If you're including the chain, the crucial quality is that it must be broken; the quantity is immaterial: you can add a few links or an entire broken necklace.

3. Shake vigorously. Saturate a cotton ball with the formula and carry it in your pocket or in a mojo bag, until your luck turns.

The Old Egg-in-the-Earth Spell

For when you are overwhelmed and weighed down with troubles and/ or frustrated desires, especially those that cannot be spoken aloud. This is among the most ancient and widespread of spells.

1 egg

A little privacy

Be careful what kind of energy you attach to your spell. Coloring containing toxins may deliver the wrong message. Just assume with good faith that Earth is really sick of humans burying toxic materials within her.

Take one uncooked egg and tell it your secrets. You can speak to the egg or you can speak into the egg, as if it were a tape recorder, whatever works for you. When you have emptied your heart, take the egg and bury it in Earth, who hears the dreams, desires and wishes of her children. Walk away, with the confidence that Earth, your mother who wishes you well, will receive your message. Watch patiently for signs.

That's it. That's the basic spell. You don't need to do anything else. However, various suggestions for embellishing and personalizing this spell exist, all basically for the purpose of intensifying delivery of your message, making it louder and clearer.

- Consider location: some try to bury the egg in an area of Earth possessing greater psychic receptivity; others prefer to bury the egg near the grave of a loved one, particularly a parent.

- Decorating, coloring or writing on the egg may enhance the spell. This must be accomplished without breaking the egg. It must be a whole, raw egg, not a shell with the insides blown out. Try making a paste from henna or turmeric or using lemon juice to create invisible ink. Gently use a toothpick as a writing implement. Some women color their egg with menstrual blood so that Earth won't confuse their message with anyone else's. You can't get more personal than that. Milk from your own breasts, if you have it, is a powerful substance as well.

Write your wishes on bay leaves and burn them. The medium assists your petition to reach the spirit realm quickly and clearly.

Honey in the Jar

Do you need someone to be responsive toward you? Do you need to soften someone's heart? Is someone not returning your calls?

A small white piece of paper

Small jar with a lid

Honey

Small white candle

1. Write the person's name on a small white piece of paper.

2. Now write your own name five times over the other person's name, obliterating it.

3. Drop the piece of paper into a jar about one quarter filled with honey and put the lid on the jar.

4. Light a small, white candle on top of the lid of the jar, a tea light is ideal and concentrate on your wish.

• • •

The opposite problem may exist. Is someone thinking of you a little too much—and not in the ways you'd like? Is someone fixated on you with anger or resentment? Let's put their anger in the freezer.

Chill Out 8pell

Write the angry person's name on a piece of paper. Drop the name into a small, unbreakable container half filled with water and place it in your freezer. New York photographer, Aris Dervis, recommends a film canister, which has the additional advantage of being able to be sealed shut, but any small container that won't shatter when frozen will do. In theory, if you have a lot of enemies, you could line them up in an ice cube tray. Leave in the freezer until you feel the coast is clear, then thaw slowly.

Tarot Card Growth Ritual

This spell requires fourteen consecutive nights and is used to draw toward you whatever you need. Begin at the new moon.

Tarot cards are used to predict the future but they can also be used to provide for you in the present. Modern Tarot cards are the amalgamation of two distinct decks: the major and minor arcana. Many use the major cards alone for meditation and visualization. They are usually considered to be more powerful than the minor, hence their name, however, this next spell harnesses the power of the minor cards instead.

Use any deck you already have or buy one that appeals to you. (Regular playing cards will leave you short one card, the knight.) The classic Rider-Waite deck works well because all the cards are illustrated, unlike some decks which only provide illustrations for the court cards. The Rider-Waite images, painted by artist Pamela Colman-Smith, are especially evocative, however not all the images on the cards are pleasant. If you find that certain images distract you from your goals, then choose another deck.

You will need fourteen small candles (votive size, perhaps) to go with the fourteen suit cards, one candle per card. All candles should be of an identical type and color. Color-coordinate the candles to match your desire.

Remember, you can always use white candles.

- Use cups for love or peace in the family: yellow, red or pink candles

- Use coins for money and prosperity: green, brown or yellow candles

- Use wands for new employment: green, red or brown candles

- Use swords for creative inspiration: black, blue, red or white candles

1. Light the first candle.

2. Lay down the ace of the appropriate suit so that it's directly in front of the candle and facing you. Each of the Rider-Waite aces depicts a celestial hand offering its gift: cup, coin, sword or flowering wand. Visualize yourself accepting that gift. Stay with the candle until it burns out.

3. On the second night, light another candle and lay down the second card in the suit. Meditate upon the implications of the image until the candle burns out. (If your deck provides no images for the numbered cards, visualize yourself attaining your goal instead.)

4. Repeat this with successive cards each night. The ten of each suit represents that the culmination of your goal is within reach. (The Rider-Waite ten of swords depicts a man prostrate and pierced with swords:

it indicates resurrection, not death, success despite all odds. If you examine the image closely, you'll observe the sun rising on a new day, while the man presumed dead, signals with his hand that he still lives. The card promises improved fortune and new beginnings.)

5. Following the ten, continue with the court cards: page, knight, queen and king, in this order. They represent the power of ancestors, spirits and Earth herself. Each offers you a gift of joy and prosperity. Visualize yourself accepting their gifts.

• • •

Do you feel unappreciated, disrespected, taken for granted, perhaps? Dried calendula blossoms in your bath attract respect from others and stimulates the self-confidence needed for success.

The "I Deserve Respect" Bath

1 cup dried calendula blossoms

Throw the dried blossoms into a warm bath, watching as the water attains a pretty yellow hue. Soak in the tub and rub your body with the dried blossoms.

Stay Put Spell

Is your home being sold out from under you? Do you really not want to leave your rental? This spell grounds you solidly in your property, making any attempt to remove you very difficult.

One caveat: if your desire is to stay put just long enough to find another dwelling, don't use this spell. It tends to bind you so completely to your present home that, while its power is in effect, even your own attempts to leave are met with failure.

1 charcoal

1 rock, preferably from your home property

Benzoin*

1. Grate a small quantity of your charcoal into a mortar and pestle.

2. Grate a bit of the rock into the mortar and pestle, as well. A regular metal food grater may be used.

3. Pound them together.

4. Add a bit of benzoin. (Benzoin is a very solid, sticky resin. It may be difficult getting it out of the bottle. In theory, you can liquefy it a little: place the bottle gently in some warm water for a few moments. In reality, even liquid benzoin has a tendency to harden as soon as it makes contact with air. I've found my best success by pulling bits of benzoin out using a turkey truss.) Mash together with the rock and charcoal dust. It should form tiny balls.

5. Scatter across all doorways or entrances to your home.

6. Repeat whenever you feel the threat reemerge, using the same charcoal and the same rock.

When the charcoal is gone, you may substitute another, but once the rock is all ground up, if the threat remains, it's time to find another solution.

• • •

The feet and the footprint are believed to reverberate with one's personal power. Reflecting this, a Hoodoo tradition evolved, known as "Foot Track Magic," involving magic spells using dirt from footprints. While some are fairly malevolent spells, this one is intended to help you broaden your social circle, find friendship, romance and better business.

---

* Although benzoin is a resin, you'll find it classified and sold with essential oils.

Best Foot First

Dirt from your own footprint

Crumbled, dried patchouli leaves

Ground cinnamon

1. Step in bare dirt on a warm, dry day and make a deep footprint. (If the weather isn't cooperative, wet the ground until it's slightly muddy, step in it barefoot until you've formed a footprint and wait for it to dry so that you can collect the dirt.)

2. Gather the dirt from that footprint. You may use a plastic bag, although an earthenware container is better.

3. The quantity of patchouli leaves depends upon the quantity of gathered dirt; there should be no less than one quarter the amount of patchouli and as much as equal parts.

4. Grind the patchouli and dirt together and add a sprinkling of cinnamon.

5. Go to where the walkway up to your house naturally begins and sprinkle the powder up to your front door to draw lucky, happy people toward you.

• • •

North African wisdom suggests that if people have been quarreling, oil poured over the spot where the quarrel took place will dissipate a tense, malevolent atmosphere. This next spell uses essential oil together with hair, seeds and flower buds to create a charm that encourages domestic peace.

Peaceful Home Charm Bag

Single strand of hair from each family member

Blue thread

Piece of angelica root

Essential oil of German chamomile

Balm of Gilead buds

Flax seeds

Lavender blossoms

Pink rosebuds

1. Make a braid with the hairs and thread.

2. Use the braid to tie a bow around the angelica root.

3. Anoint the hair and root with a few drop of chamomile oil.

4. The root, together with the other ingredients, is now placed in either a sachet or charm bag. If making a sachet, use muslin with blue thread; tie a muslin bag with a blue satin ribbon.

5. For the purpose of a good luck charm, either form is acceptable; however if there is *a lot* of domestic turbulence, make a charm bag so that you can easily add more chamomile for reinforcement.

Happy Trails Travel Charm

This charm is reputed to keep its owner from getting lost, whether on the road or during spiritual journeys.

Red flannel cloth

Earth

Coal powder

Small piece of silver: bead, charm or antique coin

1. Roll and stitch together a piece of red flannel cloth until its shape approximates a finger.

2. Stuff it with earth, coal powder and a small piece of silver.

3. Sew it together and carry it on your person.

BEAUTY SPELLS

Animal Allies: Butterfly, Peacock, Snake. Place an image of these creatures near your mirror or wherever you most usually make up your face. Allow them to encourage you to draw out and appreciate your own inherent beauty.

Spirit Allies

Freya *(Nordic)*, Oshun *(Yoruba)*, Persephone *(Greek)*: *if you ask nicely these beautiful deities will share their prized beauty secrets with you.*

Freya's Enchanting Facial

STEP 1: FACE MASK

1 tablespoon honey

Moisten your face with warm water, then apply the honey evenly to cover your face. Allow to remain on for a ½ hour (or as long as is comfortable). Remove by rinsing first with warm water, then with cold.

STEP 2: SKIN TONER

> 1 cup springwater
>
> 1 teaspoon dried cowslip blossoms*
>
> 1 teaspoon dried catnip leaves*

Cowslips are wild primroses and Freya's favorite flowers. Sharing her essence, they're reputed to bring you a clear, beautiful complexion.

1. Boil the water and pour over the herbs. Allow them to infuse for 10 to 15 minutes.

2. Strain and allow to cool.

3. Apply to your face with a cotton ball.

4. Use any remainder on your neck, body or in your bath.

- You can also refrigerate the remainder for 24 hours.

- To complete your day of beauty, prepare infused oil of primroses using the petals and sunflower oil. Full body massage with this oil is reputed to enhance and attract romance and increase both inner and outer beauty.

Persephone's Box of Beauty

Whenever the beautiful Greek goddesses feared that their beauty needed revitalizing, who did they turn to? Persephone, the compassionate Queen of the Underworld and Princess of Springtime, kept a box filled with beauty, which she would lend as needed. Ever generous, she'll help you fulfill your potential and dreams, too.

---

* You may also use fresh leaves and blossoms; both plants are easy to grow. Just increase the quantity to $1^1/_2$ teaspoons each.

A pretty box

Dried flower petals

Dried orrisroot

Dried parsley

Dried poppy seeds

Pleasing photograph or drawing of yourself

Small, shiny crystals, gemstones and metals

1. Line the box with the dried botanical material. A magic box is an ongoing project; it does not have to be completed at one sitting. Search out the prettiest potpourri flowers you can find.

2. Add pretty treasures from the Earth.

3. Add an image of yourself that pleases you, an image of yourself at your best. If you don't have one yet, start the box anyway and experiment with new photos, sketches or drawings.

4. Continue to build your box of beauty. Let Persephone inspire and encourage you.

- This spellbox assists you to transform yourself from caterpillar to butterfly. When you're feeling a bit devitalized, just take it out and play with your treasures to receive their empowering magic.

- Store hair ornaments and jewelry in your box to empower and enhance them.

• • •

Turmeric is a rhizome, a member of the ginger family and is most typically sold in the supermarket as a ground yellow powder favored in curries. Check in the supermarket's spice aisle. It's a favored spiritual purification agent in areas as widely apart as India and Hawaii. In both places, interestingly, the rhizome is also associated with their leading spiritual ladies of beauty: Lakshmi (India) and Laka (Hawaii). In addition to purifying your aura, this face mask also tones and purifies your skin. In India, it's used as a quick temporary do-it-yourself face-lift.

Golden Glow Face Mask

1 tablespoon of turmeric powder

½ cup of full-fat yogurt

Blend the turmeric into the yogurt, mixing thoroughly. Apply to your face. Leave on for at least 10 minutes or up to half an hour. It will impart a golden glow to your skin, which in India is considered very beautiful and auspicious. If you don't like the effect, do it before bedtime as it usually wears off by morning. (The golden glow will fade from your skin, however, turmeric is a potent and *permanent dye*. Watch out for carpets and clothing!)

• • •

Rosemary reinvigorates more than psychic capacity. At age seventy-two, Queen Isabel of Hungary was crippled by gout and rheumatism. Her master herbalist concocted a reviving water for her, originally only with the intent of relieving her physical pain. The water was administered in daily vigorous massage. Not only was she soon moving, *dancing* as I believe the legend goes, her former beauty and youthful aura were also revived. Hungary Water has been popular ever since. The original 14th century formula called for one-and-one-half pounds of fresh flowering rosemary tops added to one gallon of alcohol and distilled. Should you happen to have distilling equipment, you can experiment with that, but modern versions also proliferate. Here's one:

Hungary Water

1 ounce infused water of dried rosemary and vervain

4 drops essential oil of rosemary

4 drops essential oil of May Chang

2 drops essential oil of German or Hungarian chamomile

2 drops essential oil of peppermint

1 drop essential oil of neroli

8 ounces vodka or other scent-free alcohol

1 ounce orange blossom water

1 ounce rose water

1. Make the herbal infused water by placing equal proportions of dried vervain and rosemary in a metal bowl and pouring boiling water over them. Steep for 15 minutes and strain out the botanical material.

2. Blend the essential oils and add them to the vodka in an airtight bottle.

3. Next add the infused flower waters. Shake vigorously.

4. Ideally, this beauty potion should now be allowed to mature for six months (giving the bottle a good shake every week) to gain full strength, however as it's pretty hard to wait that long, give it as long as you can.

• • •

Although it lacks a historical tale to equal Hungary Water, the following bath formula can be prepared quickly and simply, perfect for when you just want to feel (and maybe appear!) a little younger. Rosemary and patchouli are both plants of profound psychic power: Both are reputed to ease the physical signs of aging as well as helping to maintain a youthful heart.

Both have powerful aromas. Adjust the formula to please your nose. You can also use this formula for bath salts, a salt scrub or body oil.

Quick Fix Youthfulness Bath Formula

5 drops essential oil of patchouli

5 drops essential oil of rosemary

Add essential oils to a full tub of warm water just prior to entering the bath.

• • •

This next bath works on two levels simultaneously. Not only do the herbs have a genuine therapeutic effect upon your skin, they also heal your self-perception. Not only is your physical appearance enhanced, more importantly, the herbs help you *feel* attractive.

Self-Confidence Ritual Bath

Calendula blossoms

Red raspberry leaves

Yellow and pink candles

A pretty teacup or mug

1. Use equal parts of the herbs. You should have a substantial quantity: at least 1 cup of each.

2. Combine the herbs in a bowl and create an infusion by pouring boiling water over them. Allow to steep for fifteen minutes.

3. Strain, reserving enough for a cup of tea. Add the remainder to a tub of warm water.

4. If your skin is dry, you may make infused oils instead, but make them separately, one infused oil of calendula and another of raspberry leaves. Add 1 tablespoon of each to the bath.

5. Float a few calendula blossoms in the water. Light the candles. Enter the tub and sip your tea. (May be sweetened with honey.)

Fumigation: Personal Incense

In ancient days, incense was burned nearby while clothes and hair were drying, to impregnate them with fragrance. This provocative incense ensures that your presence will linger, even when you are not physically present.

1. Play with botanical substances that appeal to you until you find a combination that expresses your essence. (You can always modify this; as you evolve, so will your personal incense.) You may use powdered herbs, resins and/or essential oils. Keep a written record of substances and quantities as you experiment so that you'll be able to reproduce it.

2. Pulverize dry ingredients in a mortar and pestle. Pour them into an airtight container.

3. Add oils, if you have them, stirring until a thick paste forms. This will be burned; don't allow it to get too liquid. (If it does, add more of the powdered material.)

4. If you wear a scent or perfume regularly, sprinkle a little on top.

5. Stir and shut the container tight. The mixture should be allowed to mature for at least two weeks. Sprinkle with a few extra drops of your everyday scent as needed.

- Burn personal incense to fumigate your clothes and hair.

- Sprinkle a little on a heated dry cast-iron skillet and walk the fragrant smoke through your home to leave your presence, especially when you are away!

> *Burn cloves and fumigate your body and clothes with the fragrance to halt and prevent malicious gossip about you.*

Sun Oil

An oil that brings you only the benefits of the shining sun so that you'll feel invigorated, relaxed, powerful and sexy, ready to be the center of attention.

4 drops essential oil of frankincense

4 drops essential oil of myrrh

1 drop essential oil of Roman chamomile

1 drop essential oil of cardamom

Add to a full bathtub just prior to entering. For extra enhancement, color the water with a saffron infusion, as strong as your pocketbook allows.

- This formula can also be added to body oil or bath salts.

The Milky Way Weight Loss Spell

1 carton milk

Weight loss programs are best scheduled to coincide with the waning moon. A magical weight loss program is initiated on the night of the full moon. Stand in your tub or shower and pour the milk over your head. Before you rinse off, envision yourself getting thinner in harmony with the moon. (May I suggest that you allow the milk to achieve room temperature first. A very cold splash of milk may drive even the best intentions right out of your mind!)

The flower world can assist you in your attempts at self-transformation. The aroma of essential oil of patchouli has been used to control an excessive appetite. Likewise, other oils will stimulate your appetite, whether for cosmetic purposes, to counteract an eating disorder,

depression or following an illness. These include essential oils of anise,
bergamot, black pepper, fennel and ginger.

In order for this to be effective, this spell must be accompanied by a sincere effort to lose weight, whether through exercise, diet modification or both. If you find yourself side-tracked or need reinforcement, don't be angry with yourself. Schedule another milk bath starting date for the next full moon, which will arrive shortly.

Hair represents more than virility and seduction; it is also tradition-ally considered a barometer of a person's personal power. Many cultures believe in physical indications of psychic potential. These range from the infant born with a caul or tooth, to albinos and children whose speech is delayed for no apparent cause. Power is often believed to announce itself through hair that is somehow distinctive, whether because of volume, beauty or just general unruliness and defiance. By caring for one's hair, you may be transitively enhancing and stimulating your personal power. Pre-venting hair loss has always been a popular concern. Anglo-Saxon men rubbed their heads with onions to stimulate hair growth. Rosemary oil is reputed to perform the same service.

Hair Growth Potion

1 ounce castor oil

1 ounce jojoba oil

30 drops essential oil of rosemary

Mix ingredients in an airtight bottle. Shake vigorously. Apply a little to your fingertips and massage into your scalp nightly. Start this regime to coincide with a new moon.

LOVE MAGIC

Animal Allies: Cat, Dove, Horse, Hummingbird, Rabbit

Spirits of Love: Aphrodite, Freya, Oshun. Lonely widows looking to start again may find Persephone, Greece's Queen of the Next Life, to be sympathetic and helpful.

In general, the new moon is considered to be the most favorable time for a new romance spell. The waxing moon will help you gain and preserve love. The waning moon helps in the removal of a now unwanted lover who is dragging his feet.

Love magic includes spells to find love, preserve love, improve love and get one's love back when he or she has strayed.

Aphrodite's Bower of Love

Apple, Linden, Myrtle or Pomegranate Trees, Roses, Scented Geraniums, Marjoram and Poppies

Aphrodite is Queen of Wild Nature. Decorate the garden with seashells and images from the sea. It would not be inappropriate to place a hot tub in the midst. Place images of her favorite creatures in the garden, too: doves, swans, rabbits, dolphins, deer, turtles, goats and wolves. If bees frequent your garden, you'll know Aphrodite sends her personal blessings to you. She likes company: put a bench or gazebo in your garden and enjoy.

The numbers two, five and six give extra power. Two because it symbolizes the ideal of the perfect union. Five because it's the number associated with Oshun and six because it belongs to Aphrodite. Fridays are especially beneficial for romantic spells because they belong to Freya.

MORE PLANTS FOR A ROMANTIC GARDEN

Basil, Carrots, Catnip, Chamomile, Chile Peppers, Coriander, Crocus, Gardenia, Hibiscus, Hyacinth, Iris, Jasmine, Lady's Mantle, Lavender, Lettuce, Mint, Onion, Orchid, Poppy, Rose, Rosemary, Saint John's Wort, Strawberry, Thyme, Vervain

---

Plants do more in the bedroom than facilitate sleep. Sprinkle vinca, also known as "the sorcerer's violet," around the bed to stir up passion. Powdered orrisroot sprinkled onto the sheets serves as a more direct aphrodisiac. Pulverized or powdered rosemary sprinkled under the bed and around the room keeps a couple happy and satisfied. Boughs of yarrow are hung over the bed to enhance and encourage sensual pleasures. Away for the night? A little concerned? Hawthorn leaves under your lover's pillow or more discreetly, crumbled and sprinkled around the bed helps keep the object of your affections faithful until you return.

TREES OF LOVE

Apricot, Avocado, Cherry, Myrtle, Orange

• • •

Forget your own dreams; you want to make sure someone special is dreaming of you? Give them a gift of a nice handmade dream pillow:

Lover Dream of Me Pillow

Allspice

Powdered orrisroot

Honeysuckle blossoms

Red rose petals

A lock of your hair

Essential oil of pine

Whoever lays their head upon this pillow should have sweet dreams of you.

1. Grind the allspice and the orrisroot together but leave the flower petals whole.

2. Place the botanicals in a bowl with a lock of your hair. (An old-fashioned formula would now recommend adding a drop of menstrual blood for extra power. An optional ingredient, should you choose.)

3. Sprinkle with a few drops of pine oil.

4. When dry, stuff the pillow and sew it shut.

Love-Drawing Spice Necklace

Vanilla beans

Fragrant dark Caribbean rum

Allspice berries

Whole cardamom pod

Cinnamon sticks

Cloves

Ginseng root

2 sewing needles

36 inches of strong thread, monofilament (fishline) or dental floss

This necklace draws love to you and smells so fragrant you'll feel like a goddess of love yourself!

1. Soak the vanilla bean(s) in the rum for a few days. Remove the bean, scrape it with a pin, cut it into the shape and size you desire, pierce with a thick needle for stringing and allow it to dry in the sun. (This method derives from Martinique, a place where knowledge of rum, vanilla, magic and cuisine abound, and is reputed to be the best way to enhance vanilla's fragrance!)

2. Soak the remaining ingredients overnight. The cardamom pod, if white, should be soaked alone to preserve its color. The remaining brown ingredients may be soaked together.

3. Once softened, you may cut and trim the roots to suit your design. You may also recurl the cinnamon as it may have lost its shape.

4. Thread each end of the cord through a needle. Add spices as you will, creating a symmetric pattern by using first one side of the thread, then the other. Arrange the smooth round allspice berries so that they will lie against the back of your neck, to minimize any skin irritation.

5. Remain focused upon your goals and desires as you pierce and string each spice bead.

Love Stones

Emerald, Ruby, Lodestone and Moonstone. Rose quartz *heals heartache and/or abuse and prepares you to accept new love. When you feel ready, a heart-shaped* garnet *attracts new romance.*

---

6. When each side measures 14 inches to the center, tie the ends of the thread, knot firmly and hang the necklace to air-dry.

7. Once dried, your necklace should last for years. Wear this necklace during romantic rituals or just to invoke a romantic mood.

• • •

You've found someone. Now you'd like to win their heart.

Be Mine Bath Ritual

Photograph or drawing of your beloved

½ cup calendula blossoms

1 cup pink roses

2 drops essential oil of Roman chamomile

2 drops rose attar

1. The photograph should ideally be a happy photograph of the two of you. No one else should be in the photograph; crop if necessary. (Under no condition, however, should you cut yourself out of the photo, even if you need to remove anyone else!) If you don't have a single photo or if you've had to cut one up, tape your images together side by side, even touching if possible. You may also draw a happy picture of the two of you. Your artistic ability is unimportant; what is important is that your drawing expresses your desire for unity and joy.

2. Fill the tub with comfortably warm water.

3. Tape the image to the wall across from where your head will be once you're in the water.

4. Light your love candles.

5. Add the botanicals and essential oils to the water.

6. Enter the tub, gaze at the image and repeat affirmations regarding your future happiness together.

• • •

Although typically depicted as a wizened crone, Hecate also has a history of successful seduction. Honey and lavender are the substances she recommends.

Hecate Bath

Milk

Honey

6 drops essential oil of lavender

Quantities for the milk and honey are based upon your personal preferences, but do not exceed 6 drops of lavender oil in the bath. Gently warm the milk on the stove. You can use as little as a cup or luxuriate in a quart or more. As it begins to warm, add the honey, stirring constantly. Do not allow the milk to boil; you only want to warm it up. As soon as the honey is absorbed, remove the pot from the stove. Fill your tub with warm/hot water and add the honey/milk mixture. White clouds should form on the surface. Add the lavender oil just before you enter the bath.

• • •

Be careful with love spells. You can't evoke true, healthy love from another unless you know (not believe, *know!*) you are deserving and worthy. The best love spells bolster your self-esteem, make you love and respect yourself, while all the while beckoning another.

This next bath ritual is one of the more time-consuming to prepare but that's an essential part of the ritual: You are affirming that you deserve the effort.

This bath is particularly beneficial for those who have loved and lost and also those who feel battered and humiliated, emotionally, physically or sexually.

It is also excellent for those occasions when you need to be transformed into a goddess or prior to performing any other romantic spells.

The Hibiscus "I Love Myself" Bath

Dried red hibiscus flowers*

Dried raspberry leaves

Dried red rose petals

Dried rose hips

---

*   This spell has a lot of ingredients; the hibiscus flowers are the most crucial component and cannot be left out. (No, you don't have to live in the tropics to gather them; dried hibiscus is available from most herbal vendors. Red hibiscus teabags are also popular; create an infusion from as many teabags as you need to achieve the desired color.) Otherwise, don't let the lack of any single item prevent you from accessing this magic. Substitute, omit, improvise as your intuition tells you!

Rose quartz and sea shells

5 candles: blue, brown, pink, white, yellow

Handful of sea salt

1 teaspoon pure almond extract

Assorted whole white blossoms: jasmine or rose

Red hibiscus flower essence (Green Hope)

1 drop essential oil of peppermint

4 drops either sweet orange, neroli or petitgrain essential oil

1. Make *two* separate infusions: one from the hibiscus alone, the other from the combined raspberry leaves, rose petals and rose hips. Quantities are dependent upon the color you wish to achieve. Red hibiscus will tint your water to match. The more flowers and the stronger the infusion, the deeper and brighter the color. You can tint your water anywhere from pale pink to deep crimson, whatever appeals to you. Just be aware that the infusion is further diluted once it's added to the tub, so the initial color must be deeper than what you ultimately desire.

2. The second infusion should contain about one quarter as much water and material as the hibiscus infusion. Use equal parts of the three herbs.

3. When the infusions are complete, strain and mix them together, taking the opportunity to adjust the color as needed.

4. Draw a bath of comfortably warm water. Place rose quartz and sea shells around your tub.

5. The spell calls for five candles in honor of Oshun, who heals and opens the heart chakra. Each color relates to and heals a different aspect. (Coconut-scented candles are extra beneficial, if possible.) Arrange them around the room. Light the candles, turning off other lights at some point before entering the tub.

6 Add the infused waters, along with the handful of salt and the almond extract. Swirl to distribute.

7. Float the white flowers on top of the bath and enter, adding the essential oils and flower essence once you're seated in the bath.

8. Breathe the beautiful aroma deeply and envision yourself as a beautiful water spirit in your enchanted grotto. Luxuriate as long as you like. There is little to say, although you may make affirmations if you like. Your actions are your affirmations in this ritual. This bath can be your private ritual or, if you're ready, shared with another.

Grow-a-Lover Spell

Plant an onion bulb in a flowerpot. Nurture it lovingly and it will help draw a lover toward you. (This spell only draws male lovers.) Traditional advice states that the onion be watered with your tears. I'm sure that works but who wants to spend that much time crying? If regular water doesn't seem quite strong enough, consider feeding some romantic infusions for a little extra stimulation. Bury a rose quartz or place it right beside the onion for extra oomph.

> *Another way to make your lover dream of you is to place one drop of romantic fragrance oil, ideally one you sometimes wear yourself, on a dried wormwood root and place under his pillow. And if you want to receive the dreams instead? Daisy roots placed under your pillow brings dreams of an absent lover.*

• • •

If you're lonely and in need of new romance.

New Romance Brew: A Potion for One

Balm of Gilead buds

Red wine

Steep the botanicals in the red wine on a new moon Friday evening. Toast the new moon with either a request for new love to enter your life or an affirmation stating that you are lovable and deserve a happy new romance. Drink your potion!

Love Potion #2: A Potion for Two

A love potion to enhance, stimulate and preserve true love.

Bottle of red wine

1 tablespoon of whole cardamom pods

Fistful of cloves

6 cinnamon sticks

Red hibiscus flower essence (Green Hope)

1. Choose the wine to suit your taste; the key is it must be red.

2. Pour the wine into a pot, add the spices and warm gently.

3. Allow to simmer gently for an hour, then strain.

4. Pour the wine into glasses and add one drop of flower essence per glass. Enjoy with your intended!

• • •

Oh, that matchmaking spirit! Do you know two people who would be perfect for each other or perhaps you know just the right person for you?

Apple Attachment Spell

1. Cut an apple in half horizontally to reveal the star hidden within.

2. Spread each half with honey.

3. Take a lock of hair from each person's head, braid them together and place on top of an apple half. Bring the two halves together and bind with a red ribbon, making several strong knots on top.

4. Bury the apples in Earth, preferably in a romantic spot, maybe near some romance-inducing plants or trees.

5. If it suits you, make an invocation to Aphrodite, Spirit of Love, who holds apples sacred.

Henna Love Spell

This henna spell is for lovers temporarily separated by distance. It's a very simple spell, perfect for farewells at an airport. Before separating, the woman pushes a small ball of henna paste into the center of the man's palm. He should allow it to remain for several hours before scraping it off. The resulting mark is subtle, indistinct and will not draw undue attention from others. Yet it carries spiritual protection as well as a reminder of the love that awaits him. Every time he glances at his hand, he will be reminded of the woman and her love. (Did I mention that henna is also reputed to ensure a man's fidelity?)

• • •

You've found love, but now you'd like to make sure that there's no straying from the path of true romance? This English bath potion is reputed to make you irresistible. Use as needed or just for a little extra reinforcement, to mark the new moon.

Your Eyes Only for Me Bath

Handful fresh rosemary

Handful fresh thyme

1 tablespoon powdered orrisroot

1 tablespoon powdered lovage root

1. Make a strong infusion from the rosemary and thyme.

2. After the infusion cools a bit, add the powdered roots.

3. Let the brew steep for awhile, stirring periodically.

4. Just before you are ready to bathe, strain and add the liquid to the water.

Lover Come to Me Candle Ritual

small pink or yellow candle

Romantic oil: either "Come to Me Lover" (formula follows on page 221) or any fragrance that evokes love. (Make sure you like the fragrance; you'll have to wear it!)

1. Carve a heart into the candle, preferably with a rose thorn. Inside the heart, place your own initials followed by a plus sign and then underneath a question mark.

2. Anoint the candle with the oil.

3. Light the candle in your window where it is visible to the outside, under a brand-new moon.

4. Verbally express your desire for love or invoke romantic spirits to assist you. Keep the invocation short and simple because you'll need to remember it, something like:

> *"No more loneliness for me,*
> *Mystery lover, come to me."*

5. Let the candle burn out naturally.

6. Keep a supply of the oil to use as a perfume whenever you find yourself in situations where you're likely to meet someone. Anoint yourself, affirming that you're ready to burn with passion and repeat your incantation.

Come to Me Lover Formula

2 drops jasmine attar

2 drops rose attar

1 drop essential oil of neroli or petitgrain

1 drop gardenia absolute or fragrance oil

1 heaping tablespoon apricot kernel or sweet almond oil

Blend essential oils into the tablespoon of base oil.

Your Love Belongs to Me Candle Ritual

Suitable for when you've met someone you're sure is for you but you're not sure about their level of commitment.

1. Prepare an altar of love featuring things that are relevant to your relationship.

2. Use a rose thorn to inscribe your initials and your lover's inside a heart carved into a white candle.

3. Light the candle and as it burns, think or chant: *Your love is for me.* Reflect on happy moments in your relationship and happier ones yet to come.

> *If you should find you've attracted the wrong love, the scent of camphor is reputed to drive men away and remove any romantic notions. Wear it as perfume to ward off unwanted interest.*

4. You *must* allow this candle to burn down naturally, without interruption. (If you cannot find enough happy reveries to fill the time it takes to burn this candle, perhaps you should reconsider whether this is the right spell to be doing.)

5. When the candle burns out, collect the wax along with some of the altar mementos and place them in a safe and private place. (Should you ever decide you no longer wish to maintain this relationship, dispose of the candle wax and mementos appropriately.)

> *Beware of the urge to get the largest candle you can find for intensification. Bigger is not necessarily better. You need a candle large enough to inscribe, so no tapers or birthday candles, but you'll also need to watch it burn in its entirety, so this is not the place for a 7-day or a very thick pillar. Use a mid-size candle, votive or a little larger. This is also an excellent opportunity to use a human figure candle.*

• • •

To bring lovers together, this next ritual requires figure candles.

We Two Meet as One

1. You will need two human figure candles of appropriate gender to represent yourself and your beloved. Choose whichever color resonates best for you.

2. Personalize each candle by carving initials, names, birthdays or symbols into the wax.

3. Anoint each candle with a romantic oil, something like "Come To Me Lover."

4. Place the candles at opposite ends of a flameproof rectangular pan or tray, facing each other. (Disposable aluminum baking trays are great or cover a roasting pan with aluminum foil.)

5. Light the candles, concentrating on your wish and affirmation of togetherness. Allow to burn for 20 minutes and then extinguish.

6. Twenty-four hours later, rub a little extra oil on the candles, push them 1 inch closer together and repeat the ritual: light the candles, focus on your desire, allow them to burn for 20 minutes and then extinguish.

7. This is to be repeated every 24 hours, continually pushing the candles closer together until they meet.

8. When the candles cannot be pushed any closer together, allow them to burn out in their entirety. If the wax from the respective candles blend together and become indistinguishable from each other, this is a very good sign.

(If by chance, you change your mind about this relationship in the middle of the ritual, do not stop. Just have the candles veer away from each other, like two ships passing in the night. Do not allow them to burn out until each candle has safely turned its back on the other. An effective divorce/separation spell is performed by reversing the process, i.e. starting the candles together in the center and pulling them gradually apart.)

Love Sachets and Bags

Charm bags and sachets can be used to attract romance. Muslin is the material of choice. Pink, white, yellow or blue are the favored colors.

To form a romance charm bag, a handkerchief-size muslin square is tied with either a piece of lace or a red satin or velvet ribbon.

Sachets are sewed closed. For romance sachets, use gold, white, red or pink thread. Cut two small matching squares of muslin. Sew up three sides, leaving one side open, so that you may fill the sachet, then sew the last side shut.

Charm bags and sachets are used in the same way: sleep with one under your pillow, keep it safe in a treasure box or wear it tucked inside your undergarments, against your skin. Five separate sachet/charm bag formulas follow, all time-tested components of romantic enchantment. Choose which appeals to you most.

- Bay leaves, pink rose petals and catnip

- Elecampane leaves or flowers plus 1 licorice root

- Dried lavender and violets

- Juniper berries, poppy seeds, vervain and violets

- Rosemary, sage and thyme

- If you're making a sachet, add 1 drop of rose attar to the botanical material.

- If you're using a charm bag, where you will have easy access to the botanicals, add 6 drops of essential oil of bergamot upon making the charm and then add another 6 drops every six days until love arrives.

Burst of Love Potpourri

1 ½ cups rose petals or rosebuds

1 cup lavender blossoms

1 vanilla bean and/or 1 tonka bean chopped up

2 tablespoons dried ground cardamom

Combine ingredients. (Do not grind or mash them up, just gently intermingle them.) Store them in an airtight box. Open and breathe in the fragrance before any love enchantment, before an important date or when you just need to feel the possibility that Earth truly does contain beauty and love. Use the potpourri-filled box to store and empower your love charms.

Romance Floor Wash

Floor washes are created to serve many purposes, not only cleansing and protection. This floor wash clears away the proverbial "bad vibes," while setting the stage for romance. If necessary, it sends a message to the universe that your home lacks a lover. If you already have one, its lingering aroma transmits a subliminal reminder of the pleasures of love.

1. Make a strong infusion of peppermint leaves and add to a bucket of water.

2. There's no need to add vinegar, but if you feel you need it, select a floral or mint vinegar rather than plain white.

3. Use the water to clean the kitchen, bedroom or bathroom floors or wherever you see fit.

4. For variety, try apple or chocolate mint. Compare and contrast, see what works best.

Better Sex But Only If You Come Back Home

Has your lover left you for another? Want him back? The spell was conceived in Morocco by women whose husbands had taken a second, often younger, wife. However, it has since been adapted by women whose husbands or lovers have left them for another.

The abandoned woman sleeps with one date inside her vagina for seven nights (same date; you can take it out during the daytime) at which point the object of her affections is induced to stop by for a little dinner, maybe lunch, just to talk. The date is chopped up finely and served in her beloved's food. If all goes as the spell intends, he won't be leaving after dinner.

> *Of course, the Moroccan spell presumes that you want your old lover back, cheating heart and all. What if you don't want him back, you want to move on and find a new lover, too? A Gullah ritual recommends burning a pair of your former lover's shoes: you'll soon have more new prospects of your own than you'll know what to do with. Perhaps this derives from the old injunction against giving a lover a gift of shoes: he'll only use them to walk out on you!*

- This spell, incidentally, is supposed to start working from Day 1. As soon as the date is placed inside, he'll remember his sex life with you fondly and be dissatisfied with his new lover.

• • •

There are also other, less intimate ways to call back a departed lover:

Lover, Come Back Incense

Ground cardamom

Dragon's Blood

No, no! I told you, there's nothing like eye of newt in this book! Dragon's Blood won't be found in the "bat's tongue" aisle of your local witch-market. It's actually the resin from the *Dracaeana draco* tree, available from sources that sell incense and herbal supplies. Unlike most resins, this one is red, hence the name.

1. Combine the ingredients in a mortar and pestle and burn as incense near an open window for seven nights.

2. Make up a little invocation or rhyme if you choose, something like:

"Lover, please come back to me,
This time our love will blessed be."

Our Hearts United in Love

To return a lost lover or reinforce the ties that bind.

Pink or yellow candle(s)

Paper and ink

Essential oil of either jasmine, pine or rose

1. In the center of a piece of paper, draw a large heart with your name and the name of your beloved written in the middle.

2. In each corner of the paper, draw a diamond shape with a cross inside. Draw smaller diamonds containing crosses at each side of the heart, plus one at the base of the heart, by the point and another at the top of the heart, by the indentation.

3. Place a single drop of either essential oil of jasmine, pine or rose on the very center of the paper.

4. Fold the paper over at least twice so that you can hold the paper within one hand.

5. Holding the paper tight, visualize yourself and your partner happy in love.

6. Place the folded paper in a bowl of hot water. Encourage the paper to disintegrate into tiny little pieces, basically into pulp, unreadable and barely recognizable as paper.

7. When this has been accomplished—and it may take a little while— add it to your bath water.

8. Light at least 1 pink or yellow candle, enter the tub and concentrate on true love. If the paper is visible in the water, rub your body with it. Allow the particles to flow down the drain with the water.

- This spell can also be accomplished in the shower. Follow steps 1 through 6, then bring the paper into a running shower and rub your body with the paper like soap until it completely disintegrates.

Broken Heart Solace Bath

White rose petals

Honeysuckle blossoms

Rose attar or rose quartz

Should all else fail, you can find solace alone in your bathroom shrine of love.

1. Float white rose petals and honeysuckle blossoms in your bath.

2. If you have the budget for a more potent variation, add a few drops of rose attar and/or honeysuckle absolute, however the flower petals are truly the essential part of the spell.

3. Wear your rose attar and/or rose quartz until your broken heart heals.

• • •

Other types of love exist and can be lost, beyond the romantic.

Have you lost a valued friend? Have you done everything you could but someone special still won't forgive you?

Reconsider Friend

Powdered or dried rosemary

Dried or rubbed sage

Salt Sugar

Pulverize all ingredients together, using about a pinch of each. Sprinkle on your friend's shoulders. It will resemble dandruff but should get them to cool off long enough for you to present your side effectively.

APHRODISIAC SPELLS

Isis and Osiris Eternal Love Oil

6 drops essential oil of frankincense

6 drops essential oil of myrrh

1 cup grapeseed oil

Frankincense and myrrh embody the sacred balance of divine male and female energies, respectively. Blend the essential oils into the grapeseed oil and use for massage, bathing or as you wish.

Erotic Bath

4 drops essential oil of neroli

4 drops essential oil of tuberose

4 drops essential oil of ylang ylang

- These essences added to the bath or blended into massage oil serve to put women in the mood.

- The fragrance worn on a woman serves to put men in the mood.

Erotic Bedroom Perfume Incense

Ground cinnamon

Frankincense resin

Rose petals or buds

Combine the ingredients in a mortar and pestle, leaving a few rosebuds whole, then burn.

You can also blend this formula into oil using essential oils, however, if you plan to apply it to your body, keep the cinnamon to a minimum, as it can burn your skin, and keep it away from sensitive parts of the body.

Love Beads

These handmade beads are strung on elastic cord and worn under clothing, against the skin. Traditionally, they're worn around women's waists but some modern variations place them around the necks as well. Their fragrance intensifies with body heat. No two women's beads are the same because the floral fragrance combines subtly with one's own. The waist beads are rarely removed and are considered very intimate and erotic. They are believed to please a current lover or if you're single, to entice a new one.

Here are three variations, based upon various traditions from West Africa and the Arabian Peninsula. Technique used to form the actual beads varies slightly based upon the ingredients, however, once completed, feel free to combine the beads in any way to form your chains of love.

Rosebud Beads

The quantity of rose petals depends upon the size chain you need. Pink roses are customary or you can use yellow flowers to please Oshun, Orisha of Love. Choose what pleases you.

1. Process the rose petals in a food processor or mortar and pestle until they form a paste.

2. Roll into pea-size balls.

3. Allow them to dry, ideally on screens that allow air to circulate.

4. When they are just slightly damp, pierce each bead with a large needle so that you will be able to string them.

5. Having allowed the beads to dry completely, string them on elastic cord to form a chain.

Myrrh Beads

3 tablespoons gum arabic

1 tablespoon sweet almond oil

5 drops essential oil of myrrh

1. Mix the ingredients together in a small bowl to form a paste.

2. Roll them into pea-size beads.

3. Pierce each bead with a thick needle and allow them to dry overnight. They may then be strung onto elastic cord.

> *Enhance the power and fragrance of any of these beads by rolling them in powdered orrisroot (a natural preservative possessing a divine, aphrodisiac fragrance) just before stringing. Should you get bored with your beads, don't dispose of them but burn them one by one as "Come Hither" incense. In the meantime, if you're not wearing them, store the beads in sealed containers with "Love Potpourri."*

Saffron Beads

1 teaspoon saffron threads

1 teaspoon myrrh or labdanum (rock rose) resin

1. Pearls and/or gold spacer beads (optional)

2. Pound saffron into the resin using a mortar and pestle.

3. When it is combined and malleable, roll into pea-size beads.

4. Pierce each bead with a thick needle and allow to dry.

5. String these beads onto elastic cord in combination with pearls and gold spacer beads, if you like.

MARRIAGE SPELLS

The Celestial Spirit of Marriage

Juno is the ancient Roman matron of women. She guards and guides women through all stages of their lives. Marriage is her holy sacrament and women may request her assistance in any aspect of matrimony. If she helps you, schedule your wedding or engagement in the months February or June, the two months named in her honor. (*Juno Februata*, "Juno of the Fever of Love," is among her many titles.) She'll also expect a commemorative altar to mark your wedding anniversaries. Her favorite things include roses, orrisroot and peacock feathers. Her sacred bird is the goose and her number is one.

Marriage and the Magical Wedding

Animal Allies: Dog, Dove, Fox, Goose, Swan. *These animals epitomize the virtues of loyalty, fidelity and commitment. A shrine devoted to matchmaking exists in Safed, Israel, ancient capital of Jewish mysticism and Kabbalah. Its cemeteries house the graves of wonder-working rabbis. They produced miracles during life. Why would a little thing like death prevent them from continuing their good deeds? Second century rabbi, Jonathan ben Uzziel never married but has spent the afterlife assisting others. Twenty years ago, you had to hike to his small, abandoned grave in the Galilee Mountains. Now, in testament to his success, you'll find parking facilities, restrooms and wheelchair access. (Safed also has a peaceful divorce shrine. The grave of Phinehas ben Jair is located in the Old Safed cemetery. To receive his blessing, walk around the grave counterclockwise seven times.)*

• • •

Is a desired proposal not as forthcoming as you'd like?

- Add elder flower infusion to beer or wine. If a couple drinks this potion from a shared glass, English folk tradition says they'll be married within a year.

- Tap your intended's wedding ring finger with a sprig of rosemary three times. Think of it as a little rosemary magic wand. A proposal should soon be forthcoming!

- **Emeralds** ensure love and are considered the finest choice for an engagement ring.

- Chinese wedding rings were once commonly carved from **lodestones** so that the rings would magically keep a couple united and maintain their initial attraction.

- Magnolia trees encourage fidelity; they're traditionally planted to mark wedding anniversaries.

- A myrtle tree's presence evokes Aphrodite's blessings of continuing romance and a tranquil home.

- Pines symbolize fidelity and commitment. Their presence encourages lengthy marriages.

An Enchanted Wedding

Preparing for a magical wedding involves more than selecting a caterer and deciding where to seat Aunt Suzy. In some cultures, the bride, and even occasionally the groom, must be primed for the wedding. These often include what would today be considered spa treatments, to enhance beauty and personal power and also to protect against the Evil Eye, to which brides are considered particularly vulnerable. Henna parties are given. In India, brides may be marinated in turmeric paste; the resulting golden color evokes the goddess Lakshmi, whom each bride at least momentarily embodies. In Java, cleansing and beautifying treatments can last for days (the wealthier the bride, the more extravagant and extensive the treatment). The bride's hair and body is bathed in rose water. She is placed in baths that contain almost as many flowers as water: frangipani, jasmine and roses. She is cleansed with sandalwood steam, eggs and ginger. She's exfoliated with rice, turmeric and exotic, fragrant flowers and massaged with frangipani and jasmine infused oils.

Although many cultures have evolved ornate bridal adornment rituals, some Tuareg tribes maintain another perspective. Women form a bridal bed from desert sand while men erect a tent around it. On her wedding day, the bride enters the tent, where she sits on her sand bed surrounded by female companions who chant blessings and spells. Although on any other day, she might be elaborately adorned, on this day she wears a plain everyday dress with no makeup or jewelry, to indicate that her husband chose her and accepts her exactly as Earth formed her.

Henna is most famous as a prime component of marriage rituals. Just prior to the wedding, so that there is enough time for the henna to set and be at its best, a henna party is thrown in the bride's honor. She is the center of attention. Although all the women may have their opportunity to be decorated, the most beautiful, intricate designs are reserved for the bride. This renders her immobile for many hours and gives her female friends and relatives plenty of time to fill her in on the facts of life and assorted husband-pleasing tips they think she should know.

- On the subcontinent, a marriage's future balance of power is believed to lie in the henna. The groom's initials are hidden somewhere in the designs on his bride's body. It's up to him to find them on the wedding night; otherwise, the bride will always hold the upper hand!

- To ensure that the bride will always know sweetness, joy and prosperity, Yemenite Jews stick a gold coin into the center of her hennaed hand and seal it with honey.

BRIDAL BOUQUETS

The bridal bouquet was originally another magical charm. Choose your flowers wisely.

- **Basil:** grants happiness, prosperity, fertility and romance. Invokes Lakshmi, goddess of marriage and all good fortune.

- **Jasmine:** brings romance, fertility and prosperity.

- **Orange Blossoms:** evoke happy romance and fertility. Their fragrance calms stressed nerves, too. (These must be thrown away before they wilt or before the month is over, whichever comes first, or they'll foster sterility within the marriage bed. Every spell has two sides, however: if you're looking to reinforce contraception, hold on to those blossoms!)

- **Queen of the Meadow:** also known as bridewort, this flower ensures romantic love and relieves stress.

- **Rose:** Juno's favorite flowers encourage romance and fidelity.

- **Rosemary:** traditionally carried by English brides or worn as a crown to represent their love and loyalty. Rosemary, lest we forget, also provides protection. Anne of Cleves wore a rosemary crown when she wed King Henry VIII and she was the only one of the four wives of whom he wearied to live happily ever after.*

- **Saffron Blossoms:** ancient Greek and Roman brides wore these blossoms, which were also used to decorate the marriage bed. (Grow your own, they're impossible to find. Only saffron threads are typically available.)

- **Stephanotis:** its Hawaiian name means "marriage flower"; the fragrant white blossoms are favorites for marriage bouquets and leis.

- **Vervain:** even just a sprig of vervain in the bridal bouquet is said to ensure the new groom's fidelity!

- **Yarrow:** ensures seven years of happiness.

• • •

Bouquets can also be created to invoke the power of beneficent spirits of love and marriage. These bouquets will not only draw blessings to the bride and groom, when the bride throws her bouquet it will serve as a true marriage amulet for the woman who catches it.

An Aphrodité Bouquet

Carry a selection of the following flowers, all beloved by the goddess of love:

Apple blossoms

Linden blossoms

Marjoram

---

* Yes, yes, Henry VIII is notorious for his six wives! However, one survived him and one died following child-birth. Of the remainder, two were divorced and two beheaded, most famously Anne Boleyn, whose criminal charges included bewitching the king.

Myrtle leaves

Scented geraniums

Yellow roses

Juno's Bouquet of Eternal Love

Purple iris

Roses

Peacock feathers (cut to size)

Do you dread throwing the bouquet? There are ways around it. A British custom provides equal opportunity and evokes less hostility than throwing a single bouquet. The bride gives each bridesmaid her own myrtle plant or cutting. If she plants it and it takes root, the bridesmaid should be married soon, too. A Swiss ritual eliminates throwing the bouquet: following the ceremony, the bride's floral wreath and/or bouquet is set aflame. If it burns quick and bright, it's considered very auspicious for the bridal couple's future.

Ariadne and Dionysus Loving Couple Bouquet

This divine couple epitomizes the ideal of marriage as a joyful, respectful and equal partnership. Carry their bouquet as a good luck charm!

Holly leaves (preferably with some berries)

Ivy leaves

Pine boughs and cones

Happy Marriage Charm

Take nine dried yarrow flower heads on stalks. Bind them together with green ribbon. This charm is most powerful when made on a Friday with a waxing moon. Hang over the bed to ensure joy and romance.

Many rituals tap Earth's powers to ensure happiness and stability to the bride and groom. Friends of a Czech bride may secretly plant and decorate a new tree for her, decorating it with ribbons and painted eggshells. Tiered wedding cakes in Bermuda are topped not with miniature brides and grooms but with tiny saplings: a gift to be planted in the newlywed's home to ensure future love and peace. Not that tiny marital dolls are to be mocked: their roots lie in ancient fertility spells. Real dolls resembling the couple were originally used and later entrusted to the bride, to be cared for as called for. Wedding rituals are replete with fertility rituals, hearkening back to times when progeny, rather than love, was considered the sole purpose for marriage.

Something old, something new, something borrowed, something red?

1. Cowrie shells attached to bridal garments, necklaces and headpieces link us to our earliest ancestors: they are among the most ancient and widely spread amulets of all. Cowries are believed to provide not only personal fertility but prosperity and protection, too. Because their shape echoes the vulva, they are believed to evoke primal, protective female power, the strongest power of all.

2. Horseshoes are lucky, not only because of their association with horses, but because they, too, are believed to resemble the female generative organs. English brides sew small silver horseshoes to the hems of their gowns for luck.

One clove of garlic is traditionally carried in the bride's pocket or sewn into a little red bag and attached to her underskirt: it brings good fortune and wards off the Evil Eye.

---

3. Other cultures use the code of color to evoke this power: brides are dressed in red or a red ribbon may be hidden under her white dress.

4. A Czech custom also evokes the female generative force, albeit symbolically: right before the ceremony, the groom is wrapped in his new bride's cloak, indicating her primal link to this power.

Although wedding rituals and bridal decorations are studded with fertility-inducing enchantment, this may not always be desirable. The traditional Rumanian bride wishing for some years of childlessness, stuffed as many roasted walnuts into her bodice as the years she wished to remain childfree.

Magical Wedding Gifts

Anyone can give the bride and groom toasters, sheets and dishes. You can give the gift of magic.

- Frankincense and saffron to increase the bride's fertility and her personal power (Bedouin)

- Horseshoes for good luck, protection and a happy marriage (Ireland)

- Carved jade butterflies ensure lasting love (China)

Party favors given to the attending guests also bestow magical blessings:

- In Egypt, guests are given small balls of henna paste to hold during the ceremony, so that they may keep their hands on good fortune.

- In Malaysia, guests are given beautifully decorated hard-boiled eggs, to invoke new beginnings and fresh starts for all, not only the bridal couple.

The Wedding's Over and the Party's Begun!

The ceremony may be over, the bouquet tossed, the garter caught, but marital rituals have only just begun. The space in time between the ending of the wedding and the couple's arrival at their new home is a threshold fraught with vulnerability and opportunities for magical good luck!

- Hawthorn, a cousin of the rose, has long associations with romance, fertility and fairy magic. A Roman bridegroom waved a hawthorn sprig as he led his new bride to the nuptial chambers, which was illuminated with hawthorn torches.

- In Switzerland, an older married couple is sent to prepare the boudoir before the couple arrives: they arrange the marriage bed romantically, with luxurious bedding and romantic flowers and fragrance, and leave behind some lucky charms: coins, bags of rice, sesame seeds and a tomcat.

- These days it's customary for the groom to carry the bride over the threshold. What happens then? Well, among many European traditions, the bride's first action upon entering her home as a wife must be to break an egg, to ensure her happiness and prosperity.

FERTILITY SPELLS

Fertility magic isn't limited to wedding symbolism.

Frog Fertility Spell

1. Place two porcelain frogs in a bowl and cover them with water.

2. Put the bowl under your bed.

3. Put two whole, uncooked eggs around the bowl. (Replace the eggs every week or as soon as you can smell them. Bury them in Earth: do not eat.)

4. Keep the frogs wet and pray that a child be sent to you.

Animal Allies: cat, donkey, frog, goat, pig, rabbit, scorpion, snake. *All these are animals possessing great fecundity. The scorpion is able to reproduce under even the harshest conditions. Contemplate these creatures, surround yourself with their images, with the hopes that some of their lush reproductive power will rub off on you!*

Spirit Allies

Because conception creates something new (someone new) from existing energy, it's very closely tied to enchantment. In general, spirits who promote magic also promote and regulate fertility. These spirits include:

- **Baba Yaga** (Slavic) **Freya** (Norse) **Hecate** (Eurasia) **Isis** (Egypt)

- **Kali** (India, Nepal)

- **Tlazolteotl** (Aztec)

- **Persephone** (Greece) assists with matters concerning contraception

- **Kapo** (Hawaii) is among the deities most involved with contraception and abortion. She may also be appealed to for renewed fertility should you desire a child, although you shouldn't bother her in this instance unless it's established that you really have a problem.

• • •

Artemis, the powerful Greek lunar spirit, is associated with all facets of women's reproductive power. She bestows fertility, guards pregnancy and eases labor pains.

Artémis Fertility Altar

Doll(s) from your own childhood

**Figures of Her beloved animals: deer, dogs, bear and particularly wolves
(Artemis is Queen of All Wild Beasts)**

Dried or fresh mugwort and/or Dittany of Crete Silver charms

A moon-shaped candle

Decorate the altar as a living petition for fertility. Leave it standing, at least until your goal is met. Feel free to light the candle for added intensity and enhancement, whenever needed.

• • •

Yemaya is the Yoruba matriarch of the sea, women and fertility. She is particularly sympathetic to those who struggle with infertility.

Yemaya Fertility Ritual #1

Watermelon (it must be the type with seeds)

Small blue or white candle

1. Bring a small watermelon to the beach.

2. Cut a well into the watermelon.

3. Dress the candle, if you wish. Hold it in your hands, charging it with your desire and your intent.

4. Insert the candle into the watermelon's well, light it and send it out to sea, making your petition to Yemaya all the while. (Make sure the candle is biodegradable and environmentally friendly, sending toxins into Yemaya's holy sea won't earn you any points.)

Yemaya Fertility Ritual #2

1 pomegranate

Honey

Paper (dioxin free, please!)

1. Go to the beach, bringing your supplies.

2. Slice the pomegranate in half and spread honey over both sides.

3. Write the name of the person who wishes to conceive on a small piece of paper and place between the halves of the fruit.

4. Bring the halves together, sealing the paper within.

> *Yemaya despises any form of domestic violence and will not send a child into that environment. Should her trust be abused, she may later remove the child. If this in any way resonates for you, the first step of any fertility petition to Yemaya is to divorce yourself completely from the violence. Request her assistance.*

5. Bind the pomegranate closed with a string of seaweed, if you can find one. (It's considered auspicious if you can.) If not, just press the halves together tight; the honey should serve as glue.

6. Make your petition to Yemaya and send the pomegranate out to sea.

Fertility Magnet Trees

- Almond

- Apricot

- Ash

- Date Palm

- Fig

- Myrtle

- Pomegranate

- Willow

In Mediterranean regions, armfuls of fragrant basil are hung over the conjugal bed to promote fertility and enhance conception.

Egg Trees

Egg trees are often erected at Easter, but like that bunny delivering eggs, the roots stretch back to Pagan Europe. The traditional egg tree involves wrapping the trunk and branches of the tree with cotton batting and festooning it with eggs. Creation of such a tree is thought to bring fertility to the childless. Birch and cherry trees are the traditional trees utilized but any tree bearing allusions to fertility, especially fruit or nut trees, may be substituted. Do the best you can. If you only have one tree available, use that one, but remember, you increase your power through details. Buy a small fertility-related tree. Maintain it after the spell to signal to the powers that be what fine parents and caretakers you would be. Keep the tree in a pot if you have nowhere to plant it.

- Plain eggs may be used but dyeing the eggs red when wishing for fertility is traditional.

- Incorporate fertility motifs into the decorations as an extra boost: triangles, cats, rabbits or fruit-bearing trees.

- A Greek variation incorporates hanging small dolls instead of, or in addition to, the eggs.

Conception Spell Box

Line the bottom of your box with dried corn, chamomile flowers and rose-buds. Add some cowrie shells and one or more crystals associated with conception. Add some animal power now: charms or fetishes representing the appropriate animals. You can add anything that has personal resonance and significance for you. Get a tiny baby doll and make it a soft bed from half a walnut shell. Make it a little cover, so that it will stay warm. Make it as simple or as elaborate as you wish. A spell box is a work in progress: add to it, play with it, any efforts are part of the spell. When your wish is fulfilled, bury the box and its contents in Earth or pass it on to another person.

Conception Crystals

Carnelian *and* **red coral** *stimulate both men's and women's reproductive systems. Blood red coral is the most popular material for amulets that protect and stimulate male reproductive capacity. Wear a single piece around the neck, either jagged and uncut in the Berber style or carved into a horned hand in Italian tradition.*

Fertility-Drawing Oil

1 lapis lazuli chip or a very tiny lapis crystal

2 tablespoons sweet almond oil

3 drops essential oil of basil

2 drops rose attar

2 drops jasmine absolute

2 drops essential oil of myrrh

1 drop essential oil of patchouli or vetiver

1 drop pomegranate flower essence (Desert Alchemy, Flower Essence
Project, Pegasus)

Place the crystal in a glass vial or container, followed by the almond oil and
then the essential oils and the flower essence, in that order. Use to dress
your fertility candle.

• • •

Lunation

Sometimes the border between science and magic is very fine. This is a
process that has been successful in reestablishing ovulatory and menstrual
cycles to nonmenopausal women whose current cycles are irregular, infre-
quent or even absent.

1. Determine the first day of your last period. Estimate if you must. If
    your cycle is so irregular or absent that you can't, use the true new
    moon (look at the calendar) as day one and count the number of days
    until the next new moon.

2. Except for days 14 through 17, sleep in an absolutely dark room.
    Absolutely dark means complete darkness, no artificial light whatso-
    ever. No little teeny glow from your alarm clock, no tiny little red light
    from the VCR. Shut the shades well to block out streetlights.

3. From the 14th to the 17th day, however, keep a light on all night. Use a
    100-watt light bulb placed in a lamp to disperse light onto the ceilings
    and walls but still minimally disturb your sleep. Placing the lamp on
    the floor is recommended.

4. Ovulation should occur during the light period. Expect the process
    to take anywhere up to six months for success. (In a study of almost
    two thousand women with irregular cycles, more than half the
    subjects achieved regular twenty-nine day cycles using the process of
    lunation alone.)

5. Those who wish to conceive should make love during the three light
    nights. Those who do not should be careful.

• • •

To enhance chances of conception, English folk healers recommend making love by the light of burning red candles. Once the sexual act is complete, the candles should be extinguished.

ANTIFERTILITY SPELLS

Remember, this is very important: contraceptive spells are intended to reinforce your efforts to remain childless. They are not meant to enable you to challenge nature nor should you rely upon them alone.

> *English folk healers recommend hawthorn leaves tucked under the mattress as a contraceptive enhancing device.*

Ancient Moroccan Contraceptive Spell

One dried fig*

A few drops of menstrual blood

To be effective, this spell must be performed cooperatively by a man and a woman.

1. Cut the dried fig lengthwise.

2. Sprinkle the blood into the cut.

3. The man then hides the fig in a secure place unknown to the woman. Theoretically, she is supposed to remain sterile for as long as the fig remains unseen.

---

* The fig may be replaced by a bead; however, there is no substitute for the other ingredient.

4. To break the spell, the man removes the fig from its hiding place and displays it to the woman.

• • •

Keys and locks are traditional magical ingredients, particularly useful for working with sex, fertility, contraception and all sorts of reproductive issues. In an attempt to preserve and/or time conception, a traditional Serbian woman would arrange a lock and key on the floor, walk in the space between them, turn around and while turning state, "When I open the lock again, I shall successfully conceive." The magically charged lock and key must be kept in a safe place, away from other hands.

PREGNANCY PROTECTION AND ENHANCEMENT SPELLS

- Animal Ally: Cat

- Crystals: Amber, Coral, Lapis lazuli

Traditional midwives did more than just assist at a birth. They provided for all facets of a woman's reproductive health and were expected to be familiar with protective enchantment for mother and child. General magical wisdom recommends that a couple refrain from advertising the pregnancy much before it visually announces itself, as a protective gesture against jealousy and malice. Magical rituals, however, may begin early in pregnancy.

Childbirth

Psychic safety and enhancement of the birthing chamber is considered magically crucial. The room may be purified. Special incense can be burned, particularly this one that provides protection and a welcoming aroma that bids the baby come forth.

Water is the element most associated with fertility and childbirth. As soon as a traditional Haitian woman knows she is pregnant, she goes to a healer for a series of magical baths. Aztec women took steam baths, supervised by an herbalist. Water can be beneficial throughout pregnancy: Hawaiian women were encouraged to gently sway swollen bellies in the ocean, to loosen up the baby for a speedier delivery. Underwater births call on beneficial water spirits to serve as spiritual midwives.

Welcome Baby Incense

Lavender blossoms

White, pink or yellow rosebuds or petals

Grind some of the flowers together in the mortar and pestle, leaving at least a few whole. Then burn.

Fertile Crescent Childbirth Incense

This incense formula focuses on easing the mother's discomfort. Galbanum resin, known as the "Mother resin," was used in ancient Egypt and Mesopotamia for pain relief during childbirth.

Anise seeds

Galbanum resin

Pound together in a mortar and pestle and burn.

• • •

Crystal Childbirth Charms: Wear bloodstone during delivery or bring some into the delivery room. They may also be used for massage during the birth.

Bedouin Childbirth Spice Necklace

This perfumed necklace may soothe and encourage the laboring woman. If it's not comfortable to wear it, then hang it nearby so that the aroma can provide comfort and protection.

Dried cloves

Seeds or dried fruits of the Mahaleb cherry (perfumed cherry tree)*

Ambrette seeds or essential oil of ambrette **

Red thread and a needle

A crystal arrow worn as a pendant is believed to stimulate quick, uncomplicated labor.

---

1. Soak cloves and seeds overnight to soften them.

2. If you are using only solid materials (cloves, seeds and/or fruits), pierce them with a needle, and string onto the red thread, leaving enough room at the ends to tie the necklace comfortably. It should be loose and comfortable when worn, not tight and constricting.

Drumming echoes Earth's heartbeat. The drumming of our mother's heartbeat was the first rhythm any of us ever felt. Many traditional childbirth rituals attempt to exploit this welcoming rhythm to enhance

---

* If you do not have your own perfumed cherry tree (and the tree does grow in parts of the United States), the dried seeds may be obtained from Middle Eastern or Indian groceries. Although this particular tree bears little reputation for danger, be aware that it comes from the family of trees from which cyanide derives and, in theory, any seeds or fruit may be toxic, if taken internally. This necklace is meant only to be worn, not eaten. If you cannot obtain Mahaleb, make the necklace with only cloves and ambrette.

** Ambrette, also known as musk seed, is widely used in Asia and is considered by many to be the closest substitute for the famed fragrance derived from endangered musk deer. The seeds may be obtained from a Middle Eastern grocery store.

*the safety of mother and baby and speed the delivery. A female hand
drummer may be hired to attend the birth, her rhythm directing and
encouraging the baby's journey through the birth canal. An experienced
belly dancer may also attend, to transfix and distract the mother,
providing encouragement and healing rhythms.*

3. If using the essential oil, moisten your fingers with the oil and rub the
cloves and seeds gently before stringing them onto the thread. You may
also add 12 drops of ambrette oil to a spray bottle full of springwater and
spray the solid material lightly. (Make sure you wash your hands thoroughly before touching your eyes after handling essential oils and cloves.)

*Birch trees symbolize new beginnings in Northern Europe, planted to
celebrate a new birth or carved into protective cradles.*

PROTECTION FOR INFANTS
AND CHILDREN

Infants and children are universally perceived as needing protection. A
child's name may connect it to powerful forces. A name can connect to the
protective power of an ancestor, deity or animal. Sharing a name is believed
to impart a little of the elder's essence to junior. You are also entitled to call
upon the blessings of any spiritual entity whose name you share.

Coral, jade and jet are favored amulets for children, as are the ubiquitous eyes and hands. Fish charms fastened to the hair protect a child while
traveling over water.

Rose quartz is the stone of childhood and innocent love, promoting
and protecting an open, trusting heart chakra. Its energy is extra beneficial
for children, providing nurturing, loving, creative, protective energy. Rose
quartz helps adults, too, by healing long-buried childhood trauma and
abuse. A rose quartz bracelet nurtures and protects a child; adults wearing
it for healing purposes might want to wear it against their heart.

Special Protectors of Pregnant Women and Children

Though there are many such spirits, Egyptians Bastet, Bes and Taweret are particularly devoted. Place their images in the birthing room or in a child's room. It's not likely you'll get an argument from the kids; these images tend to please them, if only for amusement. Bastet appears as a pretty cat who sometimes wears hoop earrings. Bes is a fierce but lovable lion-headed dwarf and his wife, Taweret, is a big-bellied pregnant hippo who sports women's breasts and a crocodile's tail! All are exceptionally devoted to women and children and bring joy and protection.

Henna for the Baby

In the Middle East, henna's magical and therapeutic properties are called on as soon as a baby is born. A paste of henna, flour and water is painted over the newly cut navel to stimulate healing and serve as a disinfectant. This first contact with henna is also believed to provide psychic safety, beauty and future wealth. Children are rarely elaborately painted with henna; however, the plant's therapeutic properties are more frequently relied upon. A feverish child is given a small moist ball of henna paste to hold, to help bring down the fever.

The Baby's Pillow

Mugwort is not for kids and shouldn't be a part of a children's dream pillow. A good rule of thumb for mugwort is, if you're not old enough to menstruate, you're not old enough for mugwort. Children rarely have trouble accessing their dreams anyway. What they need (or at least what their parents need!) are herbs to provide a soothing peaceful transition to dreamland.

Malachite *attached to a baby's bed encourages sound sleep while warding off any malevolent spirits. Make sure it's placed so that the baby can't choke on the hard stone.*

Baby Dream Pillow

Select one or any combination of the following:

>Calendula flowers
>
>Catnip (but not if you have a cat!)
>
>Raspberry leaves
>
>Rose petals
>
>Vervain (to bring joy and inspire a lifetime love of learning!)
>
>Chamomile flowers, hops, lavender blossoms and linden flowers promote sound sleep. (Avoid chamomile if there's a family history of ragweed allergies.)

Mix the herbs and place into a closed bag of the softest flannel. A child old enough to be out of the oral stage can sleep with it, but a baby should only be allowed to touch or handle the pillow under supervision. Otherwise place the pillow near enough so that the aromas may be inhaled but not so close that the baby can chew on the bag, potentially freeing the herbs and choking.

• • •

Should a child fall ill, a small flannel pillow shaped like a bear and stuffed with dried rosemary and lavender soothes, amuses and promotes healing. Black mustard seeds in a red flannel pillow are also reputed to boost immunity or try the Immunity Incense to keep your young one hale and hearty.

It used to be a fashion to sprinkle garlic under a child's pillow for protection during the night. Of course, those were the days when parents didn't ask kids for input. A more discreet and less aromatic alternative is to slip one clove of garlic into the very center of a child's dream pillow.

A necklace of cloves strung onto red thread and hung on the wall near the baby's bed (but far out of reach of a small child) brings good luck, protection and stimulates intelligence.

Immunity Incense

Bay leaves, chopped

Frankincense resin

Mash the ingredients together to form a paste and burn. (You may want to burn the incense without the child in the room and with the doors and windows closed. When the incense has burned down, open the windows and settle your child in the room.)

- A few drops of essential oil of eucalyptus, pine or rosemary in a pan of water near a source of heat also cleanses the air of the microbes and psychic dangers that tend to travel hand in hand.

Sweet Sibling Spell

If the new child is not the first, elder siblings may experience some jealousy. To prevent jealousy, just before the siblings are formally introduced, a few grains of sugar are placed in the infant's hand (*never* substitute honey, which even in small doses may be harmful to an infant). The elder siblings lick the sugar off the baby's hand. It must be swallowed immediately for the spell to be effective.

MONEY MAGIC

If money could be earned solely by magical means, there'd be an awful lot of rich fortune-tellers. If those magical techniques have been uncovered, they remain under heavy guard. Magic can, however, provide for your needs if not for all your material desires. Magic can protect against poverty, and if you find yourself in need of a specific sum of money, there are spells to help.

Consider 2 the number of power for money magic as it encapsulates the concept of doubling.

Money Charms: black pearl, citrine, emerald, lodestone. Worn or carried, these minerals should magnetically attract further prosperity.

Animal Allies

Cat, Dragon, Frog, Rabbit, and Rat guard Earth's treasures. In addition, each is perfectly comfortable accepting Earth's bounties. Work with their images (go back to the Animal Allies section if your memory needs refreshing) to attract prosperity and also to learn how to accept Earth's benevolence graciously and comfortably.

• • •

Money Plant bears that name because its seeds resemble coins. Money Plant flower essence (Pegasus Products) helps provide insight regarding barriers to prosperity and also helps adjust any inner obstacles that prevent you from achieving prosperity.

A Money Garden

These plants growing in your garden or within your home invoke and maintain prosperity: **alfalfa, basil, camellia, chamomile, cinquefoil, dill, heliotrope, honeysuckle, jasmine, lettuce, marigold, mint, morning glory, nasturtium, onion, Oregon grape.**

Burn alfalfa and scatter the ashes around your property for prosperity. Alternatively, burn alfalfa and carry the herb in a medicine bag to ease financial woes. Buckwheat, cascara sagrada (*Rhamnus purshianus*)[*] and nuts, particularly walnuts, added to the bag will enhance the power.

Money Trees

- Almond

- Banana

- Horse chestnut

- Oak

• • •

A Romany recommendation for cash growth is pots of marigolds placed near your doors and windows. The power is enhanced if you can find a golden pot or something golden in color to place the marigolds upon, a brass tray, perhaps? Use any type of marigold you like, however French marigolds call in the power of the ancestors for assistance.

More Money Spice Necklace

Wear this necklace to attract money and to evoke an inner acceptance of prosperity.

Allspice berries

Cinnamon sticks

Cloves

Ginseng root

Nutmeg

---

[*] Native American tree, decimated by white settlers. Very endangered, find out how it is obtained before using.

sewing needles

36 inches of strong thread, dental floss or monofilament (fishline)

1. Soak the spices and roots overnight to soften them.

2. Once softened, you may trim and cut the roots and cinnamon sticks to suit your taste or recurl the cinnamon, if it's lost its shape.

3. Thread each end of the cord through a needle. Add spices as you will, creating a symmetric pattern by using first one side of the thread, then the other. Reserve some of the smooth, round allspice berries for the ends of the necklace, so that this will be what lies against your neck, minimizing any irritation.

4. When each side measures 14 inches to the center, tie the ends of the thread, knot firmly and hang the necklace to air-dry. Once dry, your necklace should last for years.

Grow Some Money Spell

• Place some fenugreek seeds in a jar and add a bit more daily. When your jar is full, bury it in Earth.

Despite its modest, mundane appearance, fenugreek is believed to be a plant of tremendous, dynamic potency. An herb of abundance, its key word is increase. Fenugreek tea is given to nursing mothers to increase their milk supply. Turkish harem women drank and bathed in infusions hoping to increase their bust size. Fenugreek provides wealth and protects against poverty. In addition to the above spell, there are other methods of harnessing this power.

• Scatter fenugreek seeds discreetly around your house.

• Soak the seeds in the water that you use to clean your house. (Strain before cleansing.)

Spirits of Financial Prosperity

Hermes (Greece), **Lakshmi** (India), **Oshun** (Yoruba)

Oshun, Orisha of Sweet Waters provides material comforts (and cash!) for her devotees. Like the most powerful spirits, she offers assistance in all departments: romance, health, beauty and prosperity.

Oshun's traditional offering, whenever you wish to invoke, petition or thank her, is a glass of springwater and a dish of honey. You must always taste any honey offered to Oshun, every time. An attempt was once made to poison her with honey. She will not accept any untasted offerings and may, in fact, look upon you with suspicion rather than love. Her colors are yellow and orange. Her metal is brass. Her sacred birds are peacocks, parrots and vultures. Her number is 5.

Oshun Prosperity Incense

Brown sugar

5 dried orange leaves

Orange zest

1. Pound the ingredients in a mortar and pestle until roughly pulverized.

2. Place in a cast-iron pan and set aflame.

3. Let it burn for a minute or so, then smother the flames. It should smoke fairly heavily, allow the aroma to fill the room.

4. Offer some pure springwater and honey to Oshun and tell her what you need.

A Money Dream Pillow

The stuffing encourages creative financial dreams and inspiration.

2 ounces dried basil

4 ounces dried chamomile blossoms

2 ounces dried fenugreek

If you need a refresher, return to the Dreams section, for detailed instructions on making dream pillows.

Prosperity Potpourri

1 cup cedar shavings

1 cup oak moss

1 tablespoon ground nutmeg

1 teaspoon ground cinnamon

Pinch of ginger

Essential oils of patchouli and vetiver

Combine the potpourri in a box with a tightly fitting lid. Keep it closed except when you need financial inspiration and/or encouragement. Then open the box and inhale. A little of this potpourri carried in a charm bag also serves as a money talisman.

Money Magnet Oil

To attract money, rub two drops of essential oil of bergamot on the palms of your hands, in your wallet, inside your pocket or wherever you carry your cash.

Milk and Honey Prosperity Bath

1 cup coconut milk

1 cup cow's milk

1 cup goat's milk

1 cup sheep's milk

1 cup holy or springwater

1 cup honey

This bath is reputed to draw money toward you. It's guaranteed to make your skin feel wonderful. Add the ingredients to the bath water. You can increase the quantity of the ingredients, if you wish, as long as all proportions remain equal.

Money Salt Scrub

1 cup of sea salt

½ cup oil, preferably safflower or sweet almond

4 drops essential oil of basil

4 drops essential oil of cedarwood

2 drops essential oil of cinnamon leaf

2 drops essential oil of patchouli

If you don't recall how to make a salt scrub, turn back to the Protection Spells section for detailed instructions.

Make your bathroom as luxurious and comfortable as possible. Dim the lights, burn some green candles. Rub the scrub on your body with gentle, circular motions and see yourself financially comfortable, prosperous and secure.

• • •

Many merchants frame their first earned dollar bill or some other significant cash bill for good luck. If you'd like to use that money, but still would like to see it grow, there are alternative techniques. To celebrate a first earning or a windfall and encourage more, sprinkle powdered ginger on the bills.

Family Full of Cash

A Hungarian spell invites new money to get comfortable with you and bring the relatives on over, too. Hold the lucky money in your hand and spit on it. Hungarians say: "Ápàd, Ányàd, *Idejöjon,*" which literally means "Daddy, Mommy, come here quick!" Use their words or make up your own.

Green Ribbon Money Growth Spells

A length of green silk cord

1. Visualize clearly and distinctly what it is that you need (a specific amount, something you need to buy).

2. Say this out loud in the form of a wish, in simple, clear, unambiguous language.

3. Now make 9 knots in the green silk cord. As you form each knot, repeat your wish.

4. Keep your cord in a safe place: a charm box or bag, in a dream pillow amidst money-attracting herbs or simply bury it in Earth.

Money Miracle Mantra

If your fortunes need a drastic upswing, try repeating this mantra for won-drous results:

"A money miracle happens to me today."

1. Start your day with this phrase and watch the miracles roll in.

2. Remember, miracles come in many shapes and sizes, small or large, accept each one graciously and await the next.

3. Repeat the phrase to suit your needs. Say it once a day or once every hour. I know someone who wrote it 100 times a day, detention-style and someone else who repeated it every time she was stopped at a traffic light.

4. You'll know when you no longer need the mantra because all of a sudden you'll realize that you've forgotten it for days.

- Always state the mantra in the present tense.

- This mantra may be used in combination with any other money spell or ritual for enhancement.

- If you need a different type of miracle, maintain the mantra's form but substitute your desire: "A love miracle happens to me today."

Should you need an exact amount of money, you owe $231.43 for instance, write the amount on a piece of paper. Drip a little basil oil on the paper, fold it in half twice and bury it in a pot of Earth. Ideally, you should then plant basil, marigolds, thyme or some other botanical associated with cash in that pot but if you fear that you'll kill the plant and really depress yourself, stick in a sturdy cactus.

New Orleans Money Magic

New Orleans and its surrounding environs are the capital of American magic. The Crescent City was the crucible where African enchantment met the magic practices of Native America and Europe.

Creole Antipoverty Spell

1 cup white sugar

1 cup salt

1 cup white rice

1 safety pin

Combine the first three ingredients together in an open bowl. Stick an open safety pin in the center and keep the bowl on a counter in full view.

New Orleans Better Business Formula

1 pint water

½ cup fresh basil leaves

Basil is particularly associated with prosperity and increase. It's also used in fertility rituals and love spells but most especially to attract greater business and profits. Prostitutes in Spain and Mexico rub their bodies with the fragrance when they need extra customers. In New Orleans, merchants and shopkeepers use it as a floor wash.

1. Infuse the basil in the water for 3 days.

2. On the 4th day, strain the herb out, retaining the water.

3. Sprinkle at the entrances of your place of business, in the corners and near the cash registers, basically in any spot you perceive as vulnerable. This formula should attract customers and prevent theft.

Quick Fix Better Business Formula

1 pint of water

12 drops essential oil of basil

Quick Fix is not quite as powerful as regular Better Business Formula; it lacks the visual component (the soaking basil leaves resemble cash), so you'll have to concentrate your focus a little harder. But it does have the advantage of being a very fast spell: you can perform it in minutes if needed. Just add the oil to the water and either sprinkle or add to a plant mister and spray throughout the room.

Basil Prosperity Bath

Water

Bunch fresh basil

1. Boil sufficient water to cover the basil.

2. Roughly chop most of the basil, but leave a handful of leaves whole.

3. Place the chopped basil in a bowl and cover with boiling water.

4. Let it sit for roughly 15 minutes, then strain and add the liquid to your bathtub filled with water.

5. Basil's visual imagery is powerfully inspirational: float the remaining whole basil leaves in the bath.

(If you need some extra inspiration to figure out where your cash will come from, throw in a few whole bay leaves as well.)

HIGH JOHN MONEY MAGIC

The king of American root magic goes by the name High John the Conqueror. Named for a legendary African-American slave hero, this root provides good fortune of all kinds. It is potent left whole, whether carried alone or added as a prize ingredient to a charm bag. The powdered root brings fortune and removes a curse. (Buy a whole one so that you can see what you're getting; powder it yourself.) High John is a member of the morning glory family. An elusive plant, it answers to a series of Latin names: *Ipomoea jalapa, Ipomoea purga* and *Convolvulus jalapa.* Reserve High John for purposes of enchantment only. It should never be eaten as it is an extremely powerful laxative and purgative.

High John's Finest Fruits

This charm attracts all Earth's finest fruits: health, wealth, love and success.

> 1 whole High John root or a piece
>
> Essential oil of bergamot
>
> Essential oil of vetiver

1. Anoint the root with the essential oils. Allow your nose to tell you how much oil to add: adjust the fragrance so that you find it pleasing.

2. Carry the root in a charm bag or in your pocket. You can also place it within a charm box.

3. Enhance with extra oil whenever you feel the root needs reinforcing.

High John's Money Roll

Essential oil of basil

1 cash bill*

1 High John the Conqueror root

Red or green thread

1. Rub a cash bill with basil oil and roll it tightly around the High John root.

2. It's important that when you wrap the root, you roll the money toward you, not away from you.

3. Bind the little money roll with red or green thread. Carry it with you as a charm or place it discreetly near the entrance to your business. (Inside the cash register is good, too!) If things slow down, reinforce the root with extra basil oil as needed.

Money Spell Box

A box

Cinquefoil

Dried patchouli or the essential oil

Powdered basil leaves

Dried vetiver or the essential oil

Fenugreek seeds

High John the Conqueror root

---

* Any kind of cash can be used, however, a two-dollar bill is considered most especially effective because it's rare and because the number 2 embodies the concept of doubling. Alternatively, any foreign currency lying around that you don't know what to do with is perfect for this charm.

Any other financially lucky roots you are able to collect: Beth Root (Low
John) or Lucky Hand

1 lodestone and/or citrine

Lucky charms: small silver horseshoe, silver shamrock, miniature rabbit,* rat
or mouse

A spell box is a work in progress: start with whatever you have accumulated and continue to build. If you should find a four-leaf clover, it is a powerful addition. Place one bill from any windfall inside to grow.

1. Line the box with the botanicals. (If you're using essential oils, rather than dried vetiver and patchouli, use them to anoint the roots and crystals.)

2. Add the roots, crystals and charms.

3. Keep the box closed except during rituals, visualizations and spells.

4. Periodically, anoint crystals and roots with essential oils or another money-drawing oil formula.

5. Keep the box in a safe spot so that no one can play with your finances.

6. When your goal is accomplished, either save this box for future use or bury it in Earth, but mark the spot so that you can dig it up again if you need it.

Lucky 8even Charm Box

High John the Conqueror root

Low John root (also known as Beth root) or Lucky Hand root

Adam and Eve root

---

* This spell calls for a representation of a rabbit: no real rabbit's feet, please! You want the rabbit powers to feel benevolent toward you. Tiny silver charms work very well as do carved Zuni stone fetishes or Japanese netsuke carvings.

1 tonka bean, to make your wishes come true

1 whole nutmeg, plus some ground nutmeg

Essential oils of patchouli and vetiver

1. Anoint the roots and beans with the oils. Place in a charm box with a lid.

2. Sprinkle with the ground nutmeg.

3. Open the box and inhale when you need financial inspiration or extra cash.

4. Carry individual pieces with you when you need some gambling luck or when you perceive that you need extra psychic protection.

TRADITIONAL NEW ORLEANS STYLE FAST LUCK OIL

Magic entered the marketing age with nineteenth and twentieth century Hoodoo formulas. Previously, spells were made at home or obtained from a local practitioner. Hoodoo practitioners, doctors of enchantment, created various formulas and potions marketed under specific names. Spells were now for sale via mail order or prepackaged in the pharmacy. Many of these formulas remain popular today, still sold under their original names through mail order and in occult supply stores and botanicas. Unfortunately, many contain nothing but colored water and artificial substances. Find an honest practitioner who still mixes up the real thing (investigate locally or check the appendix of this book for recommendations) or make them yourself. Oils are used for anointing charms, candles and roots. Some have lovely smells, but if you wish to anoint yourself, make sure they're created from real essential oils.

• • •

This formula, favored by gamblers, brings both love and money quickly, but don't expect it to last. This is an oil for when you need a quick shot, an emergency fix. Traditional New Orleans gambling lore recommends this formula for those who play slot machines, rather than slower card games.

Essential oil of cinnamon leaf

Vanilla absolute or fragrance oil

Essential oil of wintergreen

Combine equal parts of these oils. Rub on your hands, on the cash that you play with or on a High John root.

Lucky Cat Candle

1 green or black cat candle

More Money Oil (or other money drawing fragrance)

1. Dress the candle as you prefer and then anoint it with the oil.

2. Concentrate on your desire and light the candle.

3. This candle does not have to burn in one sitting; you may extinguish it, however the spell will not take full effect until the candle has been fully burned. Concentrate on your goal each time you relight.

More Money Oil

Essential oil of chamomile

Essential oil of Texas cedarwood

Essential oil of vetiver

Combine equal parts of the essential oils to anoint money candles or charms.

New Orleans Gambler's Lucky Hand

1 Lucky Hand root

High John the Conqueror root

Pinch of cinquefoil

Miniature pair of dice

Essential oil of basil or any money-drawing oil formula

Anoint the roots, cinquefoil and dice with the oil, place in a medicine bag and carry with you as needed.

Algiers Powder

Another New Orleans favorite for increased money, gambling success and love.

Cinnamon sticks

Dried patchouli leaves

Vanilla beans

Grind all the ingredients together in a mortar and pestle. Carry in a lucky pouch and sprinkle wherever and whenever you need a touch of magic.

ENCHANTMENT TO HEAL BODY AND SOUL

Once upon a time in the West, no physician was worth his salt unless he also had a background in astrology. The line between psychic and physical healing is very thin; in some cultures it's nonexistent. Instead, it's believed that healing takes place on the physical, psychic and emotional planes simultaneously in order to be truly effective. Here are a few magical tips to enhance and comfort body and soul.

> *If you have a health disorder, you might want to research which plants are most associated with your illness and grow them to cultivate an alliance.*

Animal Allies

Bear and Snake are the animals associated with healing and rejuvenation. Bear is particularly associated with herbal medicine; they are root diggers and some traditions believe that it was Bear who first revealed the medicinal secrets of roots and botanicals to human beings. Bears and snakes both burrow in Earth and are believed to be privy to the Earth Mother's most elusive wisdom. Because snakes shed their skin, appearing constantly rejuvenated and regenerated, they have long been associated with healing traditions.

A Healing Garden

Any plant may have therapeutic properties. The following plants have a metaphysically beneficial effect on health; they behave as guardians. Grow any combination of the following: **Balm of Gilead, basil, chamomile, coriander, fennel, garlic, heliotrope, lavender, melissa (lemon balm), mint, onion, poppy, rose, rosemary, Saint John's Wort, thyme, tobacco.**

TREES OF LIFE AND GOOD HEALTH

For added energy, plant trees in a circle, place a bench, seat or hot tub in the center and soak in the healing power. **Apple, Bay Laurel, Cedar, Olive, Willow.**

Healing Garlands

- **Amaranth:** worn as a crown, it hastens healing and recuperation.

- **Eucalyptus:** the fresh green seedpods are strung as necklaces to promote healing and prevent infection.

- **Ivy:** wear as a crown to soothe a hangover.

- **Mugwort:** worn across the forehead relieves headaches.

- **Rosemary:** stimulates the brain and mental processes, beneficial for those who fear Alzheimer's or dementia.

Spirits of Healing

Apollo, Baba Yaga, Fauna, Hecate, Isis. **Oshun** specifically assists women with disorders of the reproductive and abdominal areas.

Candle Healing

- Blue candles are burned to provide relief from pain and stress and for healing illnesses of the mind and emotions.

- Green candles are burned to invoke healing on the physical plane. Many have found success even with deeply entrenched illness.

- Burn brown candles if you feel your situation is just not fair!

- Dress and burn human figure candles to represent the individual for whom you seek healing.

Choose a cat figure candle if what you need are a few of those nine lives. If you are stumped for medical information or direction, burn a black or red witch candle and ask the wise woman it represents to journey to the spirit world and reveal the information you need.

Healing Energy Necklace

Angelica root

Carob root

Ginseng root

Cloves

Allspice berries Juniper berries

Nutmeg

Sewing needles

36 inches of strong thread, dental floss or monofilament (fishline)

These spices bestow a soothing fragrance. In addition, each of these spices radiates power that encourages healing on the physical plane.

1. Soak the spices overnight to soften them.

2. Trim the angelica root, carob and ginseng root to the desired length and shape.

3. You may need a small power drill to pierce the hard nutmeg, although some claim to be able to puncture the seed with a sharp needle. If this is a problem, omit this ingredient.

4. Thread each needle to one end of your thread.

5. Begin to string the roots and spices onto the thread, creating a symmetrical pattern by adding a spice first to one side of the thread, then the other.

6. Concentrate upon your goal as you pierce and string each root or spice.

7. Reserve some smooth round allspice and juniper berries for the end of the necklace so that they will rest against the back of your neck.

8. When your beads measure 14 inches to the center on each side, tie a strong knot and hang your necklace to air-dry. If cared for gently, your necklace should provide you with strength and comfort for years.

Crystals

- **Agate** relieves nausea.

- **Amazonite** relieves migraines and soothes eyes. Place the stone in pure springwater overnight and then use the water to bathe the eyes.

- Place cool **hematite** right where it throbs to soothe a headache.

- **Jade** is believed to have a beneficial strengthening effect upon the kidneys.

- **Jet** controls and alleviates migraine headaches.

- **Lapis lazuli** promotes articulate speech: autistic children, stroke victims or anyone who needs to make a speech may find lapis beneficial if worn over the throat.

- **Rose quartz** provides strength and healing for those enmeshed in eating disorders.

- Running your fingers through a bowl of loose **pearls** is believed to enhance the immune system, stimulate health and encourage long life.

Minerals to Alleviate Depression

- Amazonite

- Bloodstone

- Jet

- Pearls

Baba Yaga's Energy Potion

Based upon recipes used to assist ancient Olympic athletes increase their stamina, this potion features Baba Yaga's favorite: poppy seeds. Baba is extremely vigorous and rarely tired; perhaps a bit of her energy can be transmitted to you!

1 tablespoon of poppy seeds

Honey to taste

Glass of red wine

1. Add the poppy seeds and honey (this is not an optional ingredient, however, add as much as you like) to the glass of wine. Allow to steep for 15 minutes.

2. You may strain out the poppy seeds or drink them in the potion, whichever you prefer.

Insomnia Bath

1 cup milk

¼ cup honey

1 teaspoon pure vanilla extract

4 drops essential oil of lavender

4 drops of essential oil of marjoram*

---

*   Essential oil of marjoram can potentially create profound physical and emotional effects. Although it is very effective at combating sleeplessness, long-term use is not recommended without expert supervision. If insomnia is more than a momentary annoyance and you find yourself enjoying this bath more than just occasionally (let's say, more than once a week) simply leave out the marjoram. Essential oil of marjoram is not safe for use during pregnancy. Lavender oil, however, is among the gentlest, safest oils for most people.

> *Amethyst's legend is misunderstood: it will not protect you from getting*
> *drunk, if you set out to do so; however, it will bolster psychic resistance*
> *to alcohol and is a talisman for those in recovery programs.*

1. Warm the milk gently over low heat and stir in the honey.

2. When they are blended, remove from the heat and add the vanilla extract.

3. Pour into running warm bathwater to disperse.

4. Add the essential oils just before you enter.

Snake Healing Dream Incubation Spell

This ritual may be helpful when what ails you remains a stubborn mystery or if, though your malady can be identified, a cure remains unknown.

1. This ritual requires only the image of a snake, which must fit comfortably under your pillow: use a photograph, a drawing or a carved stone fetish.

2. Right before you go to sleep, look at the snake, tell it explicitly what you need to know and request any information it can bring you.

3. Place the snake under your pillow and go to sleep. The snake may respond via information in your dreams or via sudden inspiration while awake.

4. Repeat this ritual as needed until you have received the information you need.

DYING, DEATH, AND FUNERALS

Death is perhaps the ultimate threshold, and magic exists to ease the transition as well as to relieve the suffering of the dying or bereaved. There are few spells to *prevent* dying: Most magical cultures perceive death as part of life, not as something to be fought at any cost. The exception is for children: there are various spiritual entities who may be petitioned to preserve a child's life. These include Oya and Baron Samedi. Baron Samedi is leader of the Vodoun spirits of the dead. He prefers to see children live a long, full life. He and his wife, La Grande Brigitte, control the gates of the cemetery and either one may be sympathetic to an appeal.

Baron Samedi Altar

Baron Samedi is a prominent and complex spiritual entity from Haiti. Should you desire to petition his help you may want to become familiar with his legends so as to develop a sense of his personality and stature. His physical manifestation is extremely consistent. He appears as an elderly man dressed entirely in black with a black top hat and black sunglasses. Sardonic humor regarding death may please him: add Halloween or Day of the Dead toys to his altar. (He also enjoys ribald sexual humor.) A pair of the blackest sunglasses you can find welcomes him and makes him feel at home. Baron Samedi likes perishable offerings: he loves black coffee, dry bread and roasted peanuts. Cigars and cigarettes are very appreciated. If he has performed a favor for you, reward him with a glass of fine rum, in which you have steeped twenty-one very hot peppers.

Aids to Transition

Aquamarine worn on the body eases the transition and provides luck for the next journey. **Jet** comforts those left behind. **Angel's trumpet flower essence** (FES) eases the approach to the mystery threshold and helps provide a sense of tranquility and peace.

The sense of smell remains until the last breath for most. Fragrance may still be used to communicate even if other methods fail. Soothing, healing incense may be burned. Scented oils are applied to the body to nurture, protect and soothe. **Essential oils of myrrh and vetiver** communicate the presence of the Earth Mother whose loving arms await—and also prevent and heal bedsores. (Remember, essential oils must be diluted in a base oil before being applied to the body. If someone is physically fragile, dilute even further; as little as one drop per tablespoon of oil can still be effective.) It is traditional for the body to be anointed with scented oils after death, too. **Sandalwood** is traditional although any fragrance associated with the individual may be used.

The period between death and funeral rites is considered an extremely vulnerable threshold. Candles and incense burn constantly for protection. Candles are strategically placed, usually at the head and feet. The body is not left alone. People may sit quietly in vigil or the body may be brought in as guest of honor at a wake. In societies where there is a history of malevolent magic, human guards will also remain at the grave until a period of safety is achieved.

Botanicals have a place in funeral rites, too. In North Africa, powdered henna leaves are sprinkled in a dead man's hair while a deceased woman's hands and feet are painted to provide happiness on the other side. (No such luck for widows who are banned from henna decoration, anywhere from a few months, as in North Africa, to forever, as in India.) In Europe, rosemary is tossed into the grave to ensure the memory of both the deceased soul and the mourners. Ancient Greeks wove garlands of yew to adorn the deceased (very poisonous for anyone else!) as a botanical request for Hecate's escort service to the beyond. Fragrant smoke may also be created. In India, sandalwood remains traditional. California Indians burned sage to purify the atmosphere but also to assuage mourners' grief.

A Bower of Comfort and Grief

The following trees, flowers and herbs provide psychic comfort but they also encourage you to express your grief in a healing, constructive manner. Many of these plants have metaphysical associations with life everlasting. Create a private garden where you can find solace and peace. Arrange a bench in a shady corner and add any memorials to honor those who have departed this Earth but remain forever alive in your heart: **Lavender, Pomegranate, Poppies, Rosemary, Roses, Sage, Willow and Yew Trees.**

Animal Allies

Butterfly, Dog, Raven/Crow, Snake and **Wolf** are ready to serve as guides and partners during your spiritual journey.

A Spice Necklace to Relieve Grief

Cloves

Juniper berries

Strong red thread and a sewing needle

1. Soak the spices overnight to soften them.

2. Puncture with a strong needle and string the spices onto the thread.

3. You may find the beading motion to be soothing in itself or you may wish to concentrate upon your goals, desires or the expression of your grief as you puncture and string each spice bead.

4. When the necklace is sufficiently long, knot it tightly and hang it to air-dry.

5. In order for this to be effective, you must give the aroma the opportunity to perform its magic. Hang it near your bed at night or wear it in bed at night so that the fragrance can reach you.

Appendix

BOTANICAL CLASSIFICATIONS

Adam and Eve Root (*Aplectrum hyemale*)

Agrimony (*Eupatorium cannabinum*)

Alecost (*Chrysanthemum balsamita*)

Alfalfa (*Medicago sativa*)

Allspice (*Pimenta officinalis*)

Almond (*Amygdalis communis var. dulcis*)

Amaranth (*Amaranthus spp.*)

Ambrette (*Abelmoschus moschatus*)

Angelica (*Angelica arcangelica*)

Angel's Trumpet (*Brugmansia syn Datura, Datura candida*)

Anise (*Pimpinella anisum*)

Apple (*Malus malus, Pyrus malus*)

Ash (*Fraxinus spp.*)

Balm of Gilead (*Populus gileadensis*)

Basil (*Ocimum basilicum*)

Bay Laurel (*Laurus nobilis*)

Bee Balm (*Monarda didyma*)

Benzoin (*Styrax benzoin*)

Bergamot (*Citrus bergamia*)

Beth Root (*Trillium erectum*)

Birch (*Betula alba*)

Black Mustard (*Brassica nigra*)

Calendula (*Calendula officinalis*)

Camellia (*Camellia spp.*)

Cardamom (*Elettaria cardomomum*)

Carnation (*Dianthus caryophyllus*)

Carob (*Ceratonia siliqua*)

Cascara sagrada (*Rhamnus purshianus*)

Catnip (*Nepeta cataria*)

Cayenne Pepper (*Capsicum frutescens*)

Cedarwood (*Cedrus spp.*)

Cedarwood, Texas (*Juniperus mexicana*)

Celery Seed (*Apium graveolens*)

Chamomile, German, Hungarian (*Matricaria chamomilla, M. recutita*)

Chamomile, Roman (*Anthemis nobilis*)

Cinnamon (*Cinnamomum zeylanicum*)

Cinquefoil (Five Finger Grass) (*Potentilla reptans*)

Clover (*Trifolium spp.*)

Cloves (*Eugenia caryophyllus*)

Coconut (*Cocos nucifera*)

Coriander (Chinese Parsley, Cilantro) (*Coriandrum sativa*)

Corsican Mint (*Mentha requienii*)

Cowslip (*Primula vulgaris*)

Cypress (*Cupressus sempervirens*)

Daisy (*Chrystanthemum leucanthemum*)

Dandelion (*Taraxacum officinale*)

Devil's Shoestrings (*Viburnum spp.*)

Dill (*Anethum graveolens*)

Dittany of Crete (*Origanum dictamnus*)

Dogwood (*Cornus spp.*)

Dragon's Blood (*Dracaena draco, Daemonorops draco*)

Dream Herb (*Calea zacatechichi*)

Elder (*Sambucus spp.*)

Eucalyptus (*Eucalyptus globulus*)

Evening Primrose (*Oenothera biennis*)

Fennel (*Foeniculum vulgare*)

Fenugreek (*Trigonella foenum-graecum*)

Fig (*Ficus carica*)

Flax (*Linum usitatissimum*)

Forget-Me-Not (*Myosotis symphytifolia*)

Foxglove (*Digitalis purpurea*)

Frangipani (Plumeria) (*Plumeria spp.*)

Frankincense (*Boswellia carterii*)

Gardenia (*Gardenia augusta*)

Garlic (*Allium sativum*)

Geranium (*Pelargonium graveolens*)

Ginger (*Zingiber officinale*)

Ginseng (*Panax quinquefolium*)

Green Bells of Ireland (*Molucella laevis*)

Hawthorn (*Cratageus spp.*)

Hazelnut (*Corylus spp.*)

Heliotrope (*Heliotropium peruviana*)

Henna (*Lawsonia inermis*)

Hibiscus (*Hibiscus spp.*)

High John the Conqueror (*Ipomoea jalapa, I. purga, Convolvulus jalapa*)

Holly (*Ilex aquifolium*)

Hollyhock (*Althaea rosea*)

Honeysuckle (*Lonicera spp.*)

Hops (*Humulus lupulus*)

Hyacinth (*Hyacinthus orientalis*)

Hydrangea (*Hydrangea arborescens*)

Hyssop (*Hysoppus officinalis*)

Iris (*Iris spp.*)

Ivy (*Hedera helix*)

Jasmine (*Jasminium spp.*)

Jojoba (*Jojoba simmondsia californica*)

Juniper (*Juniperus communis*)

Labdanum (Rock Rose) (*Cistus ladanifer*)

Lady's Mantle (*Alchemilla vulgaris*)

Lavender (*Lavandula augustifolia*)

Lemon *(Citrus limonum)*

Lemon Balm (Melissa) *(Melissa officinalis)*

Lemongrass *(Cymbopogon citratus)*

Lemon Verbena *(Lippia citriodora)*

Lilac *(Syringa vulgaris)*

Lime *(Citrus acris)*

Linden *(Tilia europea)*

Lovage *(Levisticum officinale)*

Low John *(Trillium erectum)*

Lucky Hand Root *(Dactylorhyza spp.)*

Mahaleb Cherry (Perfumed Cherry Tree) *(Prunus mahaleb)*

Manuka (New Zealand Tea Tree) *(Leptospermum scoparium)*

Marigold, African, Aztec, French *(Tagetes spp.)*

Marigold, Pot *(Calendula officinalis)*

Marjoram *(Origanum majorana)*

May Chang *(Litsea cubeba)*

Milkweed (Butterfly Weed) *(Asclepias tuberose)*

Mimosa *(Acacia decurrens)*

Mistletoe *(Viscum album)*

Money Plant *(Lunaria annua)*

Moon Flower *(Ipomoea alba)*

Morning Glory *(Ipomoea spp.)*

Mugwort *(Artemisia vulgaris)*

Mullein *(Verbascum thapsus)*

Myrrh *(Commiphora myrrha)*

Myrtle *(Myrtus communis)*

Neroli *(Citrus aurantium Amara)*

Nettles, Stinging *(Urtica dioica)*

Night Jasmine (Night Jessamine) *(Cestrum nocturnum)*

Night Scented Stock *(Mathiola longipetala)*

Nutmeg *(Myristica fragrans)*

Oak *(Quercus robur)*

Oak Moss *(Evernia prunastri)*

Oleander *(Nerium oleander)*

Olive *(Olea europaea)*

Onion *(Allium cepa)*

Oracle Sage *(Salvia divinorum)*

Orange *(Citrus aurantium Dulcis)*

Oregano *(Origanum vulgare)*

Oregon Grape *(Berberis aquifolium)*

Orrisroot *(Iris spp.)*

Pansy *(Viola tricolor)*

Parsley *(Petroselinum crispum)*

Patchouli *(Pogostemon cablin)*

Peony *(Paeonia spp.)*

Peppermint *(Mentha piperita)*

Petitgrain *(Citrus aurantium Amara)*

Pine *(Pinus spp.)*

Pomegranate *(Punica granatum)*

Poppy *(Papaver spp.)*

Primrose *(Primula vulgaris)*

Purslane *(Portulaca grandiflora)*

Queen of the Meadow *(Spiraea ulmaria)*

Raspberry *(Rubus idaeus)*

Rose *(Rosa spp.)*

Rose Geranium *(Pelargonium graveolens)*

Rosemary *(Rosmarinus officinalis)*

Rowan *(Sorbus aucuparia, Fraxinus aucuparia)*

Rue *(Ruta graveolens)*

Safflower *(Carthamus tinctorius)*

Saffron *(Crocus sativa)*

Sage *(Salvia spp.)*

Sage, Oracle *(Salvia divinorum)*

Sage, White *(Salvia apiana)*

Saguaro *(Cereus giganteus)*

Saint John's Wort *(Hypericum perforatum)*

Sandalwood *(Santalum album)*

Solomon's Seal *(Polygonatum multiflorum)*

Spider Flower *(Cleome spinosa)*

Spruce *(Picea spp.)*

Star Anise *(Illicuim verum)*

Star Tulip *(Calochorus tolmiei)*

Stephanotis *(Stephanotis floribunda)*

Storax *(Styrax officinalis)*

Tagetes (African, Aztec, French Marigolds) *(Tagetes sp.)*

Texas Cedarwood *(Juniperus mexicana)*

Thyme *(Thymus vulgaris)*

Tobacco, Ornamental *(Nicotiana alata grandiflora)*

Tonka Bean *(Dipteryx odorata)*

Tuberose *(Polianthes tuberose)*

Turmeric *(Curcuma longa)*

Vanilla *(Vanilla planifolia)*

Vervain *(Verbena officinalis)*

Vetiver *(Vetiveria zizanoides)*

Vinca *(Vinca major)*

Violet *(Viola odorata)*

Walnut *(Juglans nigra)*

Water Mint *(Mentha aquatica)*

White Sage *(Salvia apiana)*

Wintergreen *(Gaultheria procumbens)*

Wormwood *(Artemisia absinthium)*

Yarrow *(Achillea millefolium)*

Yerba Santa *(Eriodictyon californicum)*

Yew *(Taxus baccata)*

Ylang Ylang *(Cananga odorata)*

Bibliography

Allende, Isabel. *Aphrodite*. New York: HarperCollins, 1998

Andrews, Ted. *Animal-Speak: The Spiritual and Magical Powers of Creatures Great and Small*. St Paul, Minnesota: Llewellyn Publications, 1995

Ann, Martha & Dorothy Myers Imel. *Goddesses in World Mythology: A Biographical Dictionary*. New York: Oxford University Press, 1993

Balz, Rodolphe. *The Healing Powers of Essential Oils*. Twin Lakes, Wisconsin: Lotus Light Publications, 1996

Batra, Sumita. *The Art of Mehndi*. New York: Penguin Group, 1999

Beckwith, Carol. *Nomads of Niger*. New York: Harry N. Abrams, Inc., 1993

Bell, Robert E. *Women of Classical Mythology*. New York: Oxford University Press, 1991

Betz, Hans Dieter. *The Greek Magical Papyri in Translation: Including the Demotic Spells*. Chicago: The University of Chicago Press, 1992

Cunningham, Donna. *Flower Remedies Handbook*. New York: Sterling Publishing Company, 1992

Cunningham, Scott. *Hawaiian Religion and Magic*. St Paul, Minnesota: Llewellyn Publications, 1994

Davis, Patricia. *Aromatherapy: An A–Z*. Barnes & Noble Books, New York 1995

Detienne, Marcel. *The Gardens of Adonis: Spices in Greek Mythology*. Princeton, New Jersey: Princeton University Press, 1994

Dunham, Carroll and Barbara Aria. *Mamatoto: A Celebration of Birth*. New York: Penguin Books, 1992

Elston, Catherine Feher. *Ravensong*. Flagstaff, Arizona: Northland Publishing Company, 1991

Epton, Nina. *Saints and Sorcerers: A Moroccan Journey*. London: Cassell & Company, 1958

Epton, Nina. *Magic and Mystics of Java*. London: The Octagon Press, 1974

Fischer-Rizzi, Susanne. *The Complete Incense Book*. New York: Sterling Publishing Company, 1998

Fisher, Angela. *Africa Adorned*. New York: Harry N. Abrams, Inc., 1984

Goodchild, Peter. *Raven Tales*. Chicago: Chicago Review Press, 1991

Gutmanis, June. *Kahuna La'au Lapa'au*. Alea, Hawaii: Island Heritage Publishing, 1997

Harris, Jessica B. *The World Beauty Book*. New York: HarperCollins, 1995

Hoffmann, David. *The New Holistic Herbal*. New York: Barnes & Noble Books, 1995

Jereb, James F. *Arts and Crafts of Morocco*. San Francisco: Chronicle Books, 1995

Johnson, Buffie. *Lady of the Beasts*. New York: HarperCollins, 1990

Karcher, Steven. *The Illustrated Encyclopedia of Divination*. Rockport, Massachusetts: Element Books, 1997

Kinsey, Robert O. *Ojime: Magical Jewels of Japan*. New York: Harry N. Abrams, Inc., 1994

Kunz, George Frederick. *The Curious Lore of Precious Stones*. New York: Dover Publications, 1971

Lavender, Susan and Anna Franklin. *Herb Craft: A Guide to the Shamanic and Ritual Use of Herbs*. Freshfields, Chieveley, Berks: Capall Bann Publishing, 1996

Leach, Maria. *Funk & Wagnall's Standard Dictionary of Folklore, Mythology and Legend*. San Francisco: Harper & Row, 1984

Lesko, Barbara S. *The Great Goddesses of Egypt*. Norman, Oklahoma: University of Oklahoma Press, 1999

Manniche, Lise. *Sacred Luxuries: Fragrance, Aromatherapy and Cosmetics in Ancient Egypt*. Ithaca, New York: Cornell University Press, 1999

Mansfield, Peter. *Flower Remedies*. Boston: Charles E. Tuttle, Inc., 1995

McIntyre, Anne. *Flower Power*. New York: Henry Holt, 1996

Morris, Desmond. *Cat World: A Feline Encyclopedia*. New York: Penguin Books, 1996

Morris, Desmond. *Bodyguards: Protective Amulets and Charms*. Boston: Element Books, 1999

Northrup, Christiane M.D. *Women's Bodies, Women's Wisdom*. New York: Bantam Books, 1994

Penner, Lucille Recht. *The Honey Book*. New York: Hastings House, 1980

Pinckney, Roger. *Blue Roots: African American Folk Magic of the Gullah People*. St. Paul, Minnesota: Llewellyn Publications, 1998

Ronck, Ronn. *The Hawaiian Lei: A Tradition of Aloha*. Honolulu: Mutual Publishing, 1997

Roome, Loretta. *Mehndi: The Timeless Art of Henna Painting*. New York: St Martin's Griffin, 1998

Ryall, Rhiannon. *West Country Wicca*. Custer, Washington: Phoenix Publishing, 1989

Saunders, Nicholas J. *Animal Spirits*. Boston: Little, Brown and Company, 1995

Seligmann, Kurt. *The History of Magic and the Occult*. New York: Harmony Books, 1948

Shealy, C. Norman. *The Illustrated Encyclopedia of Healing Remedies*. Boston: Element Books, 1998

Shlane, Leonard. *The Alphabet Versus the Goddess*. New York: Penguin/ Arkana, 1998

Style, Sue. *Honey from Hive to Honeypot*. San Francisco: Chronicle Books, 1993

Too, Lillian. *Feng Shui Fundamentals: Eight Easy Lessons*. Rockport, Massachusetts: Element Books, 1997

Unterman, Alan. *Dictionary of Jewish Lore and Legend*. London: Thames and Hudson, 1991

Weinberg, Norma Pasekoff. *Henna from Head to Toe*. Pownal, Vermont: Storey Books, 1999

Acknowledgments

Deepest gratitude to Michael Kerber, Peter Turner, Bonni Hamilton, Jane Hagaman, Kathryn Sky-Peck, Christine LeBlond, Eryn Eaton, and the rest of the brilliant staff at Weiser Books. Special thanks to Greg Brandenburgh without whom this book would not exist. I would also like to thank Mat Auryn, whose foreword made me cry (in a good way!) as well as Stephanie Rose Bird and Vajra Conjure Wright, who, over the years, have become such a big part of this book for me. Carole Murray and Adele Clough, I miss you every day. The previous edition of this book was dedicated to the memory of Zoltan, Herta, and Irma Illes, now joined in the Otherworld by my aunt Clara Fisher—all in my heart forever. As always, my love and gratitude to Rachel and Jordan.

Index of Spells

ABC Love Oracle, 187

Algiers Powder, 270

Ancient Moroccan Contraceptive Spell, 247

Angelica Floor Wash, 152

An Aphrodite Bouquet, 236

Apollo's Balls of Fortune, 185

Apple Attachment Spell, 219

Ariadne and Dionysus Loving Couple
    Bouquet, 237

Artemis Fertility Altar, 242

Aura-Cleansing Incense, 147

Avian Oracle, 189

Awaken the Spirits Incense, 182

Baba Yaga's Energy Potion, 275

Baby Dream Pillow, 253

Banish Bad Vibes Floor Wash, 153

Basic Bath Salts, 157

Basil Prosperity Bath, 264

Basil Vinegar, 164

Be Mine Bath Ritual, 213

Bedouin Childbirth Spice Necklace, 250

Best Foot First, 199

Better Sex But Only If You Come Back
    Home, 226

Broken Heart Solace Bath, 228

Burst of Love Potpourri, 225

Calling Up the Dead Incense, 183

Candomblé Cleansing Incense, 147

Chill Out Spell, 195

Coconut Cleansing Candle, 148

Come to Me Lover Formula, 221

Conception Spell Box, 245

Creole Antipoverty Spell, 263

Crystal Bead Bracelet, 90

Curse Removal Bath, 165

Devil's Shoestrings Ankle Bracelet, 168

Don't Cross My Path, 156

Don't Overwhelm Me Psychic Bath, 179

Dream Incense, 133

Dream Pillows, 122

Dried Herb Bundles, 104

Druid Herb Garden, 108

Egg Bedroom Cleanser, 150

Egg Domestic Dispute Disposal, 151

Egg Trees, 244

Erotic Bath, 230

Erotic Bedroom Perfume Incense, 230

Extra Protection Bath Salts, 157

Family Full of Cash, 261

Fertile Crescent Childbirth Incense, 249

Fertility-Drawing Oil, 245

Five Fingers Protection Bath, 177

Florida Water Formula #1, 146

Florida Water Formula #2, 146

Fly Me To The Moon: An Astral Projection
    Pillow, 128

Foot Protection Ritual, 167

Freya's Enchanting Facial, 201

Frog Fertility Spell, 240

Fumigation: Personal Incense, 207

Golden Glow Face Mask, 204

Green Ribbon Money Growth Spells, 261

Grow Some Money Spell, 257

Grow-a-Lover Spell, 217

Hair Growth Potion, 209

Happy Marriage Charm, 238

Happy Trails Travel Charm, 200

Hawaiian Aura Cleanser, 152

Healing Energy Necklace, 273

Hecate Bath, 214

Henna Love Spell, 219
Henna Paste, 115
Henna Treasure Chest, 117
The Henna Ritual, 112
Hexbreaker Bath, 165
The Hibiscus "I Love Myself" Bath, 215
High John's Finest Fruits, 265
High John's Money Roll, 266
Honey in the Jar, 194
Hungary Water, 204
The "I Deserve Respect" Bath, 197
Immunity Incense, 254
Incense Cones, 104
Insomnia Bath, 275
Insomnia Pillow, 127
Isis and Osiris Eternal Love Oil, 229
Isis Oil, 174
Juno's Bouquet of Eternal Love, 237
Lemon and Sugar, 116
Love Potion #2: A Potion for Two, 218
Love-Drawing Spice Necklace, 212
Lover Come to Me Candle Ritual, 220
Lover Dream of Me Pillow, 211
Lover, Come Back Incense, 227
Lucky Cat Candle, 269
Lucky Dream Pillow, 190
Lucky Seven Charm Box, 267
Lucky Spice Necklace, 190
Lunation, 246
Luxurious Remember Your Dreams Bath, 132
Marie Laveau Water, 175
Milk and Honey Prosperity Bath, 260
The Milky Way Weight Loss Spell, 208
A Money Dream Pillow, 258
Money Magnet Oil, 259
Money Miracle Mantra, 262
Money Salt Scrub, 260
Money Spell Box, 266
Moon Bath Salts, 176

More Money Oil, 269
More Money Spice Necklace, 256
Myrrh Beads, 231
New Home Floor Wash, 153
New Orleans Better Business Formula, 263
New Orleans Gambler's Lucky Hand, 270
New Orleans Style Psychic Enhancement Bath, 176
New Romance Brew: A Potion for One, 218
Obeah-Style Coconut Cleansing Candle, 149
Ojo de Dios, 161
The Old Egg-in-the-Earth Spell, 193
Onion Bad-Vibe Removal, 151
Oshun Prosperity Incense, 258
Our Hearts United in Love, 227
Overwhelming Anger Bath, 171
Ozark Love Oracle: The Sacrificial Mullein, 188
Peaceful Home Charm Bag, 200
Persephone's Box of Beauty, 202
Personal Jinx Removal Ritual, 170
Personal Oracle Bath Ritual, 184
Prophetic Dreams Pillow, 127
Prosperity Potpourri, 259
Protection Formula, 164
Psychic Enhancement Spice Necklace, 172
Psychic Power Incense, 174
Psychic Replenishing Bath, 178
Psychic Shield Infused Oil, 17
Psychic Stimulation Tea, 172
Pure Magic Fragrance Ritual, 99
Purification Bath, 142
Quick Fix Aura-Cleansing Bath, 142
Quick Fix Better Business Formula, 264
Quick Fix Youthfulness Bath Formula, 205
Reconsider Friend, 229
Remember Your Dreams Bath, 132
Return to Sender Doll Ritual, 169
Romance Floor Wash, 225

Rose Water, 44

Rosebud Beads, 231

Saffron Beads, 232

Salt Scrubs, 158

Sandalwood Spirit-Cleansing Face
    Mask, 144

Scandinavian House Protection
    Amulet, 163

Séance Incense, 183

Self-Confidence Ritual Bath, 206

Seven Roses Aura-Cleansing Bath, 143

Snake Healing Dream Incubation Spell, 276

A Spice Necklace to Relieve Grief, 279

Spirit Summoning Oil, 181

State of the Relationship Divination
    Oracle, 187

Stay Put Spell, 197

Sun and Moon Psychic Bodyguard Dream
    Pillow Stuffing, 155

Sun Oil, 208

Sweet Dreams Anti-Insomnia Incense, 133

Sweet Dreams Bath, 131

Sweet Sibling Spell, 254

Tarot Card Growth Ritual, 195

Uncrossing Oil, 192

Van Van Oil, 192

Vinegar Room Cleanser, 150

We Two Meet as One, 223

Welcome Baby Incense, 249

Yemaya Fertility Ritual #1, 242

Yemaya Fertility Ritual #2, 243

Your Eyes Only for Me Bath, 220

Your Love Belongs to Me Candle
    Ritual, 221

About the Author

A lifelong student and lover of the magical arts, Judika Illes is the author of numerous books devoted to spells, spirits, saints, and witchcraft. Her books include *Encyclopedia of 5000 Spells, Encyclopedia of Witchcraft, Encyclopedia of Spirits, Encyclopedia of Mystics, Saints, and Sages, Daily Magic, Magic When You Need It,* and *The Weiser Field Guide to Witches.* Judika is the editor and curator of two books of mystical fiction, *The Weiser Book of the Fantastic and Forgotten* and *The Weiser Book of Occult Detectives.* A certified aromatherapist, she has been a professional Tarot card reader for over three decades. A native New Yorker, Judika teaches in the US and internationally. Follow her on Instagram @judikailles

ALSO IN WEISER CLASSICS

The Alchemist's Handbook: A Practical Manual, by Frater Albertus, with a new foreword by Robert Allen Bartlett

Predictive Astrology: Tools to Forecast Your Life and Create Your Brightest Future, by Bernadette Brady, with a new foreword by Theresa Reed

The Druidry Handbook: Spiritual Practice Rooted in the Living Earth, by John Michael Greer, with a new foreword by Dana O'Driscoll

Futhark: A Handbook of Rune Magic, by Edred Thorsson, newly revised and updated by the author

The Herbal Alchemist's Handbook: A Complete Guide to Magickal Herbs and How to Use Them, by Karen Harrison, with a new foreword by Arin Murphy-Hiscock

Liber Null and Psychonaut: The Practice of Chaos Magic, by Peter J. Carroll, newly revised and updated by the author, with a new foreword by Ronald Hutton

The Mystical Qabalah, by Dion Fortune, with a new foreword by Judika Illes and a new afterword by Stuart R. Harrop

Psychic Self-Defense: The Definitive Manual for Protecting Yourself Against Paranormal Attack, by Dion Fortune, with a new foreword by Mary K. Greer and a new afterword by Christian Gilson

Saturn: A New Look at an Old Devil, by Liz Greene, with a new foreword by Juliana McCarthy

Spiritual Cleansing: A Handbook of Psychic Protection, by Draja Mickaharic, with a new foreword by Lilith Dorsey

Taking Up the Runes: A Complete Guide to Using Runes in Spells, Rituals, Divination, and Magic, by Diana L. Paxson, with new material by the author

The Handbook of Yoruba Religious Concepts, by Baba Ifa Karade, newly revised and updated by the author

Yoga Sutras of Patanjali, by Mukunda Stiles, with a new foreword by Mark Whitwell